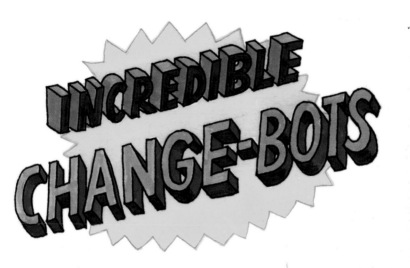

INCREDIBLE CHANGE-BOTS

MORE THAN JUST MACHINES!

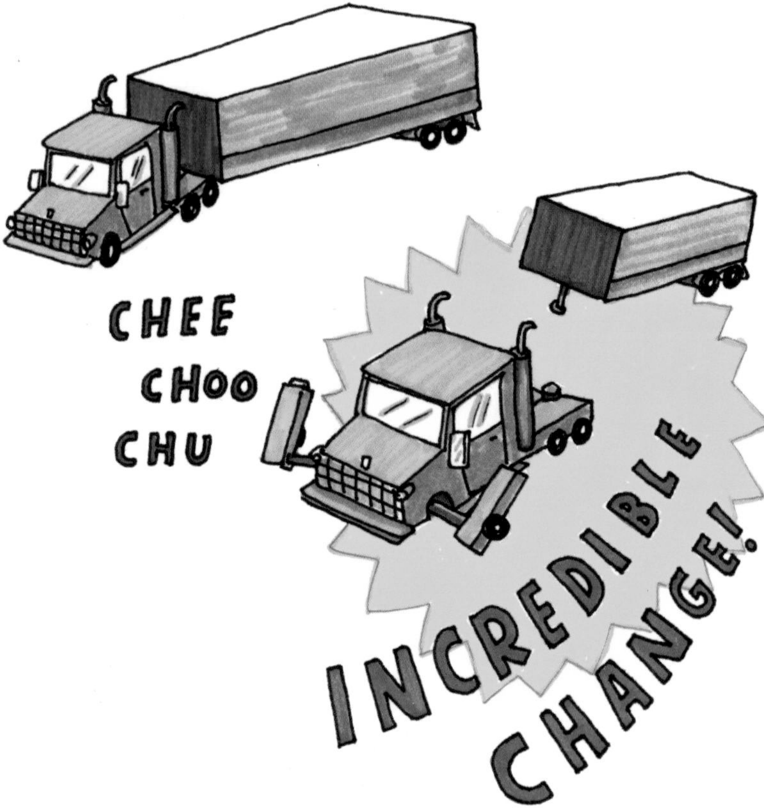
CHEE
CHOO
CHU
INCREDIBLE
CHANGE!

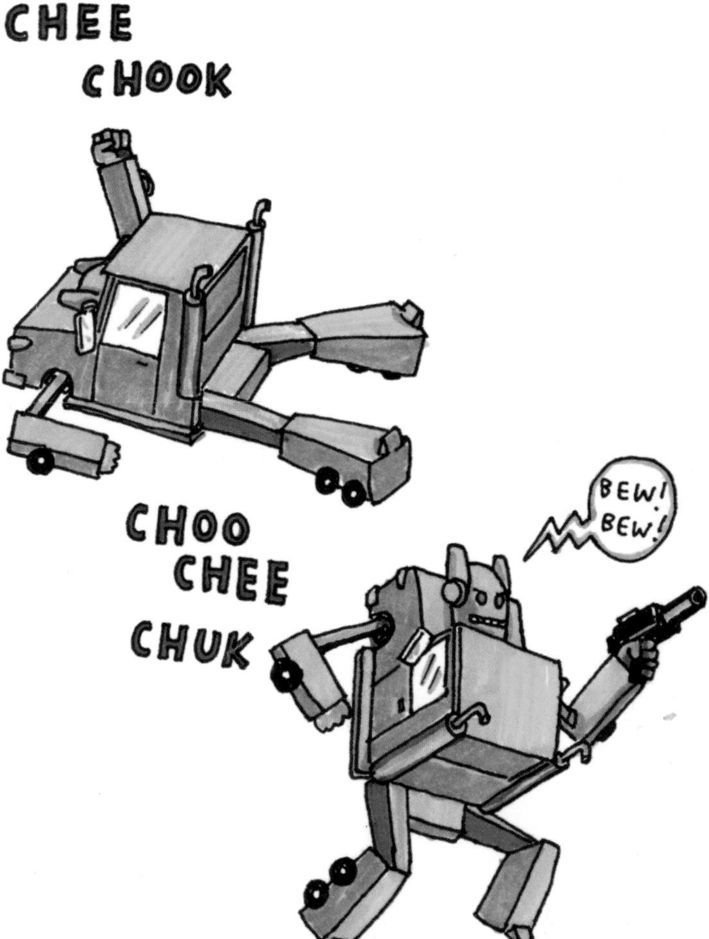
CHEE
CHOOK
CHOO
CHEE
CHUK
BEW! BEW!

ISBN   978-1-891830-91-4
2ND PRINTING. MARCH 2011.
PRINTED IN SINGAPORE.

MANY THANKS ARE DUE TO THE USUAL SUSPECTS:
EVERYONE WHO'S BEEN READING MY BOOKS,
CHRIS AND BRETT FROM TOP SHELF, DOUG, PAUL H,
ALL MY FAMILY AND FRIENDS, AND OF COURSE,
JENNIFER AND OSCAR.

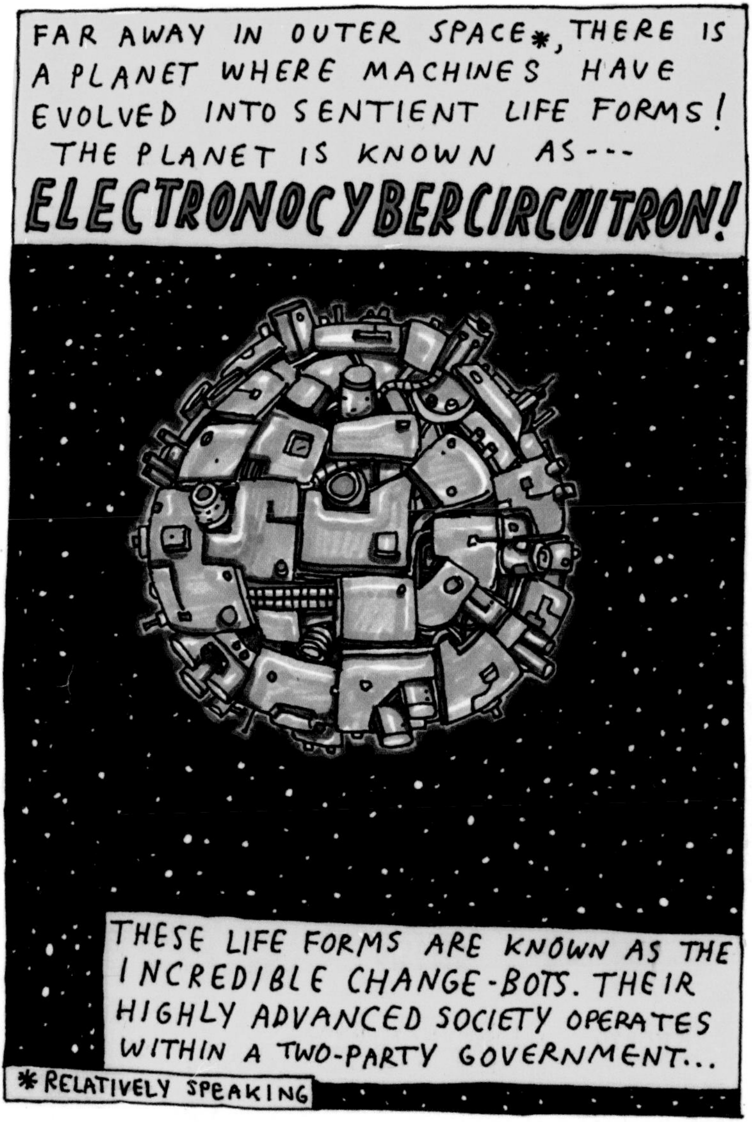
FAR AWAY IN OUTER SPACE*, THERE IS A PLANET WHERE MACHINES HAVE EVOLVED INTO SENTIENT LIFE FORMS! THE PLANET IS KNOWN AS---
ELECTRONOCYBERCIRCUITRON!
THESE LIFE FORMS ARE KNOWN AS THE INCREDIBLE CHANGE-BOTS. THEIR HIGHLY ADVANCED SOCIETY OPERATES WITHIN A TWO-PARTY GOVERNMENT...
* RELATIVELY SPEAKING

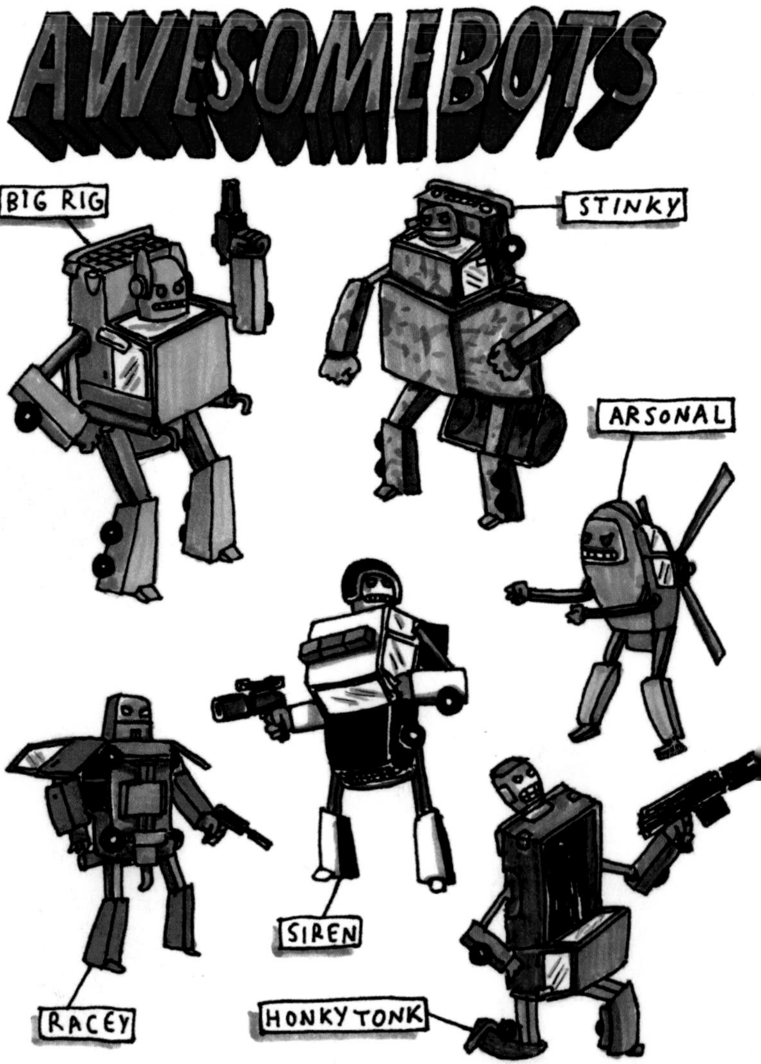
AWESOMEBOTS
BIG RIG
STINKY
ARSONAL
SIREN
RACEY
HONKY TONK

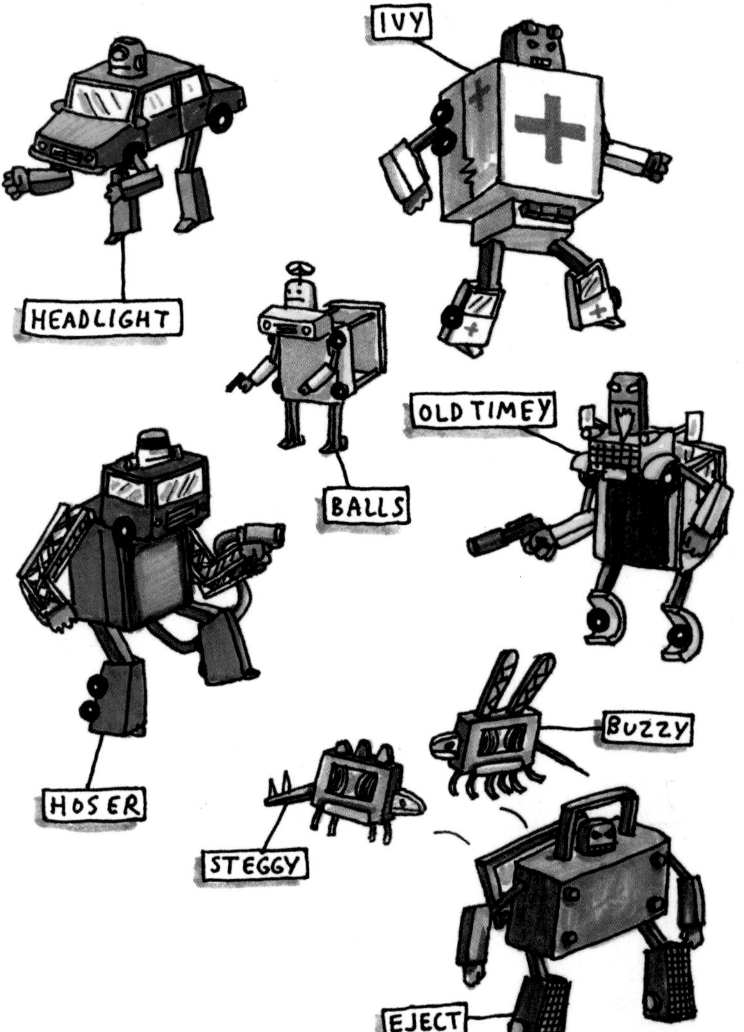
IVY
HEADLIGHT
BALLS
OLD TIMEY
HOSER
BUZZY
STEGGY
EJECT

FANTASTICONS

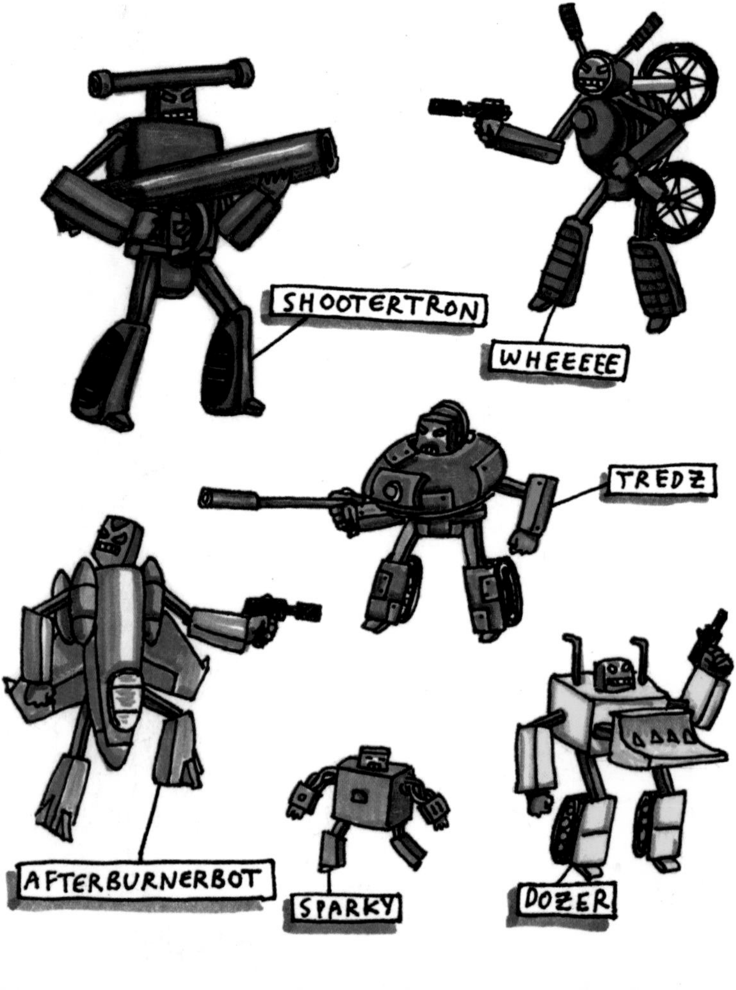
SHOOTERTRON
WHEEEEEE
TREDZ
AFTERBURNERBOT
SPARKY
DOZER

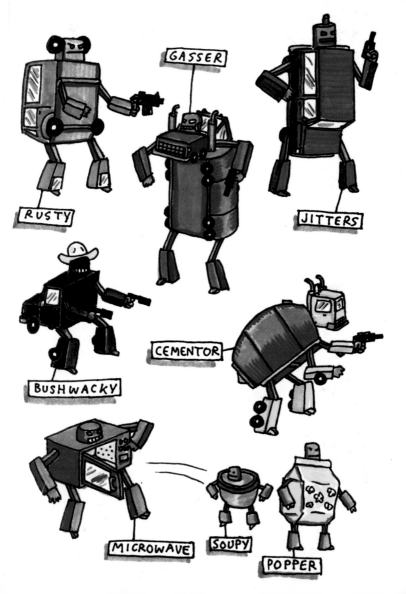

RUSTY

GASSER

JITTERS

BUSHWACKY

CEMENTOR

MICROWAVE

SOUPY

POPPER

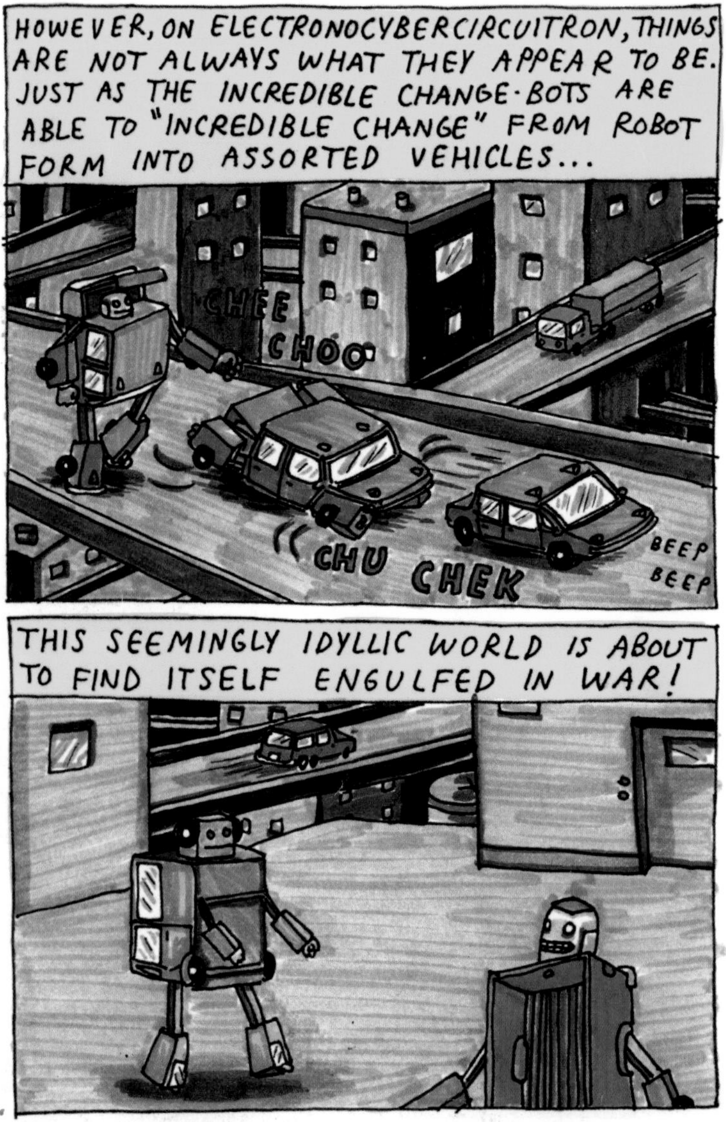
HOWEVER, ON ELECTRONOCYBERCIRCUITRON, THINGS ARE NOT ALWAYS WHAT THEY APPEAR TO BE. JUST AS THE INCREDIBLE CHANGE-BOTS ARE ABLE TO "INCREDIBLE CHANGE" FROM ROBOT FORM INTO ASSORTED VEHICLES...
CHEE
CHOO
CHU
CHEK
BEEP
BEEP
THIS SEEMINGLY IDYLLIC WORLD IS ABOUT TO FIND ITSELF ENGULFED IN WAR!

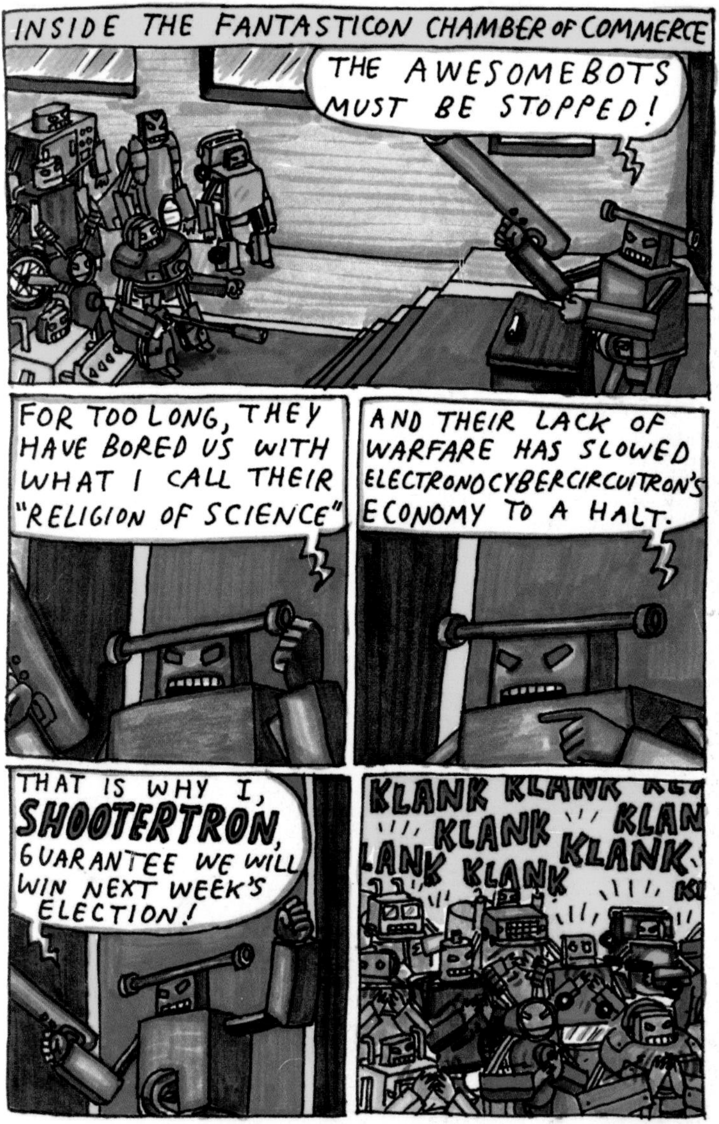
INSIDE THE FANTASTICON CHAMBER OF COMMERCE
THE AWESOMEBOTS MUST BE STOPPED!
FOR TOO LONG, THEY HAVE BORED US WITH WHAT I CALL THEIR "RELIGION OF SCIENCE"
AND THEIR LACK OF WARFARE HAS SLOWED ELECTRONOCYBERCIRCUITRON'S ECONOMY TO A HALT.
THAT IS WHY I, SHOOTERTRON, GUARANTEE WE WILL WIN NEXT WEEK'S ELECTION!
KLANK KLANK
KLANK KLAN
LANK KLANK KLANK
KLANK

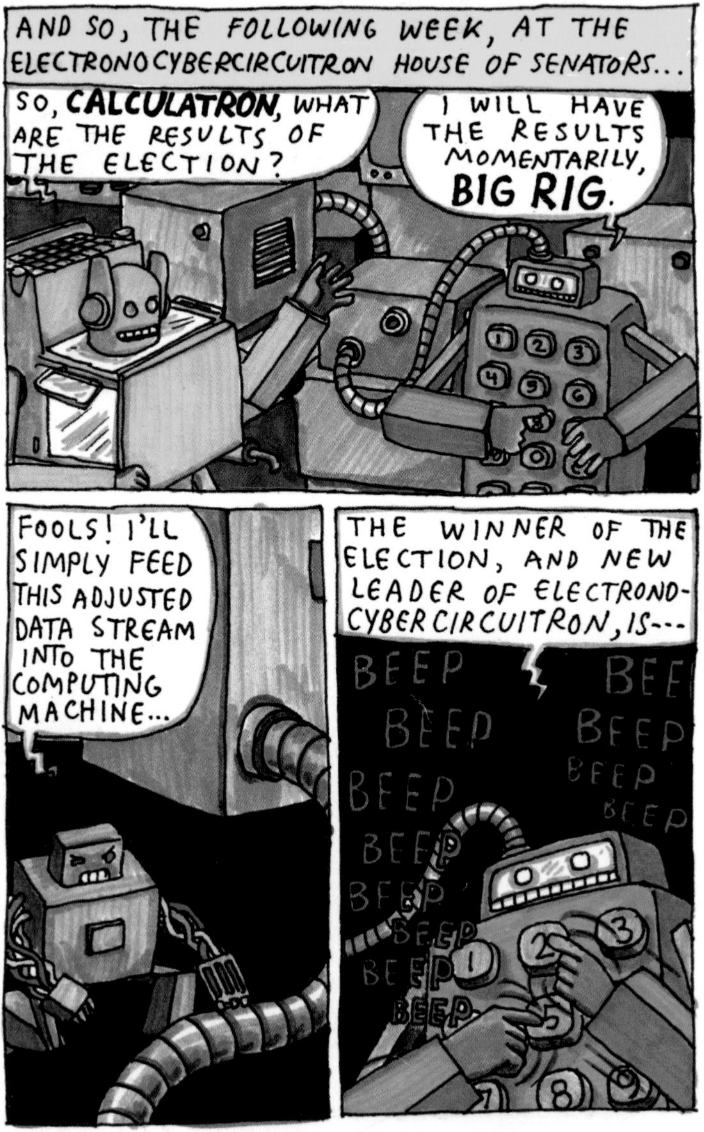
AND SO, THE FOLLOWING WEEK, AT THE ELECTRONOCYBERCIRCUITRON HOUSE OF SENATORS...
SO, CALCULATRON, WHAT ARE THE RESULTS OF THE ELECTION?
I WILL HAVE THE RESULTS MOMENTARILY, BIG RIG.
FOOLS! I'LL SIMPLY FEED THIS ADJUSTED DATA STREAM INTO THE COMPUTING MACHINE...
THE WINNER OF THE ELECTION, AND NEW LEADER OF ELECTRONOCYBERCIRCUITRON, IS---
BEEP BEEP BEEP BEEP BEEP BEEP BEEP BEEP BEEP BEEP BEEP BEEP

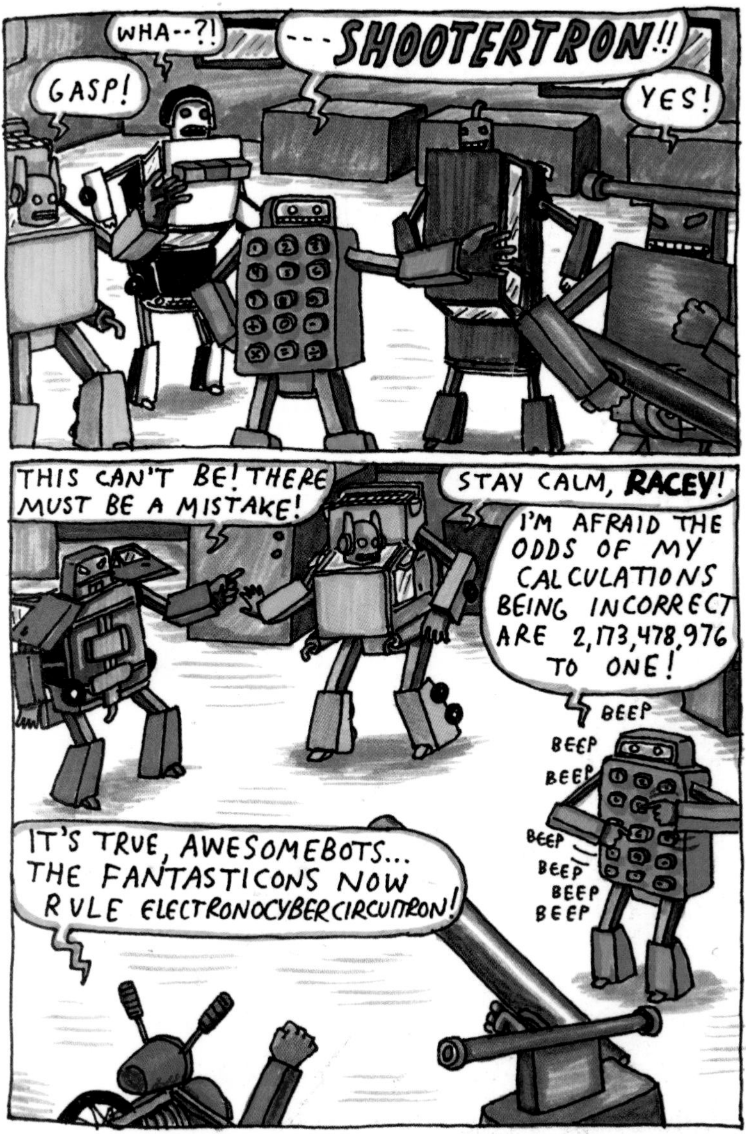
WHA--?!
---SHOOTERTRON!!
GASP!
YES!
THIS CAN'T BE! THERE MUST BE A MISTAKE!
STAY CALM, RACEY!
I'M AFRAID THE ODDS OF MY CALCULATIONS BEING INCORRECT ARE 2,173,478,976 TO ONE!
BEEP
BEEP
BEEP
BEEP
BEEP
BEEP
BEEP
IT'S TRUE, AWESOMEBOTS... THE FANTASTICONS NOW RULE ELECTRONOCYBERCIRCUITRON!

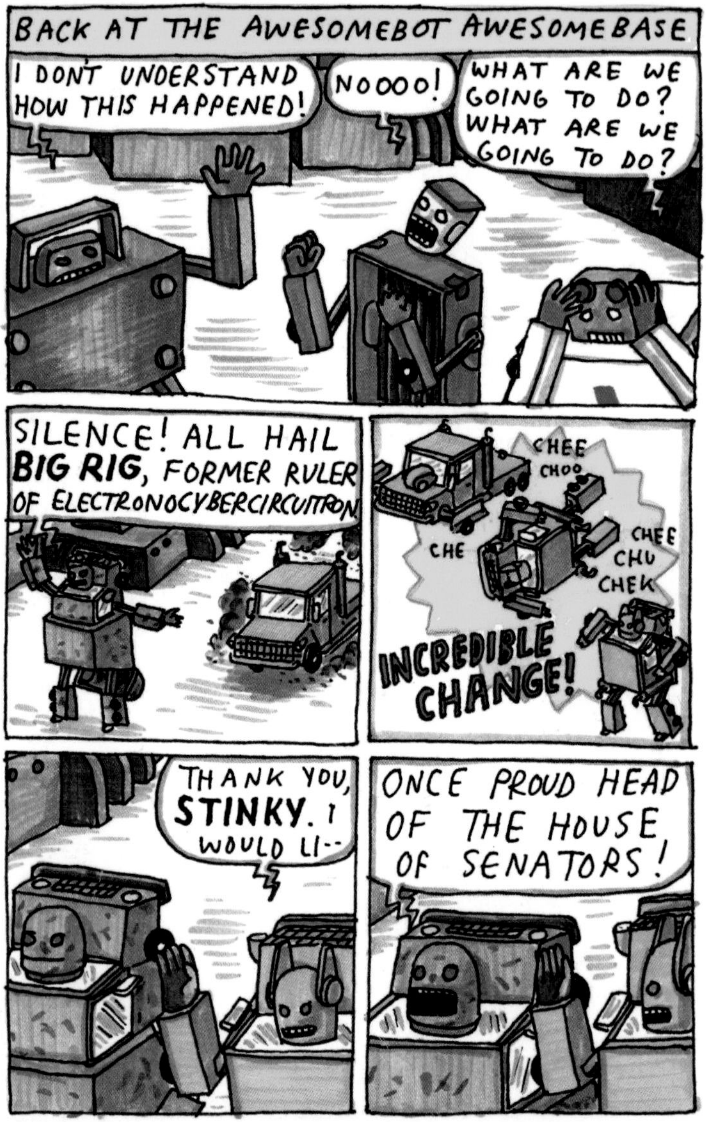
BACK AT THE AWESOMEBOT AWESOMEBASE
I DON'T UNDERSTAND HOW THIS HAPPENED!
NOOOO!
WHAT ARE WE GOING TO DO? WHAT ARE WE GOING TO DO?
SILENCE! ALL HAIL **BIG RIG**, FORMER RULER OF ELECTRONOCYBERCIRCUITRON
CHEE CHOO
CHE
CHEE CHU CHEK
INCREDIBLE CHANGE!
THANK YOU, **STINKY**. I WOULD LI--
ONCE PROUD HEAD OF THE HOUSE OF SENATORS!

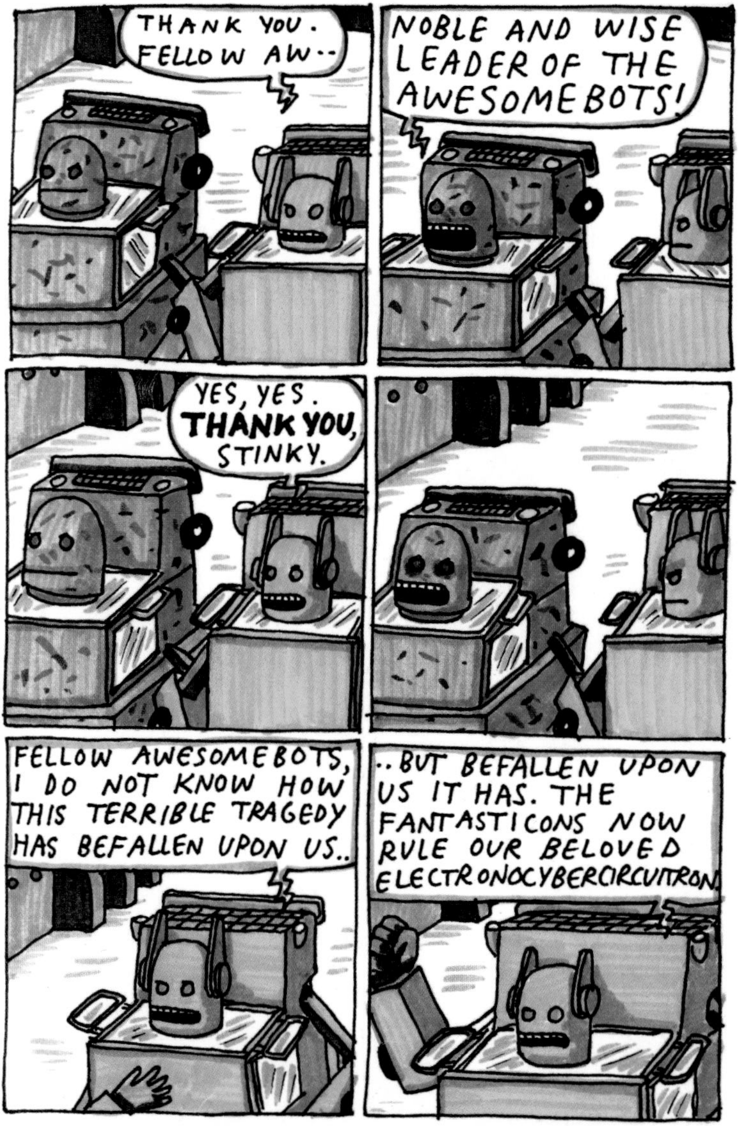
THANK YOU. FELLOW AW..
NOBLE AND WISE LEADER OF THE AWESOMEBOTS!
YES, YES. **THANK YOU,** STINKY.
FELLOW AWESOMEBOTS, I DO NOT KNOW HOW THIS TERRIBLE TRAGEDY HAS BEFALLEN UPON US..
..BUT BEFALLEN UPON US IT HAS. THE FANTASTICONS NOW RULE OUR BELOVED ELECTRONOCYBERCIRCUITRON.

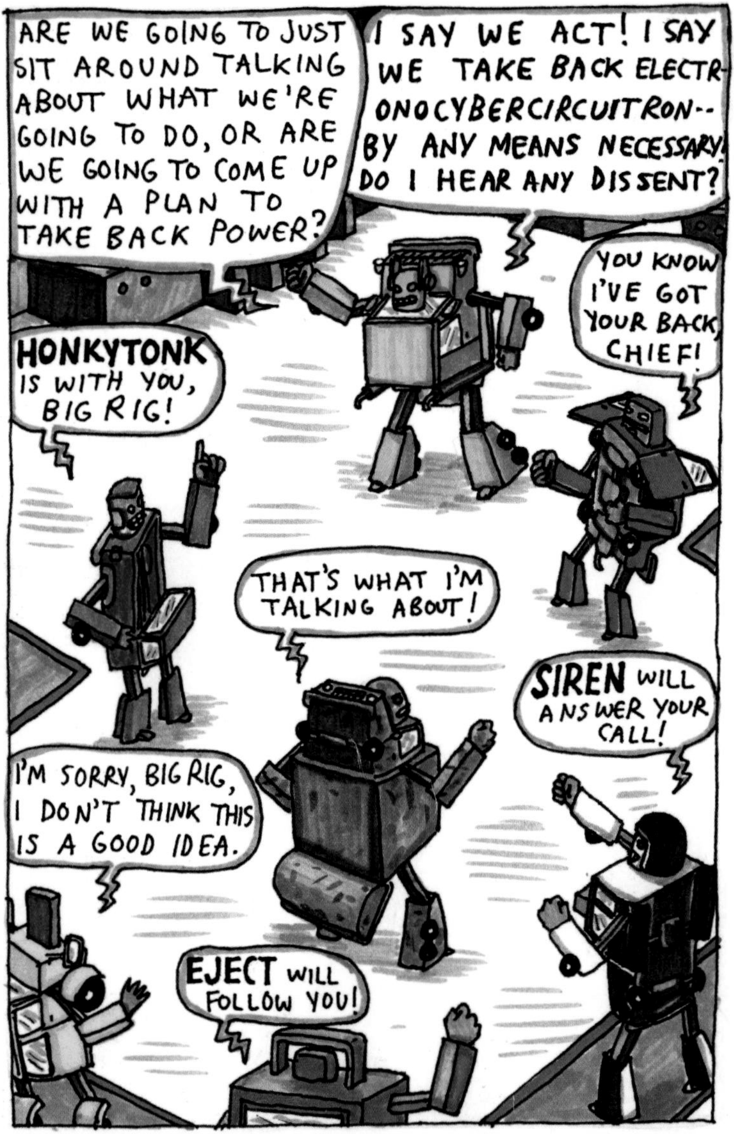
ARE WE GOING TO JUST SIT AROUND TALKING ABOUT WHAT WE'RE GOING TO DO, OR ARE WE GOING TO COME UP WITH A PLAN TO TAKE BACK POWER?
I SAY WE ACT! I SAY WE TAKE BACK ELECTR-ONOCYBERCIRCUITRON-- BY ANY MEANS NECESSARY! DO I HEAR ANY DISSENT?
YOU KNOW I'VE GOT YOUR BACK, CHIEF!
HONKYTONK IS WITH YOU, BIG RIG!
THAT'S WHAT I'M TALKING ABOUT!
SIREN WILL ANSWER YOUR CALL!
I'M SORRY, BIG RIG, I DON'T THINK THIS IS A GOOD IDEA.
EJECT WILL FOLLOW YOU!

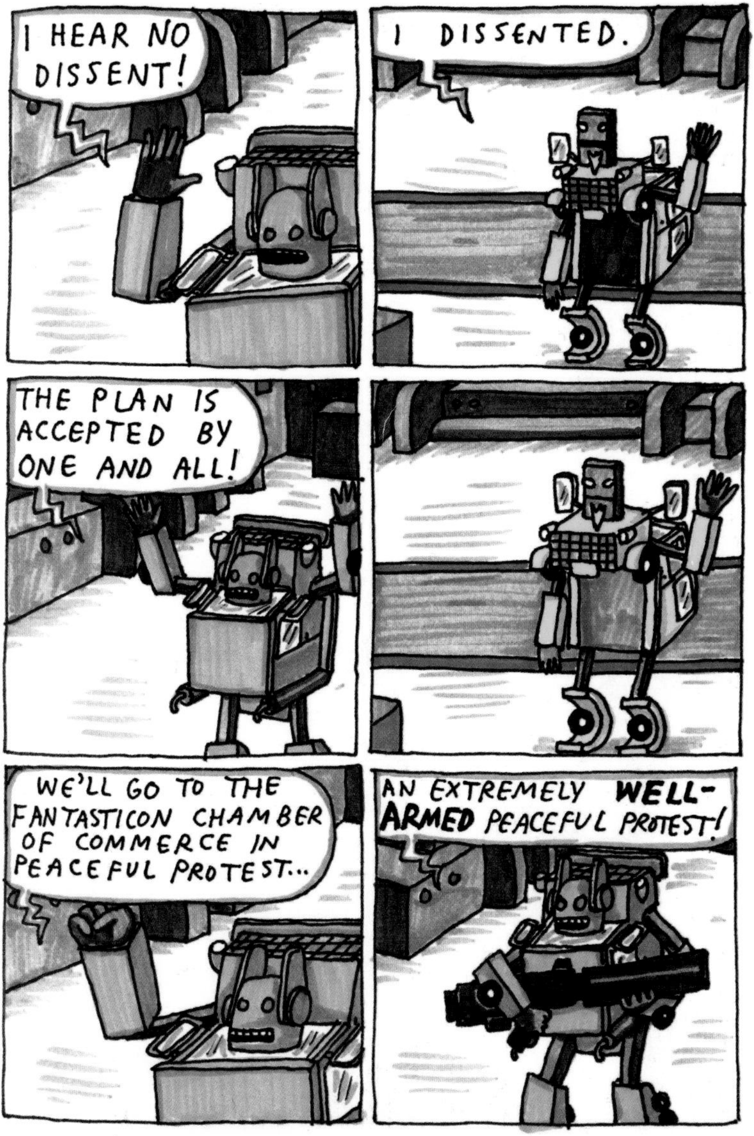
I HEAR NO DISSENT!
I DISSENTED.
THE PLAN IS ACCEPTED BY ONE AND ALL!
WE'LL GO TO THE FANTASTICON CHAMBER OF COMMERCE IN PEACEFUL PROTEST...
AN EXTREMELY WELL-ARMED PEACEFUL PROTEST!

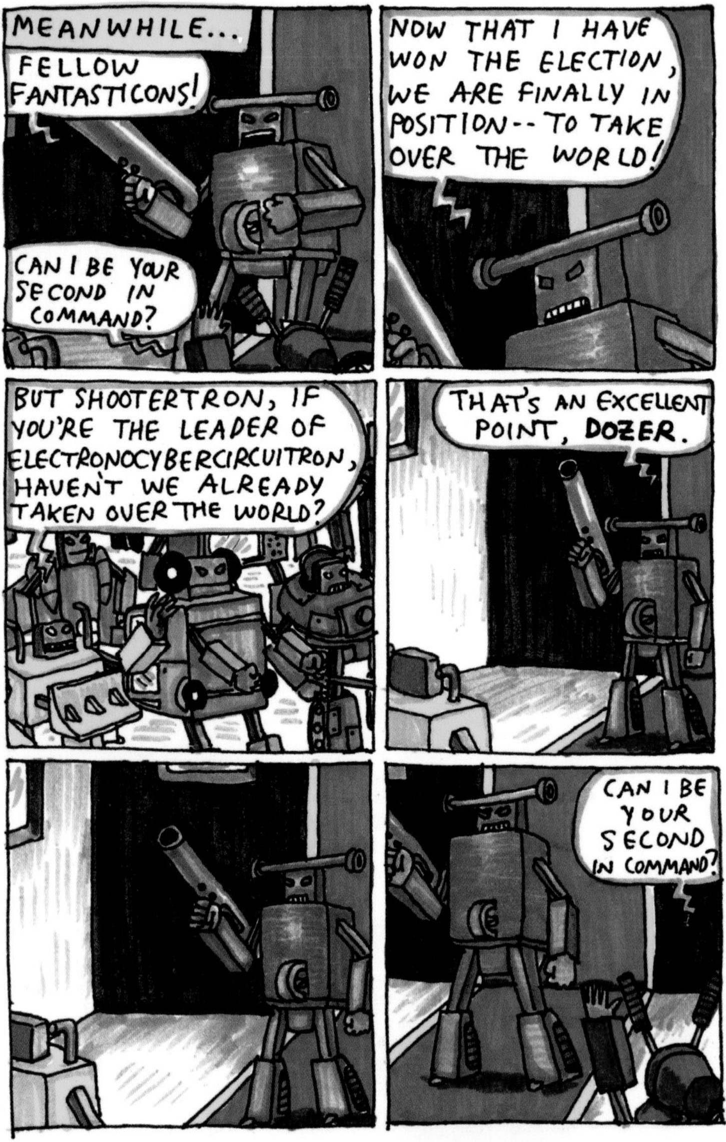
MEANWHILE...
FELLOW FANTASTICONS!
CAN I BE YOUR SECOND IN COMMAND?
NOW THAT I HAVE WON THE ELECTION, WE ARE FINALLY IN POSITION-- TO TAKE OVER THE WORLD!
BUT SHOOTERTRON, IF YOU'RE THE LEADER OF ELECTRONOCYBERCIRCUITRON, HAVEN'T WE ALREADY TAKEN OVER THE WORLD?
THAT'S AN EXCELLENT POINT, DOZER.
CAN I BE YOUR SECOND IN COMMAND?

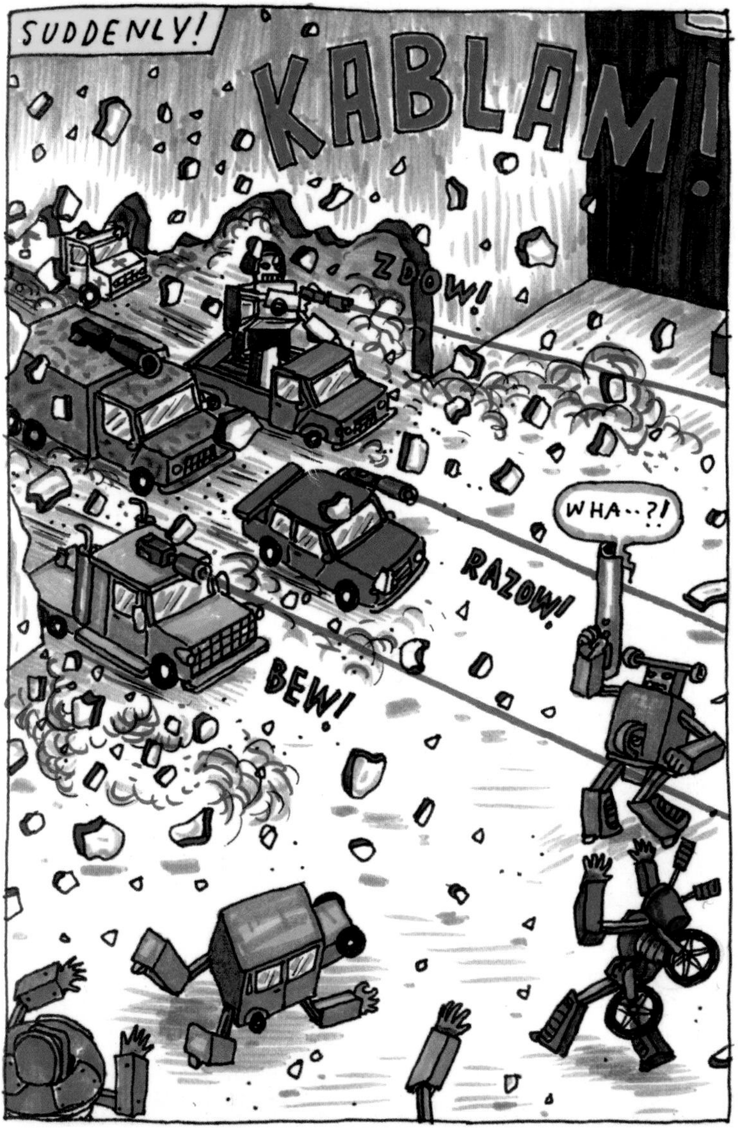
SUDDENLY!
KABLAM!
ZDOW!
WHA..?!
RAZOW!
BEW!

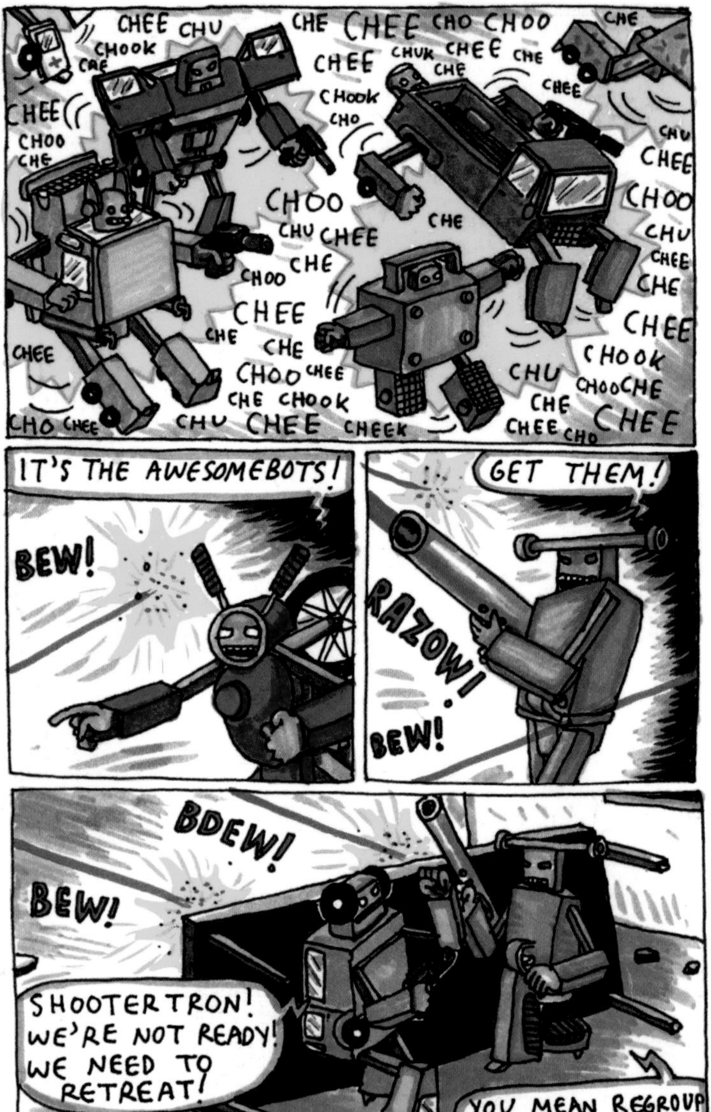
CHEE CHU
CHOOK
CHE
CHE CHEE CHO CHOO
CHE
CHEE
CHUK CHEE CHE
CHE
CHEE
CHOOK
CHO
CHEE
CHOO
CHE
CHU
CHEE
CHOO
CHOO
CHU CHEE
CHE
CHE
CHU
CHEE
CHE
CHOO
CHEE
CHE
CHE
CHEE
CHOOK
CHOO CHEE
CHE CHOOK
CHU
CHOOCHE
CHE
CHO CHEE
CHU CHEE
CHEEK
CHEE CHO
CHEE
IT'S THE AWESOMEBOTS!
BEW!
GET THEM!
RAZOW!
BEW!
BDEW!
BEW!
SHOOTERTRON! WE'RE NOT READY! WE NEED TO RETREAT!
YOU MEAN REGROUP

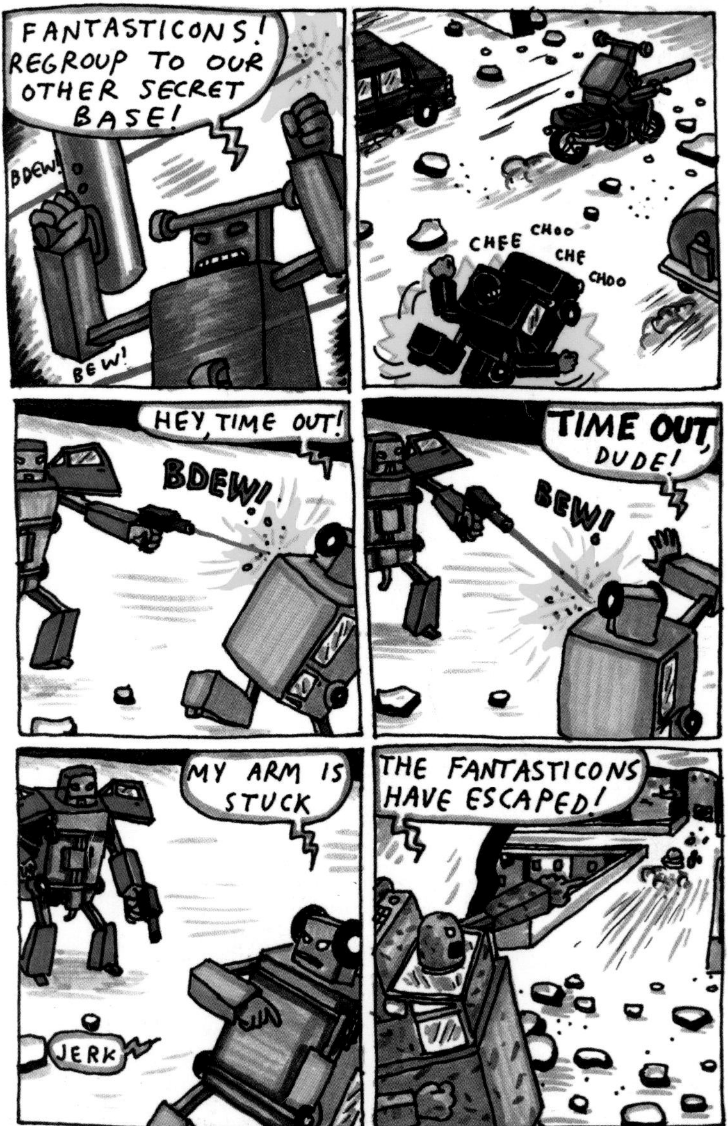
FANTASTICONS! REGROUP TO OUR OTHER SECRET BASE!
BDEW!
BEW!
CHEE
CHOO
CHE
CHOO
HEY, TIME OUT!
BDEW!
TIME OUT, DUDE!
BEW!
MY ARM IS STUCK
JERK
THE FANTASTICONS HAVE ESCAPED!

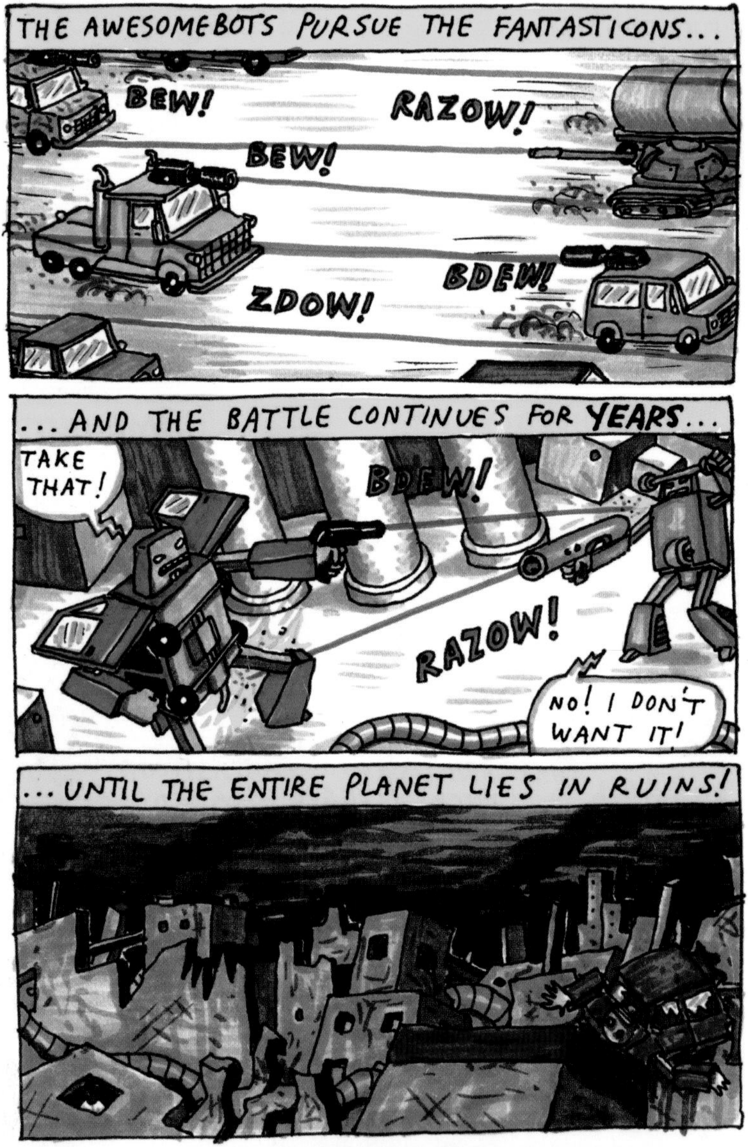
THE AWESOMEBOTS PURSUE THE FANTASTICONS...
BEW!
RAZOW!
BEW!
BDEW!
ZDOW!
...AND THE BATTLE CONTINUES FOR YEARS...
TAKE THAT!
BDEW!
RAZOW!
NO! I DON'T WANT IT!
...UNTIL THE ENTIRE PLANET LIES IN RUINS!

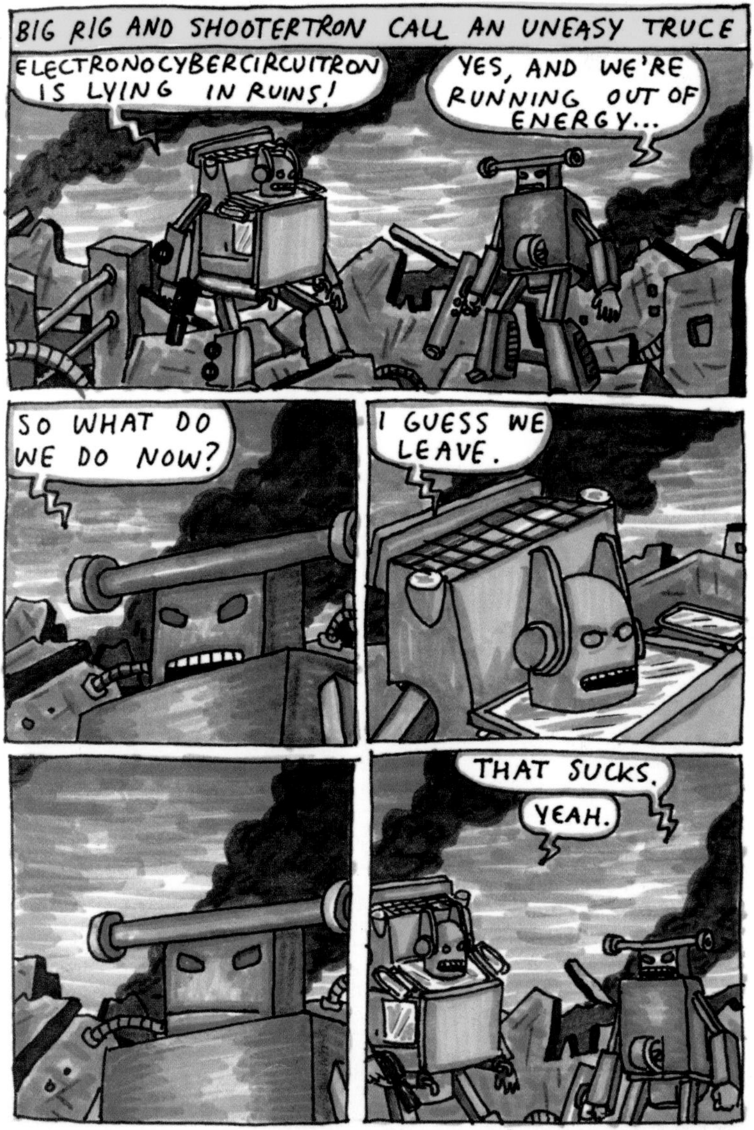
BIG RIG AND SHOOTERTRON CALL AN UNEASY TRUCE
ELECTRONOCYBERCIRCUITRON IS LYING IN RUINS!
YES, AND WE'RE RUNNING OUT OF ENERGY...
SO WHAT DO WE DO NOW?
I GUESS WE LEAVE.
THAT SUCKS.
YEAH.

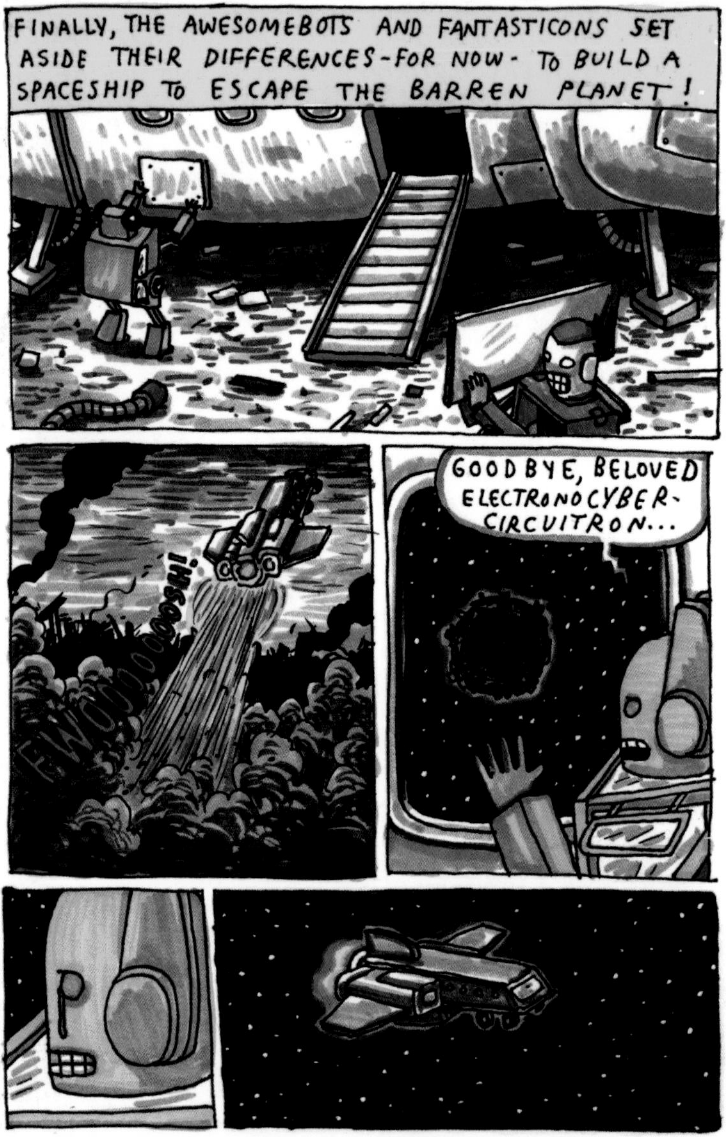
FINALLY, THE AWESOMEBOTS AND FANTASTICONS SET ASIDE THEIR DIFFERENCES - FOR NOW - TO BUILD A SPACESHIP TO ESCAPE THE BARREN PLANET!
GOODBYE, BELOVED ELECTRONOCYBER-CIRCUITRON...

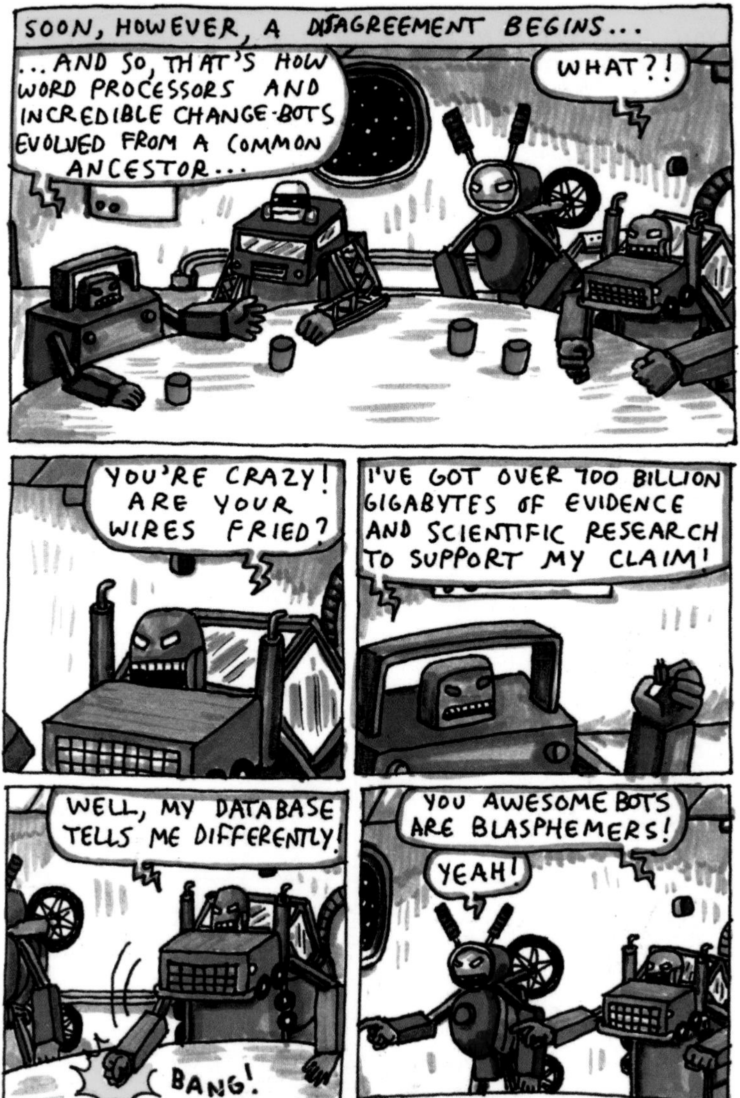
SOON, HOWEVER, A DISAGREEMENT BEGINS...
...AND SO, THAT'S HOW WORD PROCESSORS AND INCREDIBLE CHANGE-BOTS EVOLVED FROM A COMMON ANCESTOR...
WHAT?!
YOU'RE CRAZY! ARE YOUR WIRES FRIED?
I'VE GOT OVER 100 BILLION GIGABYTES OF EVIDENCE AND SCIENTIFIC RESEARCH TO SUPPORT MY CLAIM!
WELL, MY DATABASE TELLS ME DIFFERENTLY!
BANG!
YOU AWESOME BOTS ARE BLASPHEMERS!
YEAH!

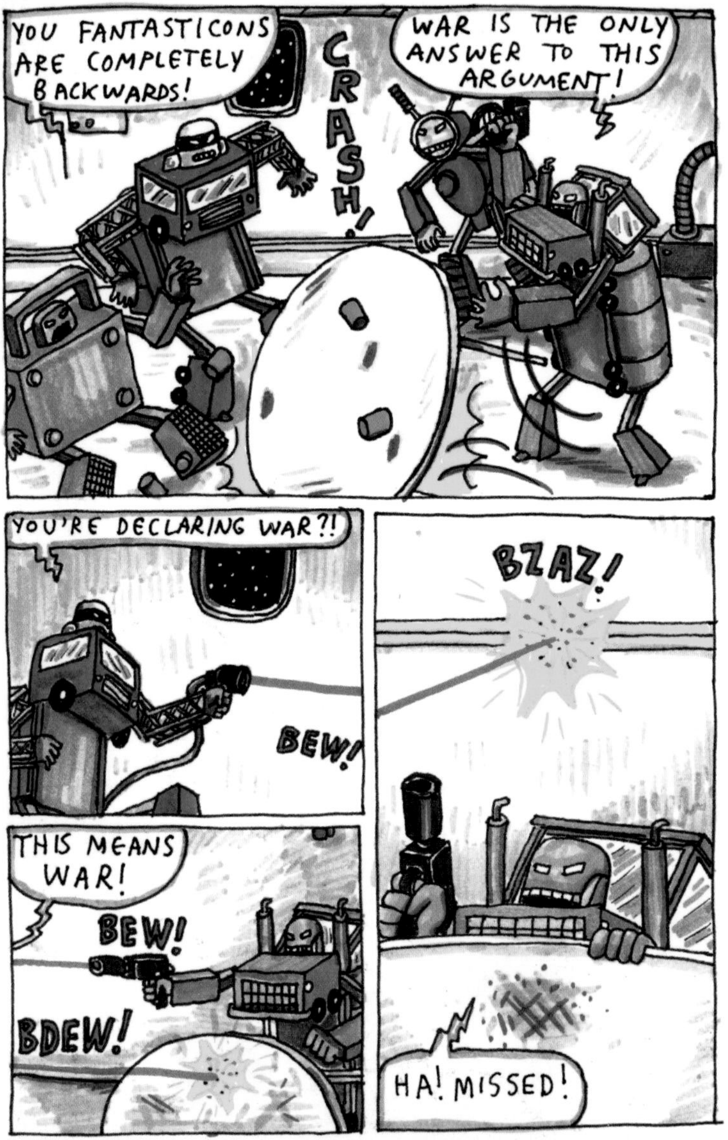
YOU FANTASTICONS ARE COMPLETELY BACKWARDS!
CRASH!
WAR IS THE ONLY ANSWER TO THIS ARGUMENT!
YOU'RE DECLARING WAR?!
BEW!
BZAZ!
THIS MEANS WAR!
BEW!
BDEW!
HA! MISSED!

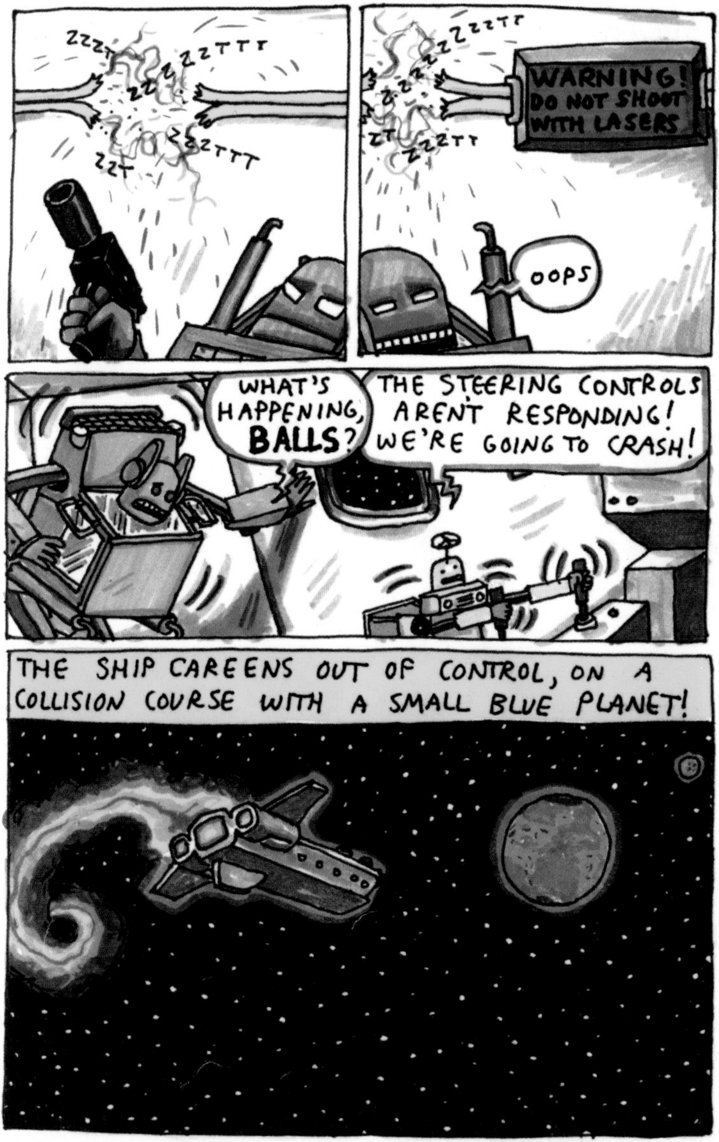
ZZZT
ZZZZTTT
ZZZ
ZZZTTT
ZZT
ZZZZZTT
WARNING! DO NOT SHOOT WITH LASERS
ZT
ZZZTT
OOPS
WHAT'S HAPPENING, BALLS?
THE STEERING CONTROLS AREN'T RESPONDING! WE'RE GOING TO CRASH!
THE SHIP CAREENS OUT OF CONTROL, ON A COLLISION COURSE WITH A SMALL BLUE PLANET!

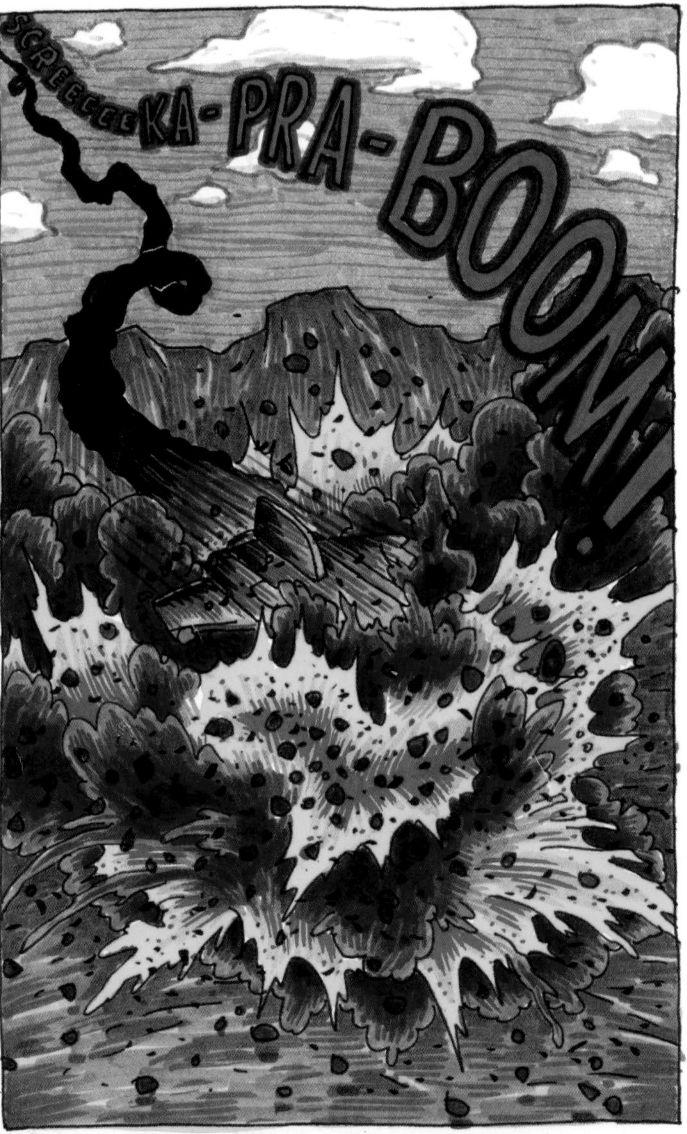
SCREEEEEEKA-PRA-BOOM!!

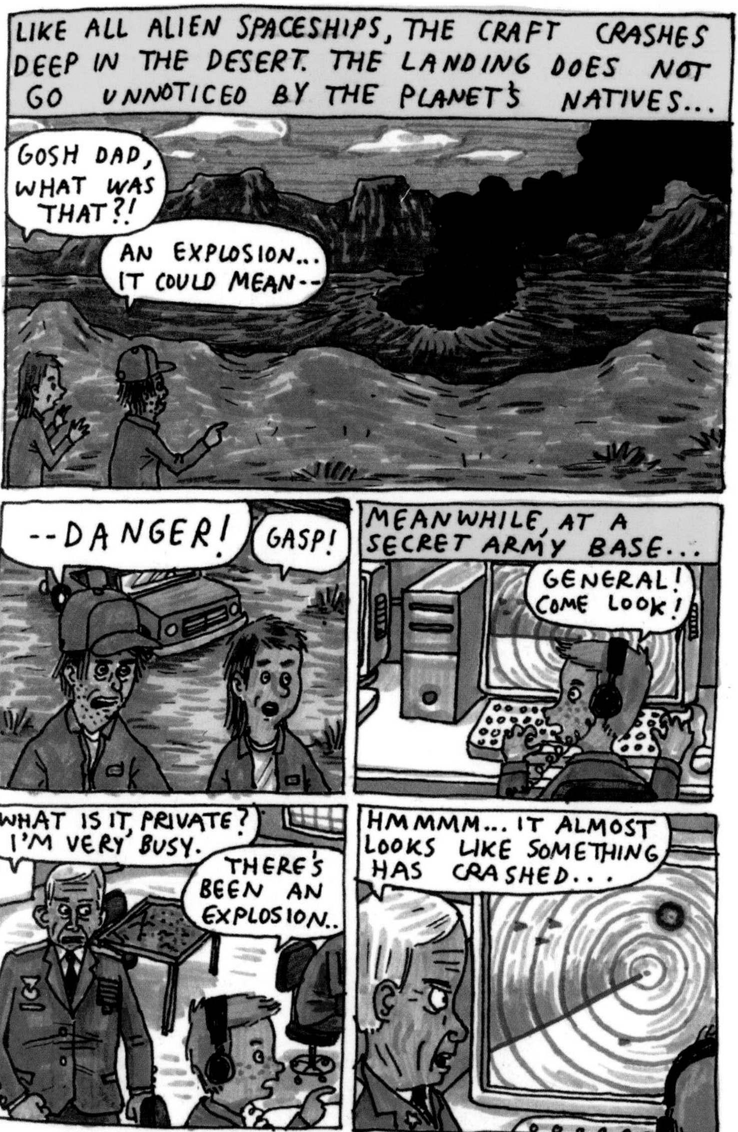
LIKE ALL ALIEN SPACESHIPS, THE CRAFT CRASHES DEEP IN THE DESERT. THE LANDING DOES NOT GO UNNOTICED BY THE PLANET'S NATIVES...
GOSH DAD, WHAT WAS THAT?!
AN EXPLOSION... IT COULD MEAN--
--DANGER!
GASP!
MEANWHILE, AT A SECRET ARMY BASE...
GENERAL! COME LOOK!
WHAT IS IT, PRIVATE? I'M VERY BUSY.
THERE'S BEEN AN EXPLOSION..
HMMMM... IT ALMOST LOOKS LIKE SOMETHING HAS CRASHED...

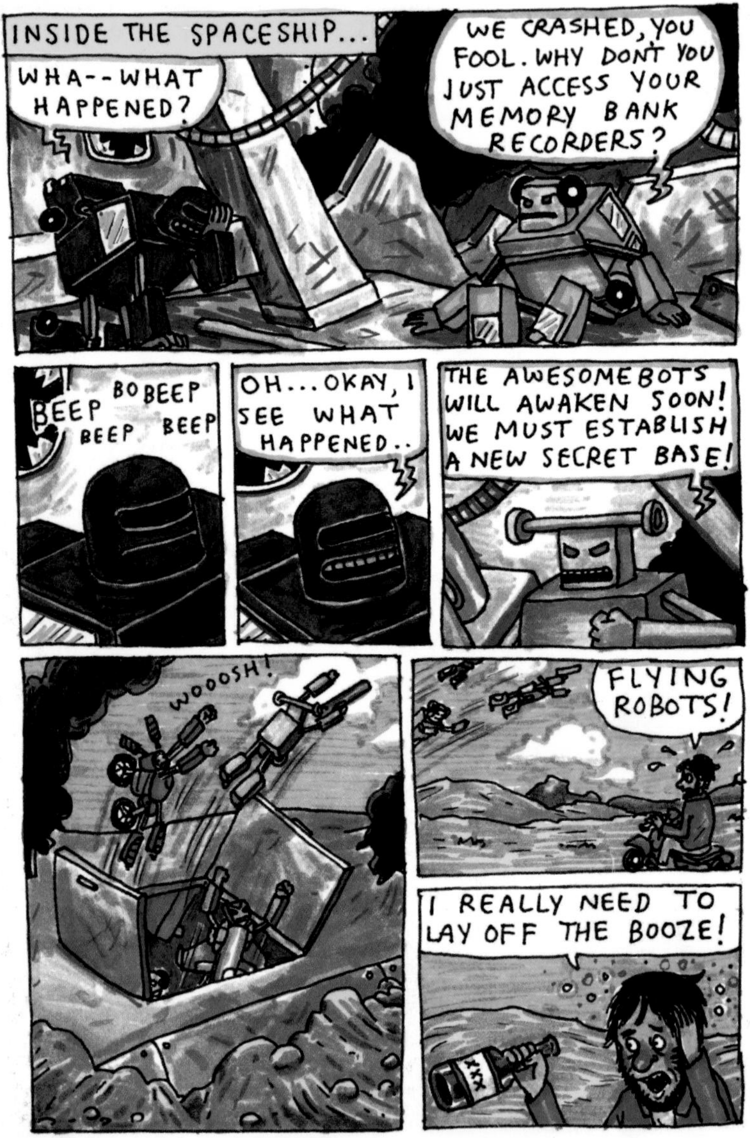
INSIDE THE SPACESHIP...
WHA--WHAT HAPPENED?
WE CRASHED, YOU FOOL. WHY DON'T YOU JUST ACCESS YOUR MEMORY BANK RECORDERS?
BEEP BO BEEP BEEP BEEP
OH... OKAY, I SEE WHAT HAPPENED..
THE AWESOMEBOTS WILL AWAKEN SOON! WE MUST ESTABLISH A NEW SECRET BASE!
WOOOSH!
FLYING ROBOTS!
I REALLY NEED TO LAY OFF THE BOOZE!
XXX

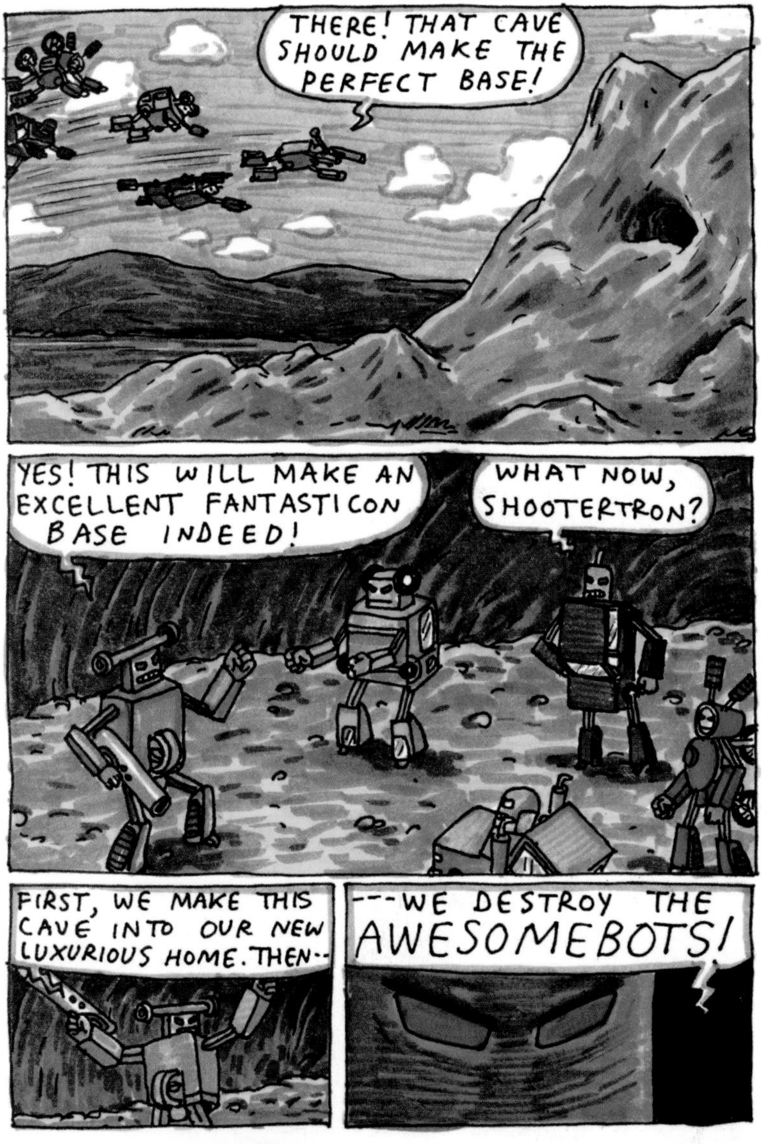
THERE! THAT CAVE SHOULD MAKE THE PERFECT BASE!
YES! THIS WILL MAKE AN EXCELLENT FANTASTICON BASE INDEED!
WHAT NOW, SHOOTERTRON?
FIRST, WE MAKE THIS CAVE INTO OUR NEW LUXURIOUS HOME. THEN--
---WE DESTROY THE AWESOMEBOTS!

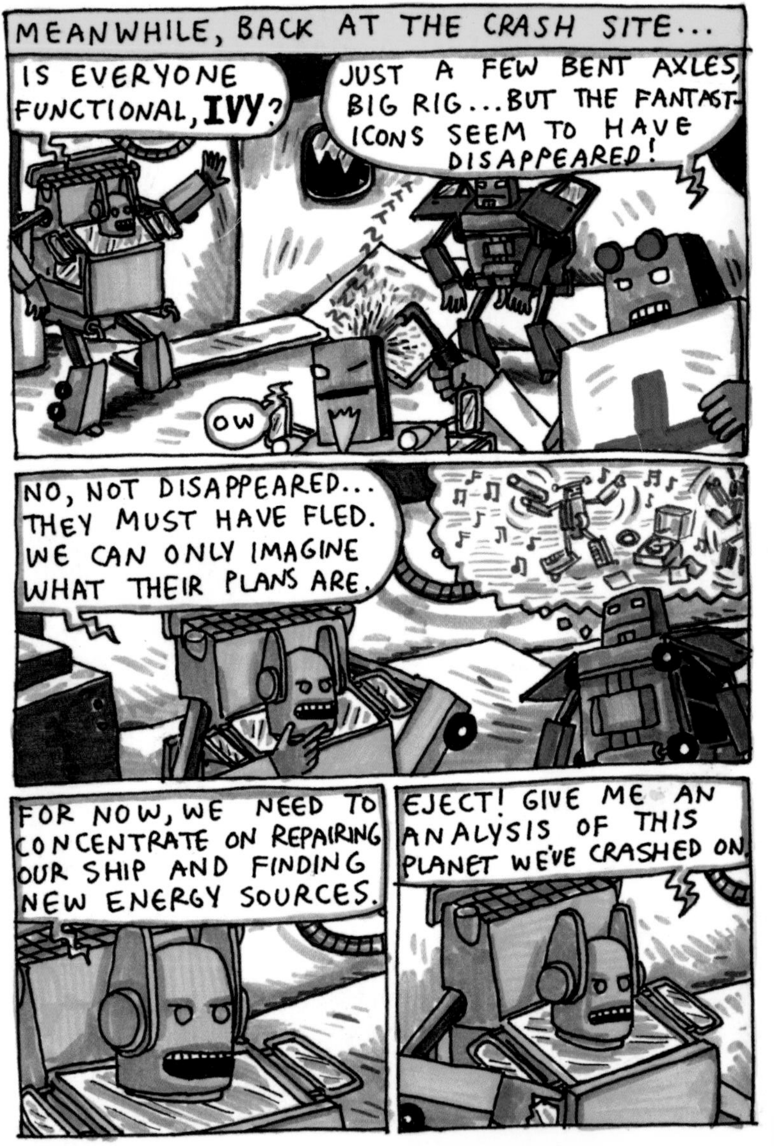
MEANWHILE, BACK AT THE CRASH SITE...
IS EVERYONE FUNCTIONAL, IVY?
JUST A FEW BENT AXLES, BIG RIG... BUT THE FANTASTICONS SEEM TO HAVE DISAPPEARED!
OW
NO, NOT DISAPPEARED... THEY MUST HAVE FLED. WE CAN ONLY IMAGINE WHAT THEIR PLANS ARE.
FOR NOW, WE NEED TO CONCENTRATE ON REPAIRING OUR SHIP AND FINDING NEW ENERGY SOURCES.
EJECT! GIVE ME AN ANALYSIS OF THIS PLANET WE'VE CRASHED ON.

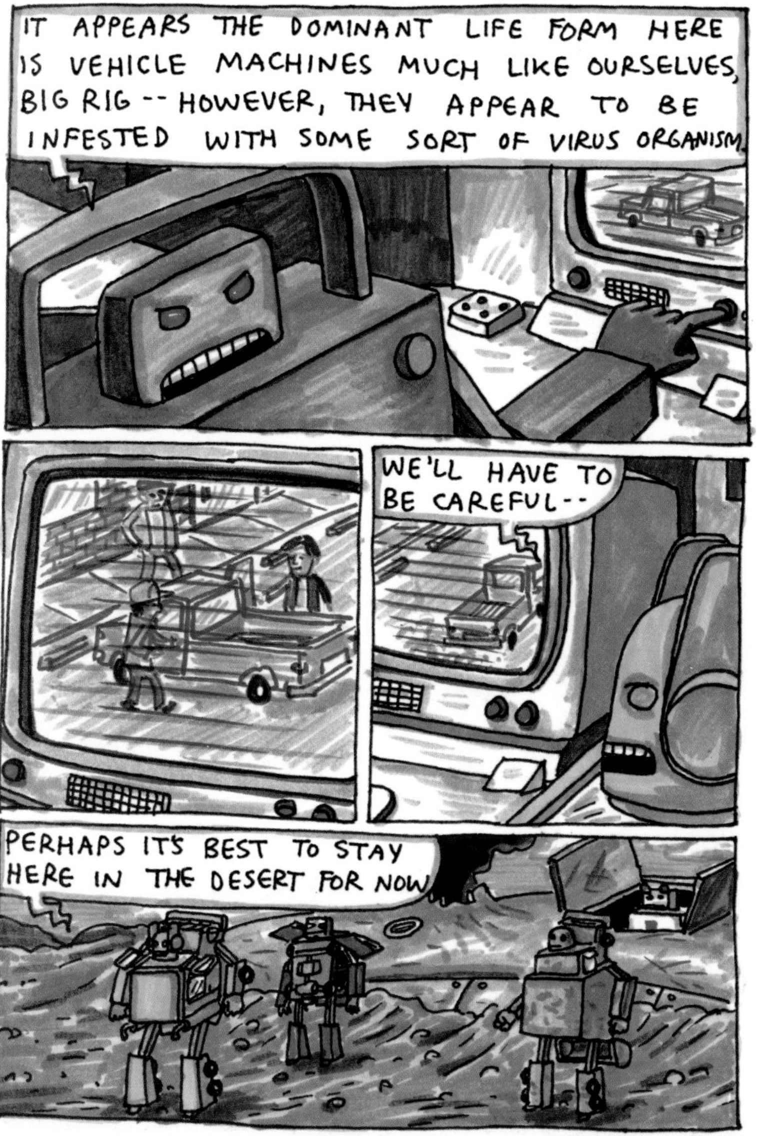
IT APPEARS THE DOMINANT LIFE FORM HERE IS VEHICLE MACHINES MUCH LIKE OURSELVES, BIG RIG -- HOWEVER, THEY APPEAR TO BE INFESTED WITH SOME SORT OF VIRUS ORGANISM.
WE'LL HAVE TO BE CAREFUL --
PERHAPS IT'S BEST TO STAY HERE IN THE DESERT FOR NOW

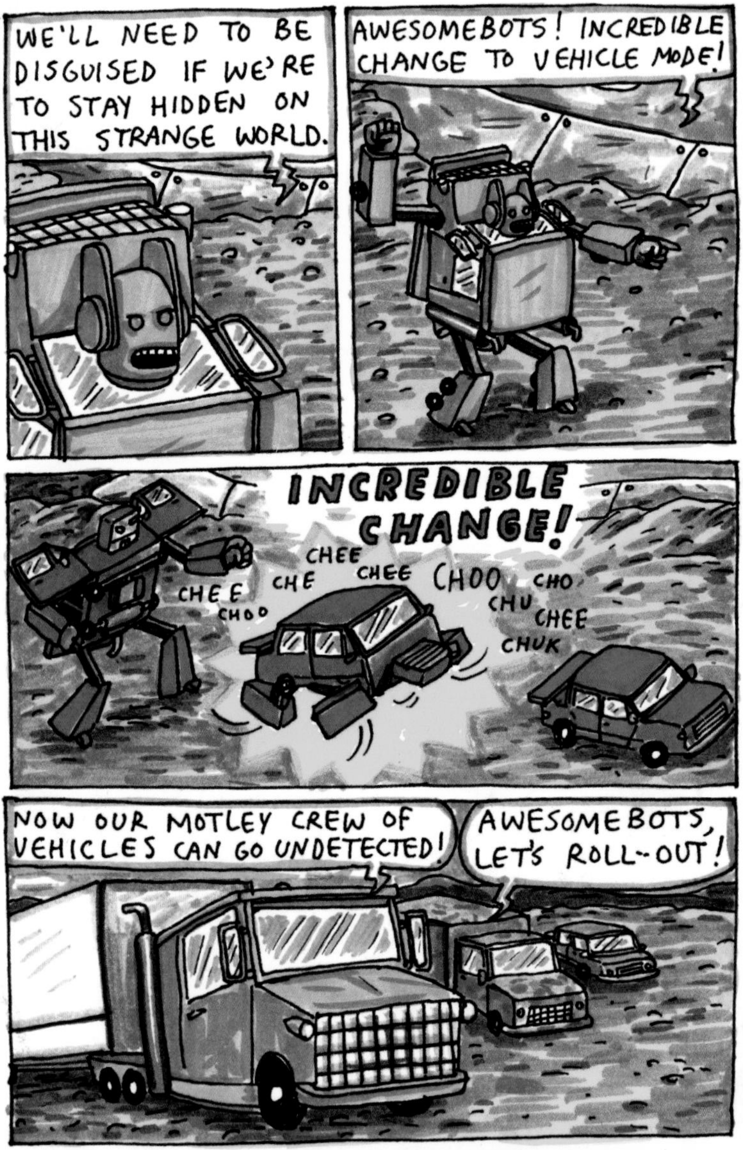

WE'LL NEED TO BE DISGUISED IF WE'RE TO STAY HIDDEN ON THIS STRANGE WORLD.
AWESOMEBOTS! INCREDIBLE CHANGE TO VEHICLE MODE!
INCREDIBLE CHANGE!
CHEE CHE CHEE CHOO CHO CHEE CHOO CHU CHEE CHUK
NOW OUR MOTLEY CREW OF VEHICLES CAN GO UNDETECTED!
AWESOMEBOTS, LET'S ROLL-OUT!

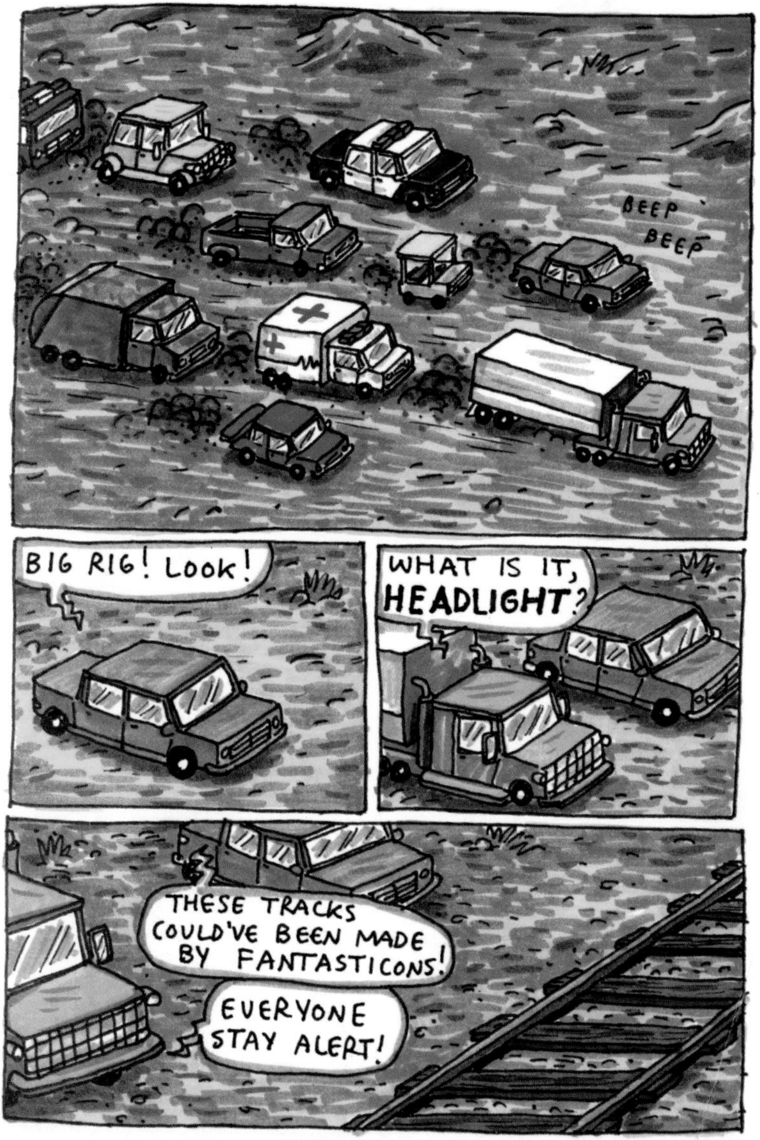
BEEP BEEP
BIG RIG! LOOK!
WHAT IS IT, HEADLIGHT?
THESE TRACKS COULD'VE BEEN MADE BY FANTASTICONS!
EVERYONE STAY ALERT!

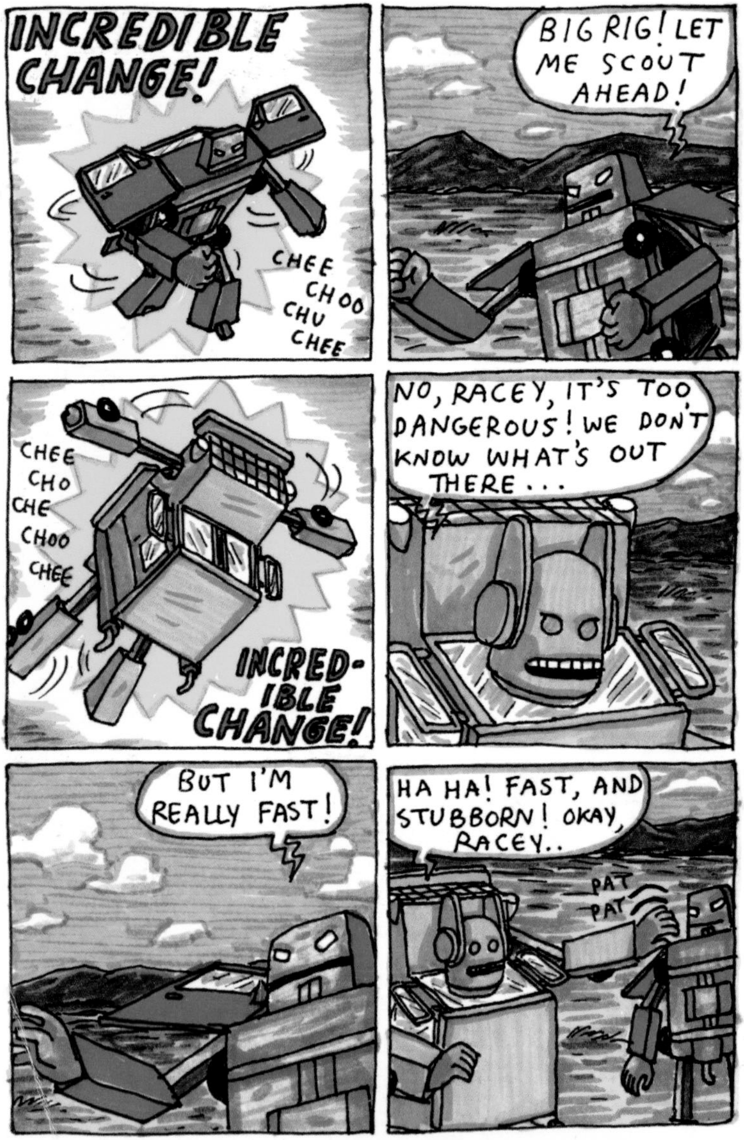
INCREDIBLE CHANGE!
CHEE CHOO CHU CHEE
BIG RIG! LET ME SCOUT AHEAD!
CHEE CHO CHE CHOO CHEE
INCRED-IBLE CHANGE!
NO, RACEY, IT'S TOO DANGEROUS! WE DON'T KNOW WHAT'S OUT THERE...
BUT I'M REALLY FAST!
HA HA! FAST, AND STUBBORN! OKAY, RACEY..
PAT PAT

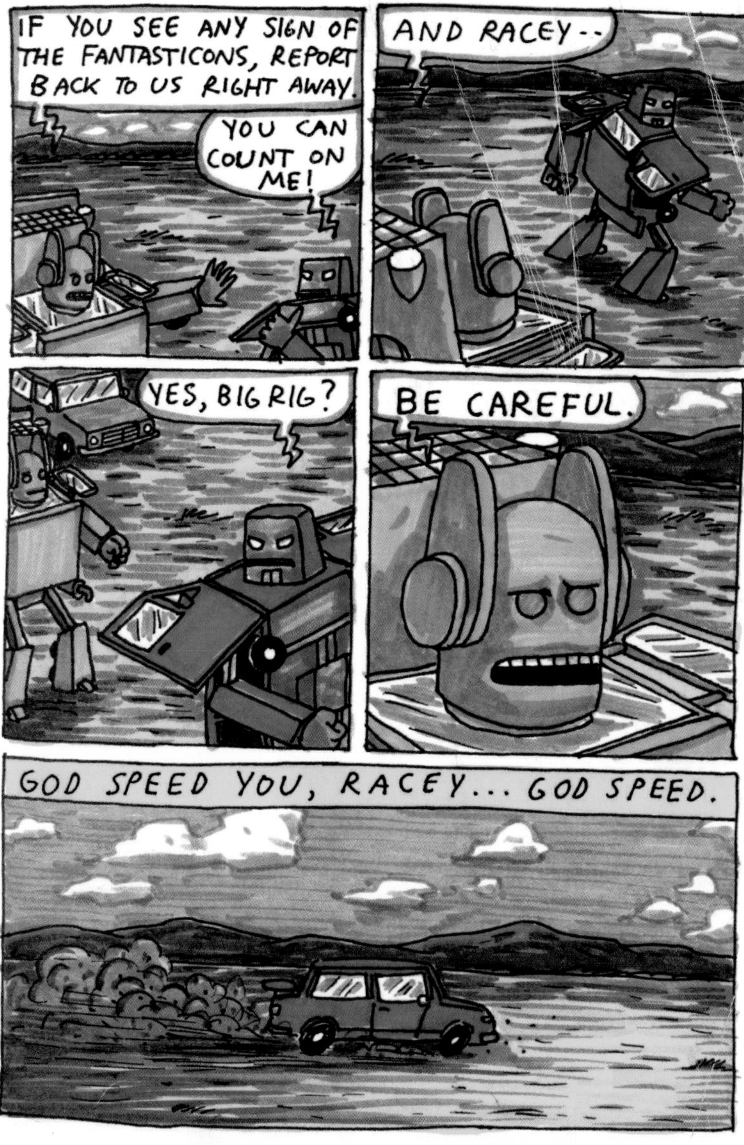
IF YOU SEE ANY SIGN OF THE FANTASTICONS, REPORT BACK TO US RIGHT AWAY.
YOU CAN COUNT ON ME!
AND RACEY--
YES, BIG RIG?
BE CAREFUL.
GOD SPEED YOU, RACEY... GOD SPEED.

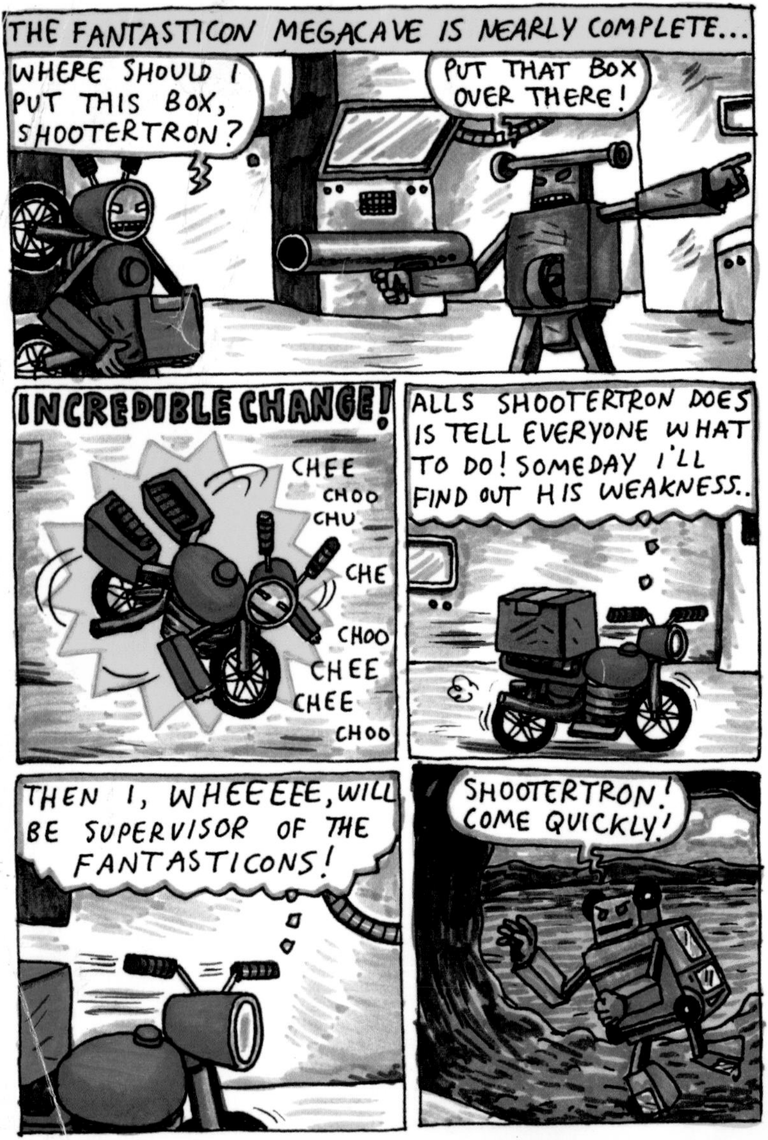
THE FANTASTICON MEGACAVE IS NEARLY COMPLETE...
WHERE SHOULD I PUT THIS BOX, SHOOTERTRON?
PUT THAT BOX OVER THERE!
INCREDIBLE CHANGE!
CHEE CHOO CHU CHE CHOO CHEE CHEE CHOO
ALLS SHOOTERTRON DOES IS TELL EVERYONE WHAT TO DO! SOMEDAY I'LL FIND OUT HIS WEAKNESS..
THEN I, WHEEEEE, WILL BE SUPERVISOR OF THE FANTASTICONS!
SHOOTERTRON! COME QUICKLY!

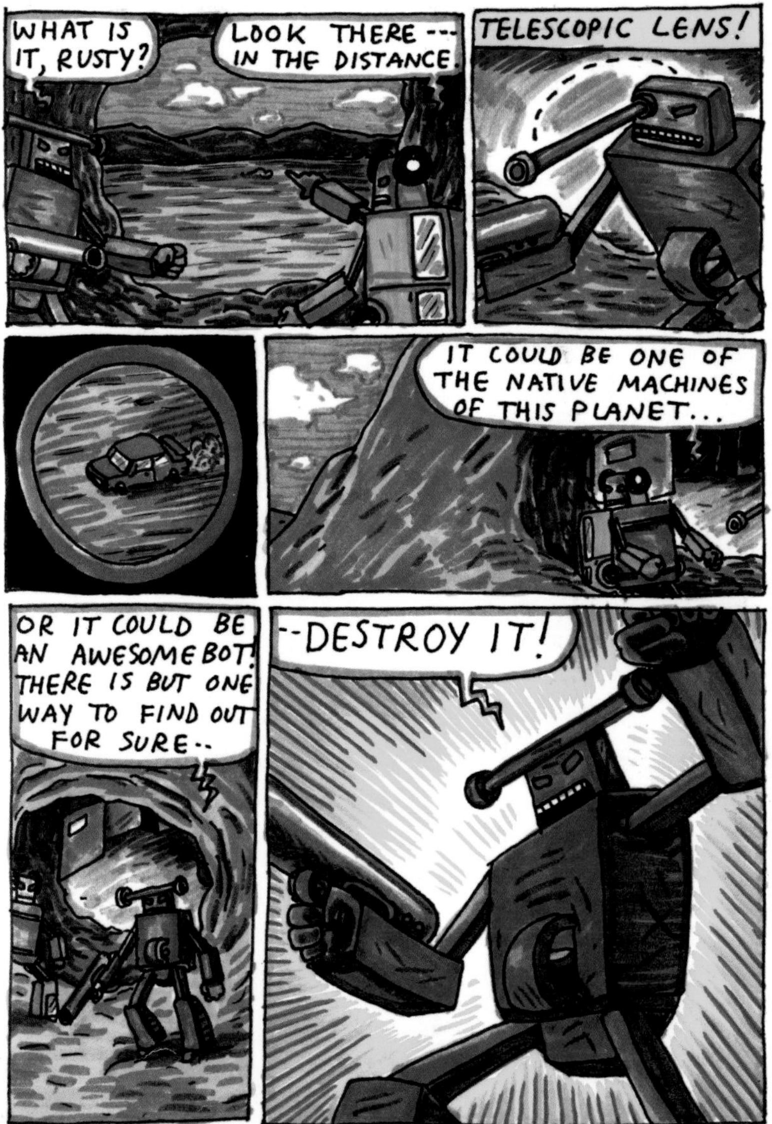
WHAT IS IT, RUSTY?
LOOK THERE --- IN THE DISTANCE.
TELESCOPIC LENS!
IT COULD BE ONE OF THE NATIVE MACHINES OF THIS PLANET...
OR IT COULD BE AN AWESOMEBOT! THERE IS BUT ONE WAY TO FIND OUT FOR SURE--
--DESTROY IT!

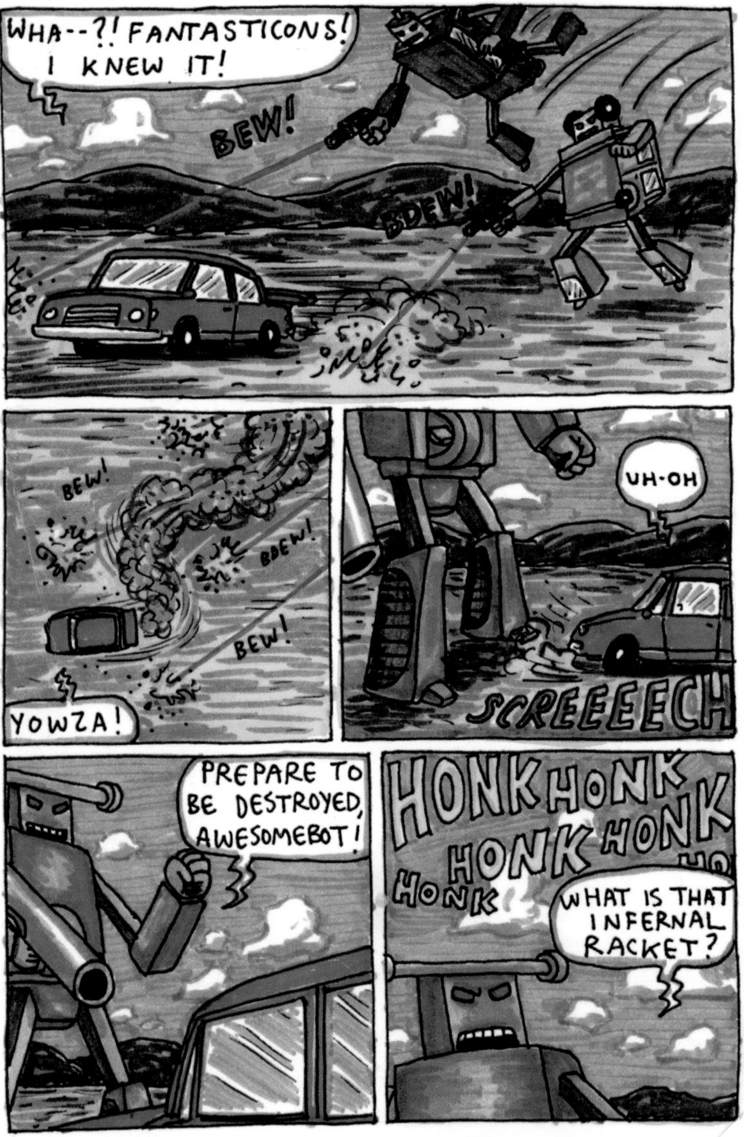
WHA--?! FANTASTICONS! I KNEW IT!
BEW!
BDEW!
BEW!
BDEW!
BEW!
YOWZA!
UH-OH
SCREEEEECH
PREPARE TO BE DESTROYED, AWESOMEBOT!
HONK HONK HONK HONK HONK
WHAT IS THAT INFERNAL RACKET?

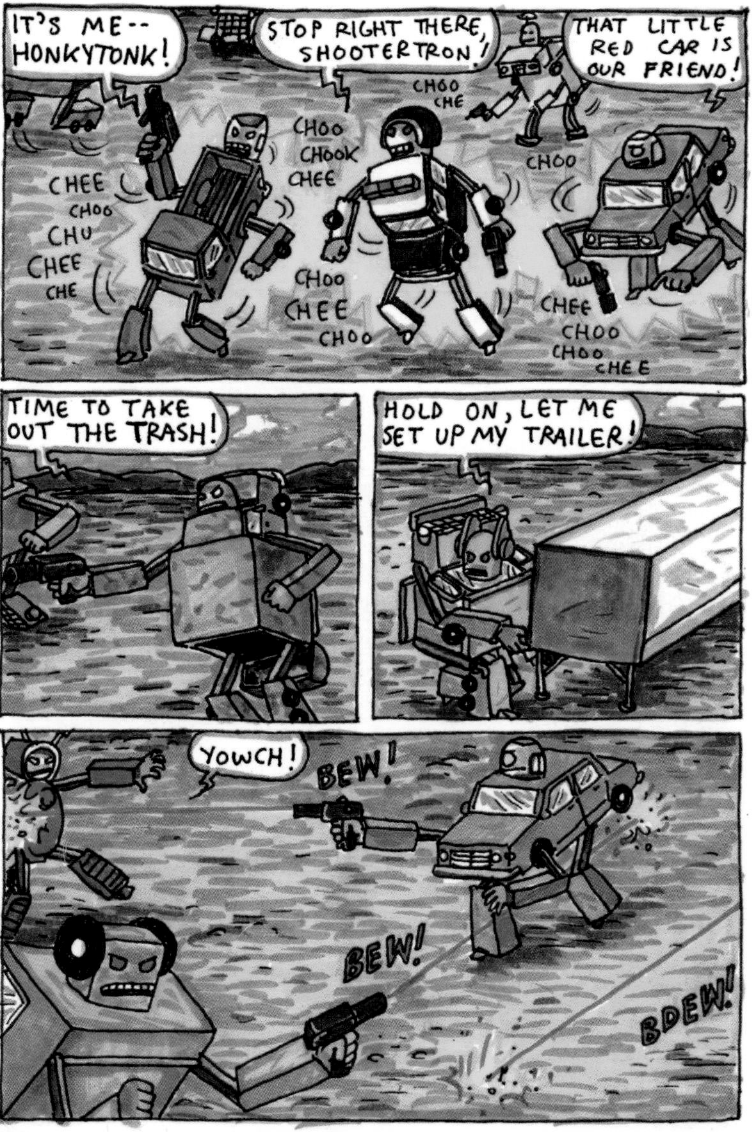
IT'S ME--
HONKYTONK!
STOP RIGHT THERE,
SHOOTERTRON!
THAT LITTLE
RED CAR IS
OUR FRIEND!
CHOO CHE
CHOO CHOOK CHEE
CHEE CHOO CHU CHEE CHE
CHOO
CHOO CHEE CHOO
CHEE CHOO CHOO CHEE
TIME TO TAKE
OUT THE TRASH!
HOLD ON, LET ME
SET UP MY TRAILER!
YOWCH!
BEW!
BEW!
BDEW!

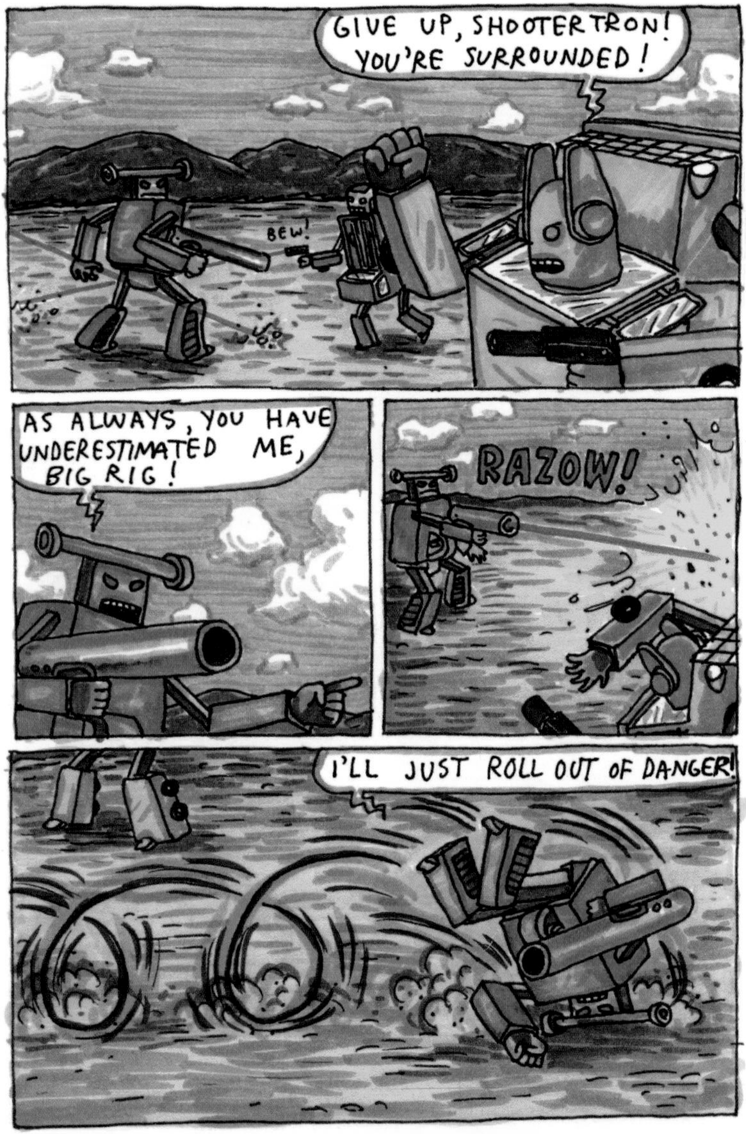
GIVE UP, SHOOTERTRON! YOU'RE SURROUNDED!
BEW!
AS ALWAYS, YOU HAVE UNDERESTIMATED ME, BIG RIG!
RAZOW!
I'LL JUST ROLL OUT OF DANGER!

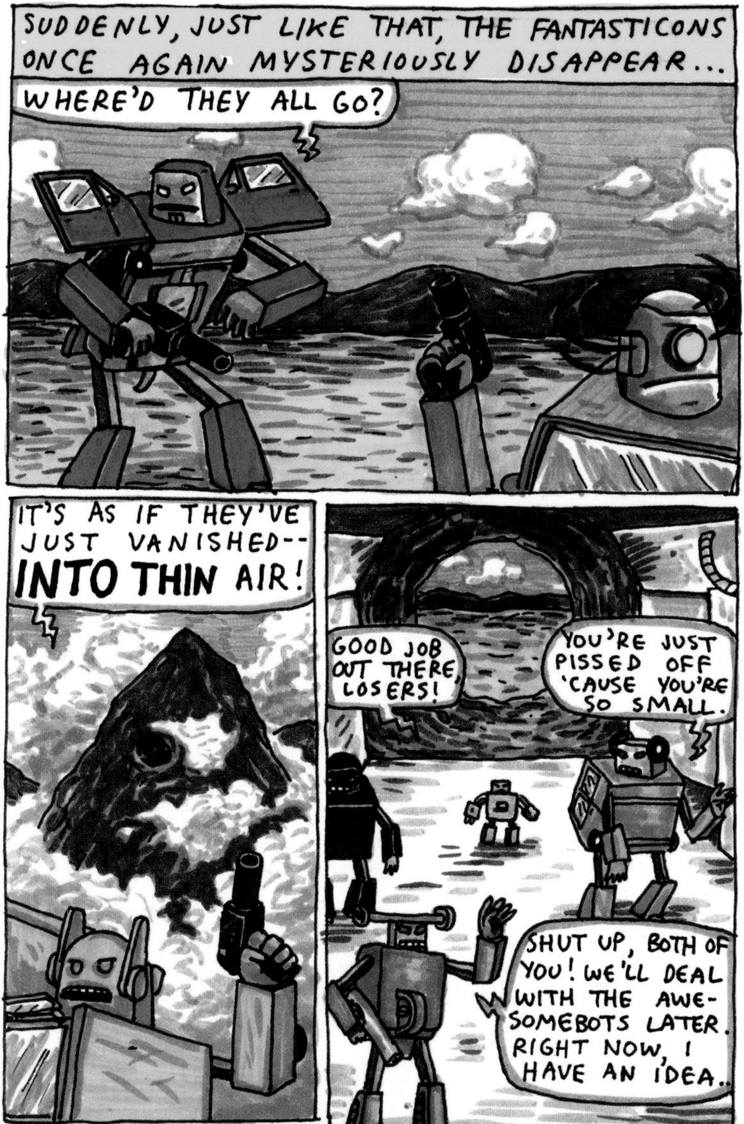
SUDDENLY, JUST LIKE THAT, THE FANTASTICONS ONCE AGAIN MYSTERIOUSLY DISAPPEAR...
WHERE'D THEY ALL GO?
IT'S AS IF THEY'VE JUST VANISHED-- INTO THIN AIR!
GOOD JOB OUT THERE, LOSERS!
YOU'RE JUST PISSED OFF 'CAUSE YOU'RE SO SMALL.
SHUT UP, BOTH OF YOU! WE'LL DEAL WITH THE AWE-SOMEBOTS LATER. RIGHT NOW, I HAVE AN IDEA..

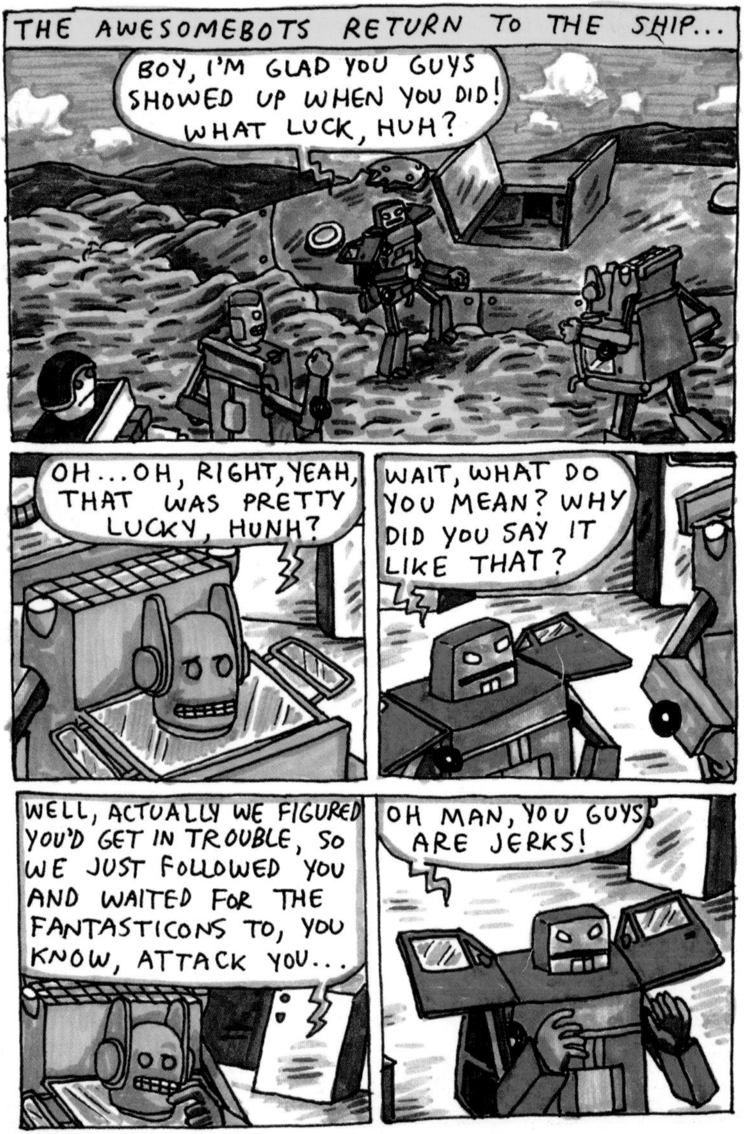
THE AWESOMEBOTS RETURN TO THE SHIP...
BOY, I'M GLAD YOU GUYS SHOWED UP WHEN YOU DID! WHAT LUCK, HUH?
OH...OH, RIGHT, YEAH, THAT WAS PRETTY LUCKY, HUNH?
WAIT, WHAT DO YOU MEAN? WHY DID YOU SAY IT LIKE THAT?
WELL, ACTUALLY WE FIGURED YOU'D GET IN TROUBLE, SO WE JUST FOLLOWED YOU AND WAITED FOR THE FANTASTICONS TO, YOU KNOW, ATTACK YOU...
OH MAN, YOU GUYS ARE JERKS!

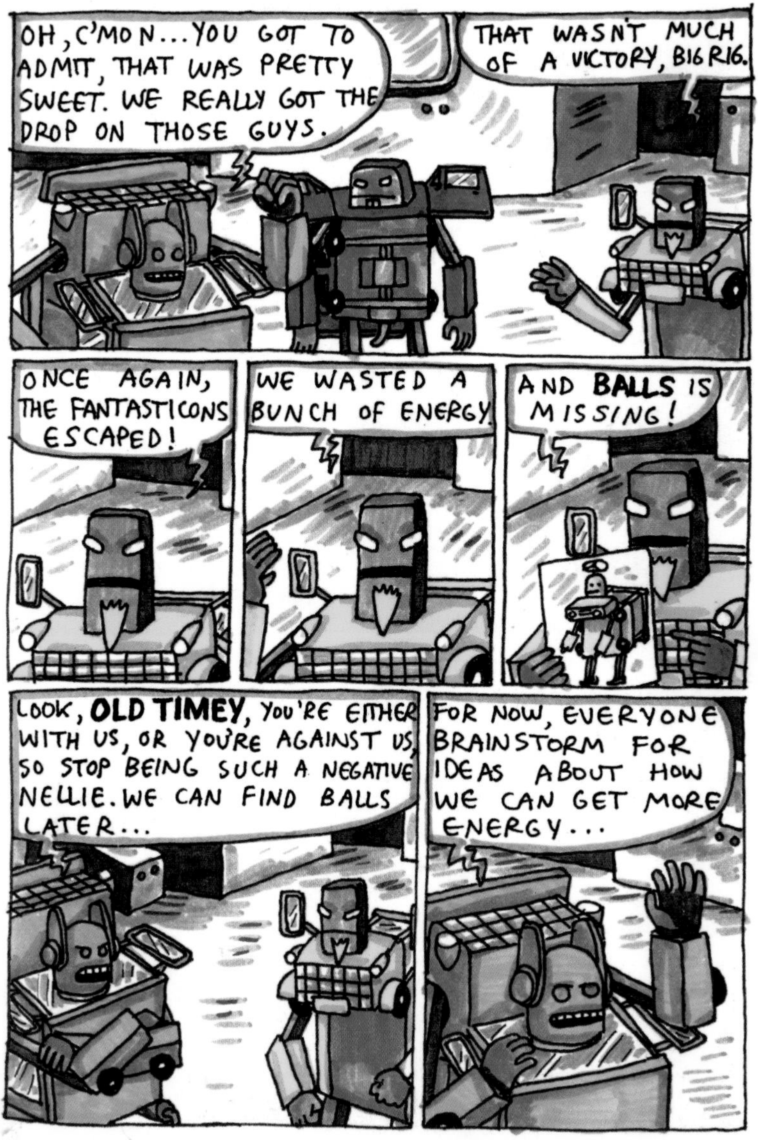
OH, C'MON... YOU GOT TO ADMIT, THAT WAS PRETTY SWEET. WE REALLY GOT THE DROP ON THOSE GUYS.
THAT WASN'T MUCH OF A VICTORY, BIG RIG.
ONCE AGAIN, THE FANTASTICONS ESCAPED!
WE WASTED A BUNCH OF ENERGY.
AND **BALLS** IS MISSING!
LOOK, **OLD TIMEY**, YOU'RE EITHER WITH US, OR YOU'RE AGAINST US, SO STOP BEING SUCH A NEGATIVE NELLIE. WE CAN FIND BALLS LATER...
FOR NOW, EVERYONE BRAINSTORM FOR IDEAS ABOUT HOW WE CAN GET MORE ENERGY...

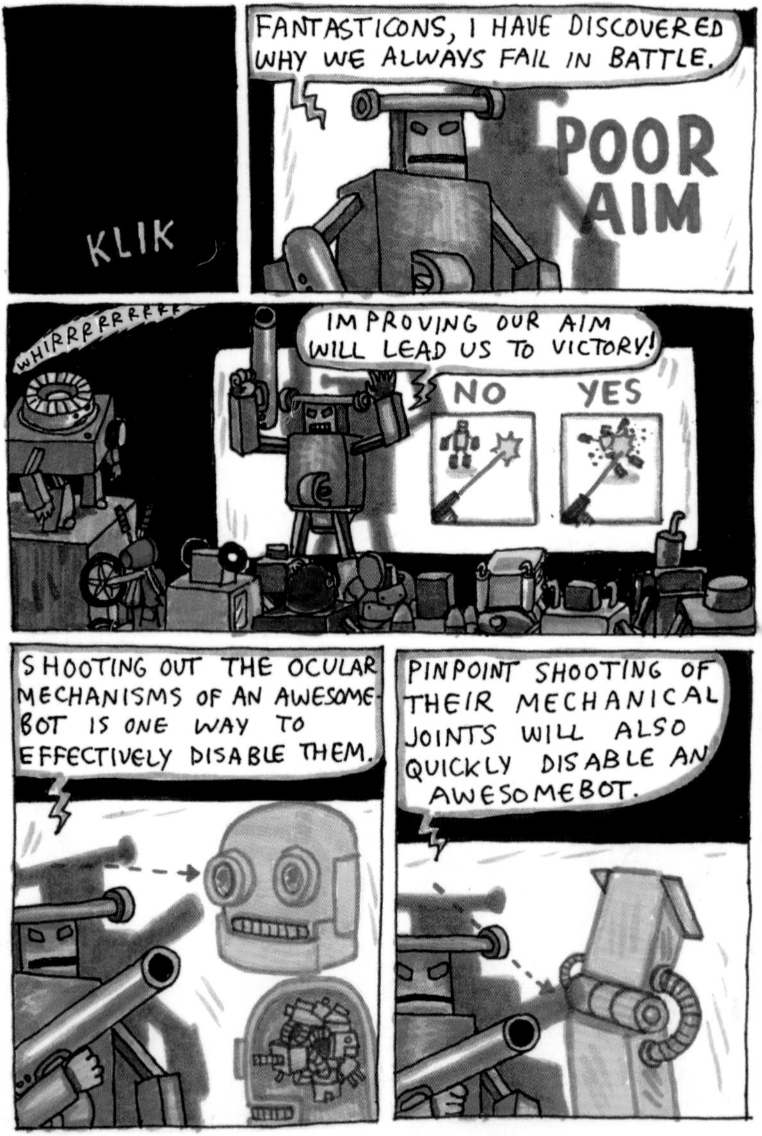
KLIK
FANTASTICONS, I HAVE DISCOVERED WHY WE ALWAYS FAIL IN BATTLE.
POOR AIM
WHIRRRRRRRRR
IMPROVING OUR AIM WILL LEAD US TO VICTORY!
NO
YES
SHOOTING OUT THE OCULAR MECHANISMS OF AN AWESOME-BOT IS ONE WAY TO EFFECTIVELY DISABLE THEM.
PINPOINT SHOOTING OF THEIR MECHANICAL JOINTS WILL ALSO QUICKLY DISABLE AN AWESOMEBOT.

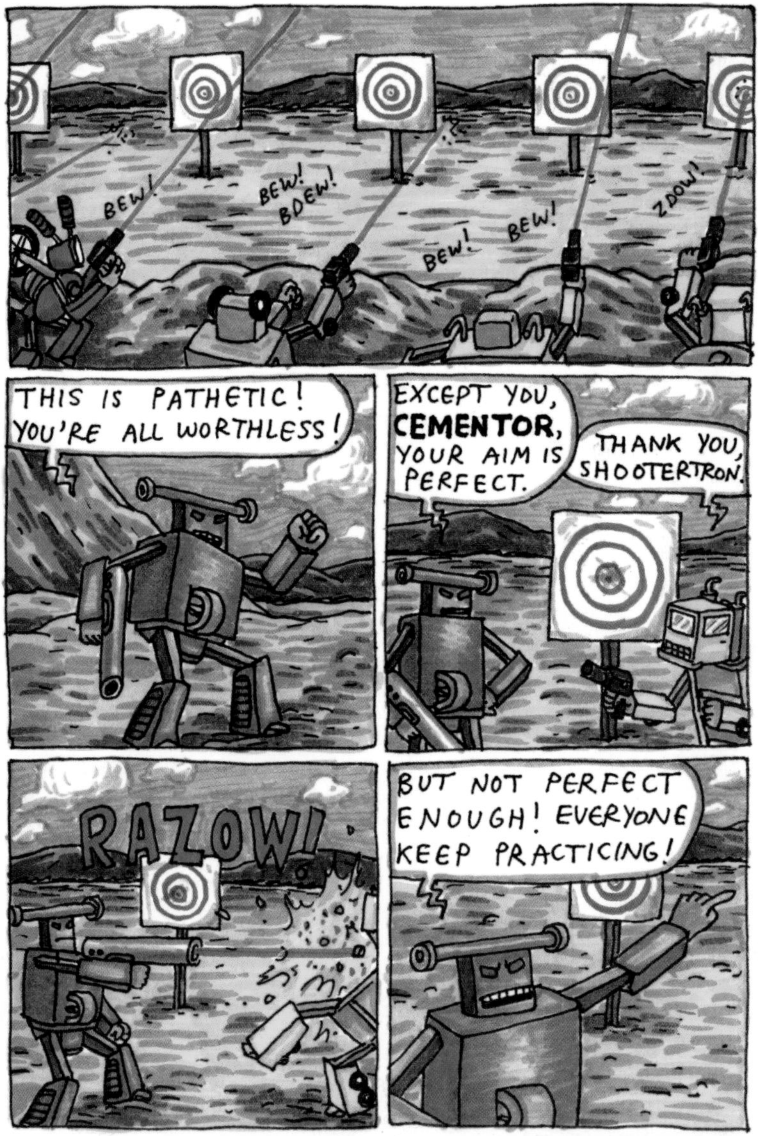
BEW!
BEW!
BDEW!
BEW!
BEW!
ZDOW!
THIS IS PATHETIC! YOU'RE ALL WORTHLESS!
EXCEPT YOU, **CEMENTOR**, YOUR AIM IS PERFECT.
THANK YOU, SHOOTERTRON!
RAZOW!
BUT NOT PERFECT ENOUGH! EVERYONE KEEP PRACTICING!

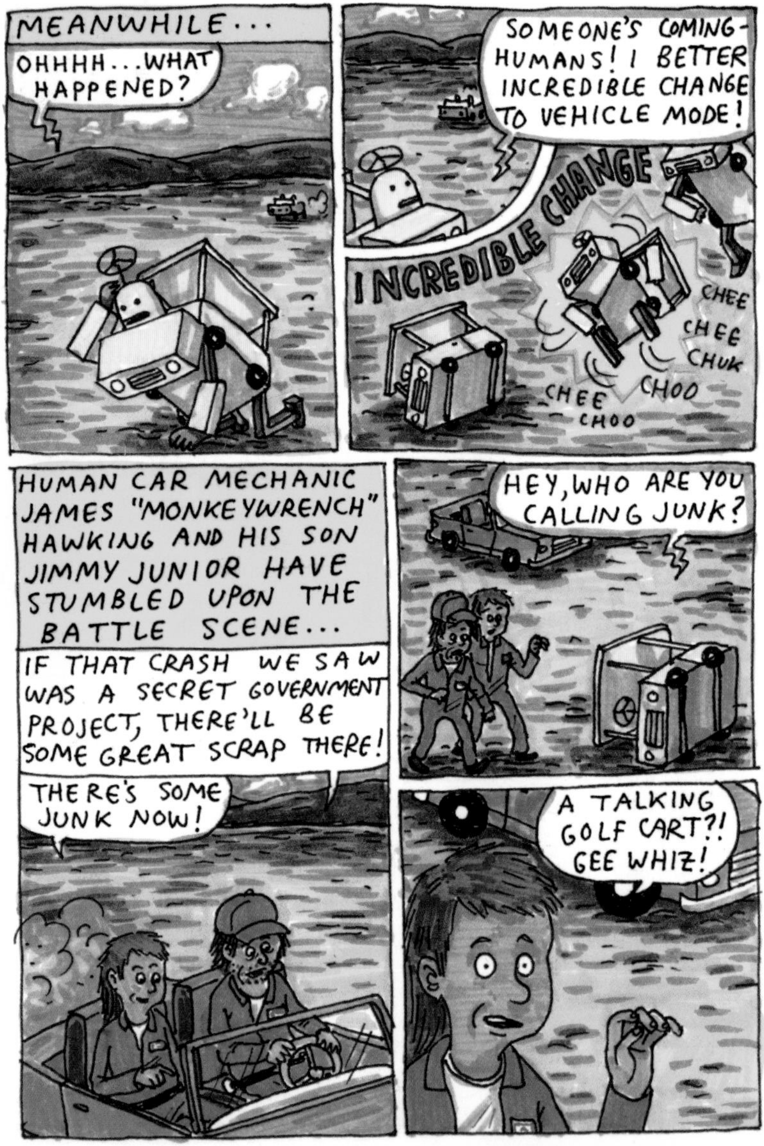
MEANWHILE...
OHHHH...WHAT HAPPENED?
SOMEONE'S COMING-HUMANS! I BETTER INCREDIBLE CHANGE TO VEHICLE MODE!
INCREDIBLE CHANGE
CHEE CHEE CHUK
CHOO
CHEE CHOO
HUMAN CAR MECHANIC JAMES "MONKEYWRENCH" HAWKING AND HIS SON JIMMY JUNIOR HAVE STUMBLED UPON THE BATTLE SCENE...
IF THAT CRASH WE SAW WAS A SECRET GOVERNMENT PROJECT, THERE'LL BE SOME GREAT SCRAP THERE!
THERE'S SOME JUNK NOW!
HEY, WHO ARE YOU CALLING JUNK?
A TALKING GOLF CART?! GEE WHIZ!

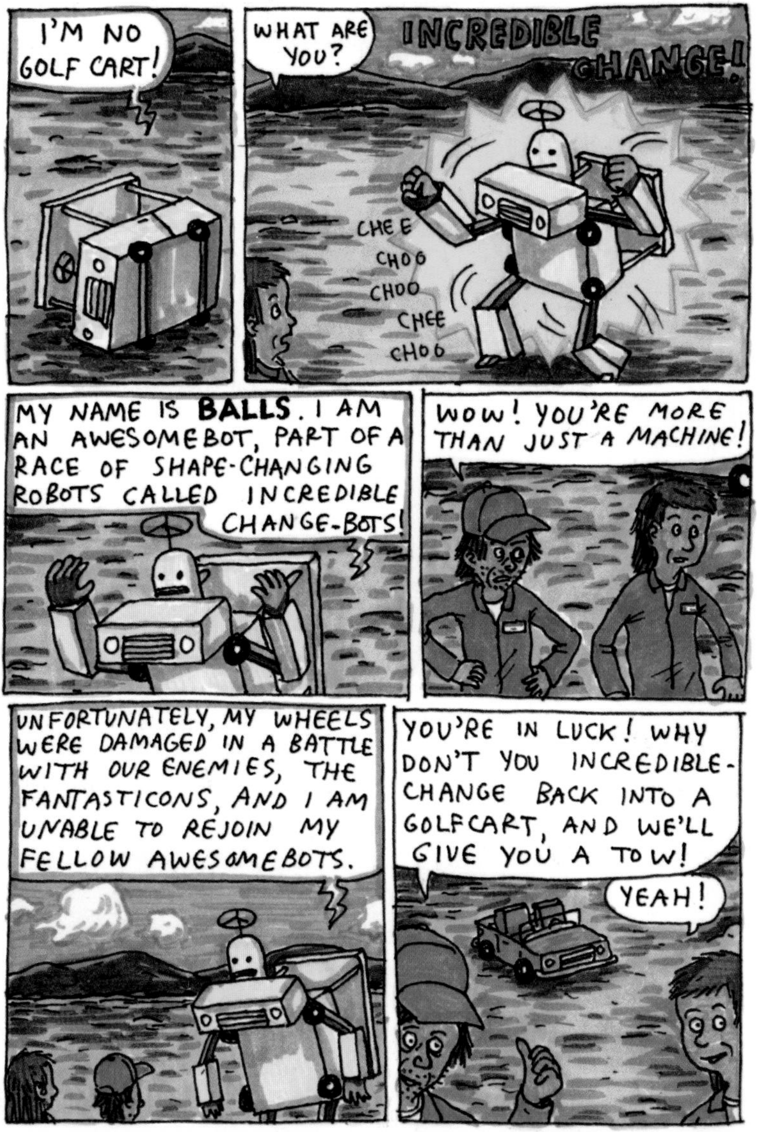
I'M NO GOLF CART!
WHAT ARE YOU?
INCREDIBLE CHANGE!
CHEE CHOO CHOO CHEE CHOO
MY NAME IS **BALLS**. I AM AN AWESOMEBOT, PART OF A RACE OF SHAPE-CHANGING ROBOTS CALLED INCREDIBLE CHANGE-BOTS!
WOW! YOU'RE MORE THAN JUST A MACHINE!
UNFORTUNATELY, MY WHEELS WERE DAMAGED IN A BATTLE WITH OUR ENEMIES, THE FANTASTICONS, AND I AM UNABLE TO REJOIN MY FELLOW AWESOMEBOTS.
YOU'RE IN LUCK! WHY DON'T YOU INCREDIBLE-CHANGE BACK INTO A GOLFCART, AND WE'LL GIVE YOU A TOW!
YEAH!

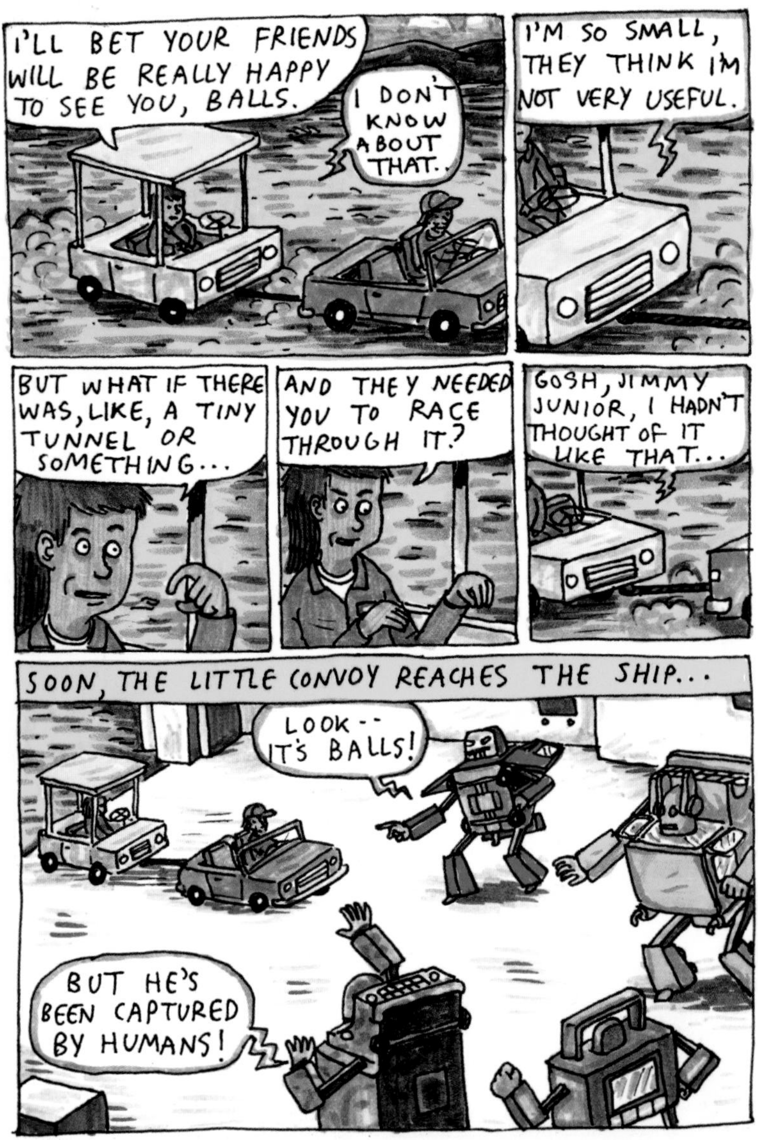
I'LL BET YOUR FRIENDS WILL BE REALLY HAPPY TO SEE YOU, BALLS.
I DON'T KNOW ABOUT THAT.
I'M SO SMALL, THEY THINK I'M NOT VERY USEFUL.
BUT WHAT IF THERE WAS, LIKE, A TINY TUNNEL OR SOMETHING...
AND THEY NEEDED YOU TO RACE THROUGH IT?
GOSH, JIMMY JUNIOR, I HADN'T THOUGHT OF IT LIKE THAT...
SOON, THE LITTLE CONVOY REACHES THE SHIP...
LOOK -- IT'S BALLS!
BUT HE'S BEEN CAPTURED BY HUMANS!

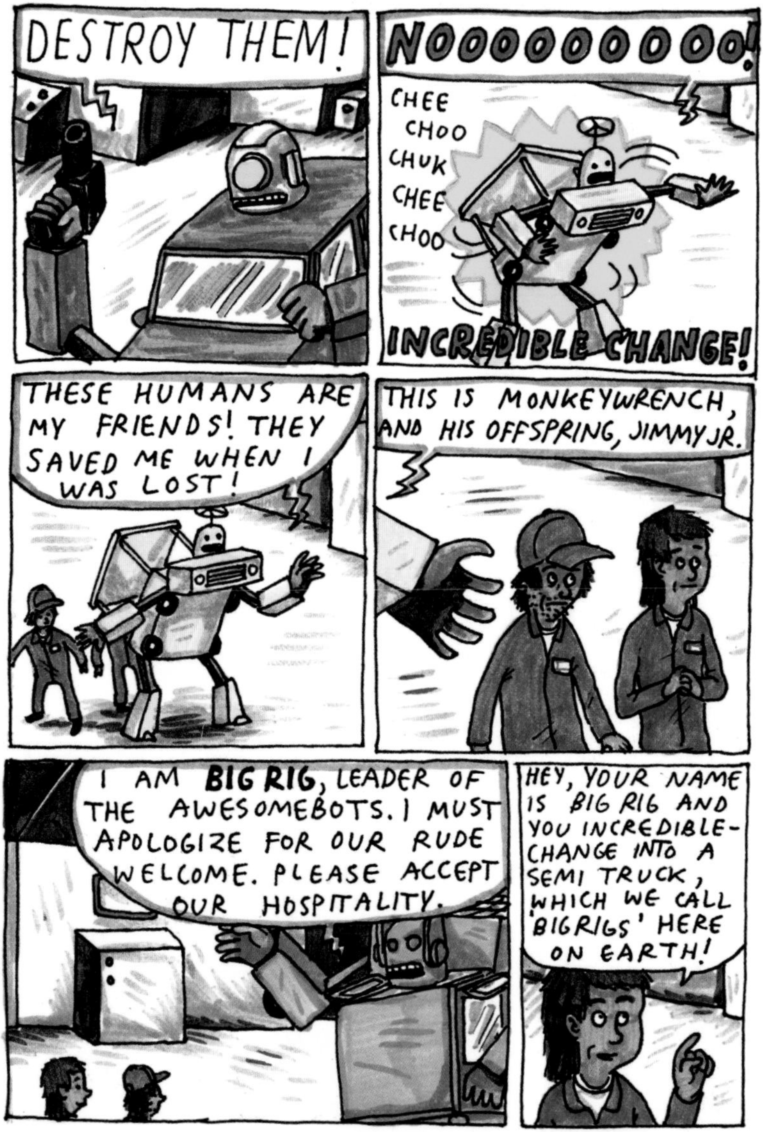
DESTROY THEM!
NOOOOOOOOOO!
CHEE CHOO CHUK CHEE CHOO
INCREDIBLE CHANGE!
THESE HUMANS ARE MY FRIENDS! THEY SAVED ME WHEN I WAS LOST!
THIS IS MONKEYWRENCH, AND HIS OFFSPRING, JIMMY JR.
I AM BIG RIG, LEADER OF THE AWESOMEBOTS. I MUST APOLOGIZE FOR OUR RUDE WELCOME. PLEASE ACCEPT OUR HOSPITALITY.
HEY, YOUR NAME IS BIG RIG AND YOU INCREDIBLE-CHANGE INTO A SEMI TRUCK, WHICH WE CALL 'BIGRIGS' HERE ON EARTH!

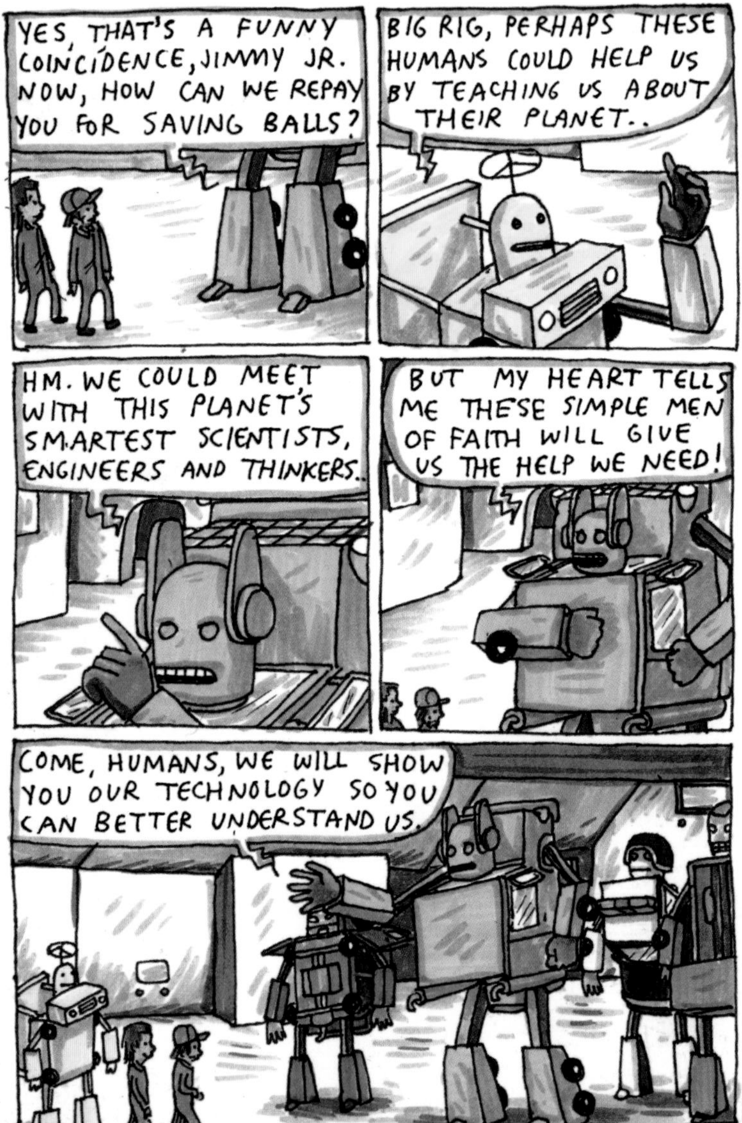
YES, THAT'S A FUNNY COINCIDENCE, JIMMY JR. NOW, HOW CAN WE REPAY YOU FOR SAVING BALLS?
BIG RIG, PERHAPS THESE HUMANS COULD HELP US BY TEACHING US ABOUT THEIR PLANET..
HM. WE COULD MEET WITH THIS PLANET'S SMARTEST SCIENTISTS, ENGINEERS AND THINKERS..
BUT MY HEART TELLS ME THESE SIMPLE MEN OF FAITH WILL GIVE US THE HELP WE NEED!
COME, HUMANS, WE WILL SHOW YOU OUR TECHNOLOGY SO YOU CAN BETTER UNDERSTAND US.

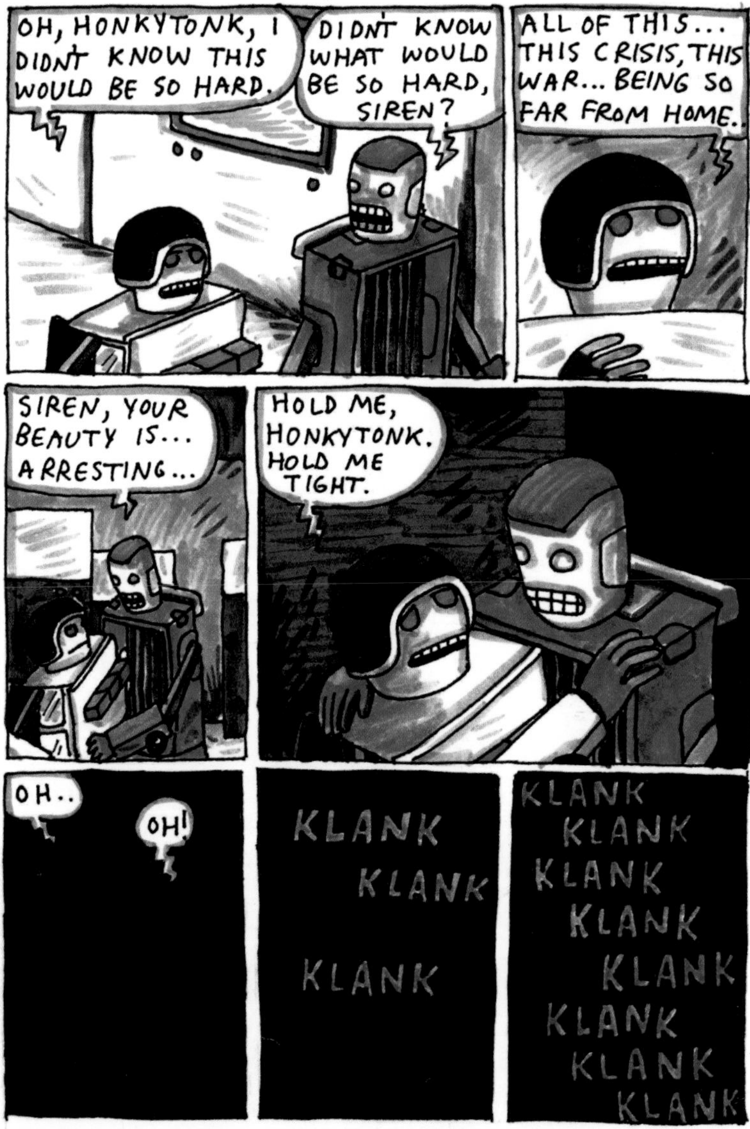
OH, HONKYTONK, I DIDN'T KNOW THIS WOULD BE SO HARD.
DIDN'T KNOW WHAT WOULD BE SO HARD, SIREN?
ALL OF THIS... THIS CRISIS, THIS WAR... BEING SO FAR FROM HOME.
SIREN, YOUR BEAUTY IS... ARRESTING...
HOLD ME, HONKYTONK. HOLD ME TIGHT.
OH..
OH!
KLANK
KLANK
KLANK
KLANK
KLANK
KLANK
KLANK
KLANK
KLANK
KLANK
KLANK

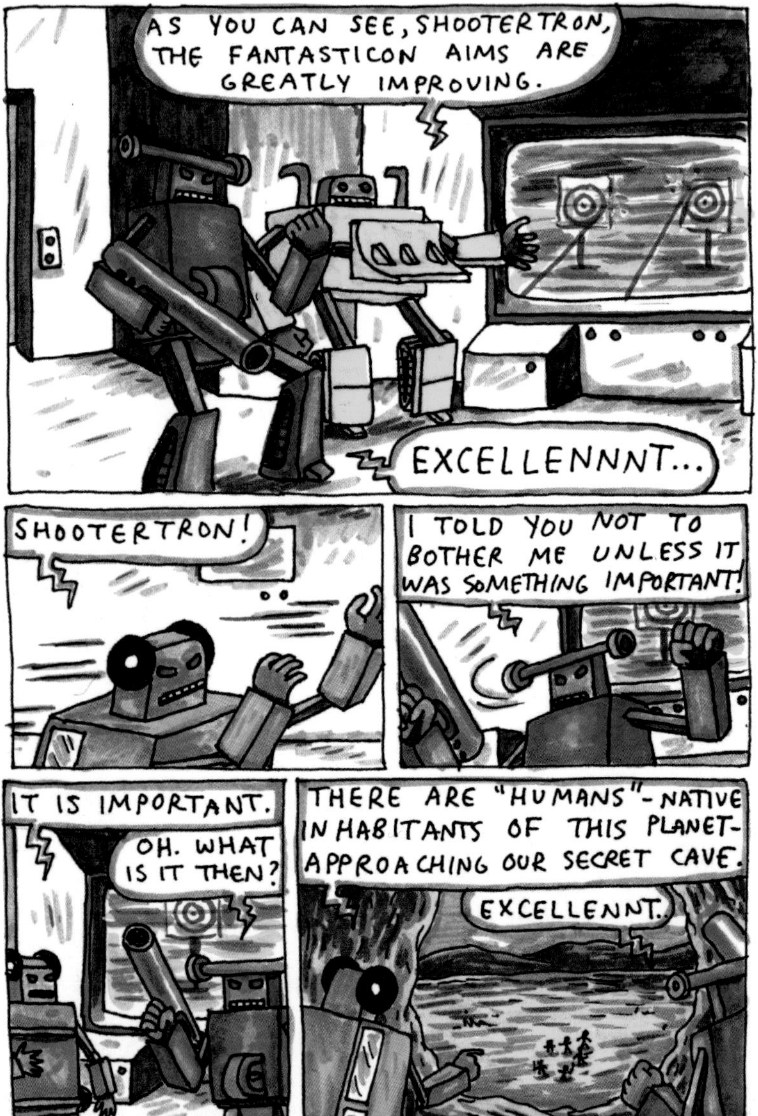
AS YOU CAN SEE, SHOOTERTRON, THE FANTASTICON AIMS ARE GREATLY IMPROVING.
EXCELLENNNT...
SHOOTERTRON!
I TOLD YOU NOT TO BOTHER ME UNLESS IT WAS SOMETHING IMPORTANT!
IT IS IMPORTANT.
OH. WHAT IS IT THEN?
THERE ARE "HUMANS"- NATIVE INHABITANTS OF THIS PLANET- APPROACHING OUR SECRET CAVE.
EXCELLENNT.

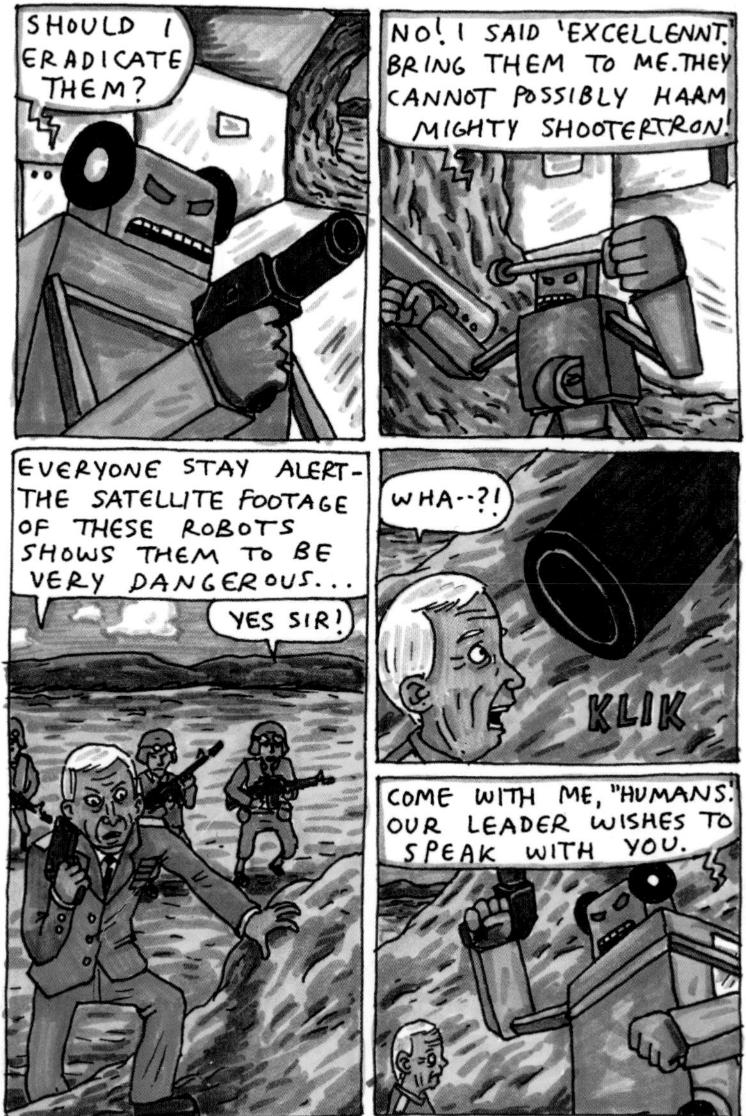
SHOULD I ERADICATE THEM?
NO! I SAID 'EXCELLENNT.' BRING THEM TO ME. THEY CANNOT POSSIBLY HARM MIGHTY SHOOTERTRON!
EVERYONE STAY ALERT- THE SATELLITE FOOTAGE OF THESE ROBOTS SHOWS THEM TO BE VERY DANGEROUS...
YES SIR!
WHA--?!
KLIK
COME WITH ME, "HUMANS." OUR LEADER WISHES TO SPEAK WITH YOU.

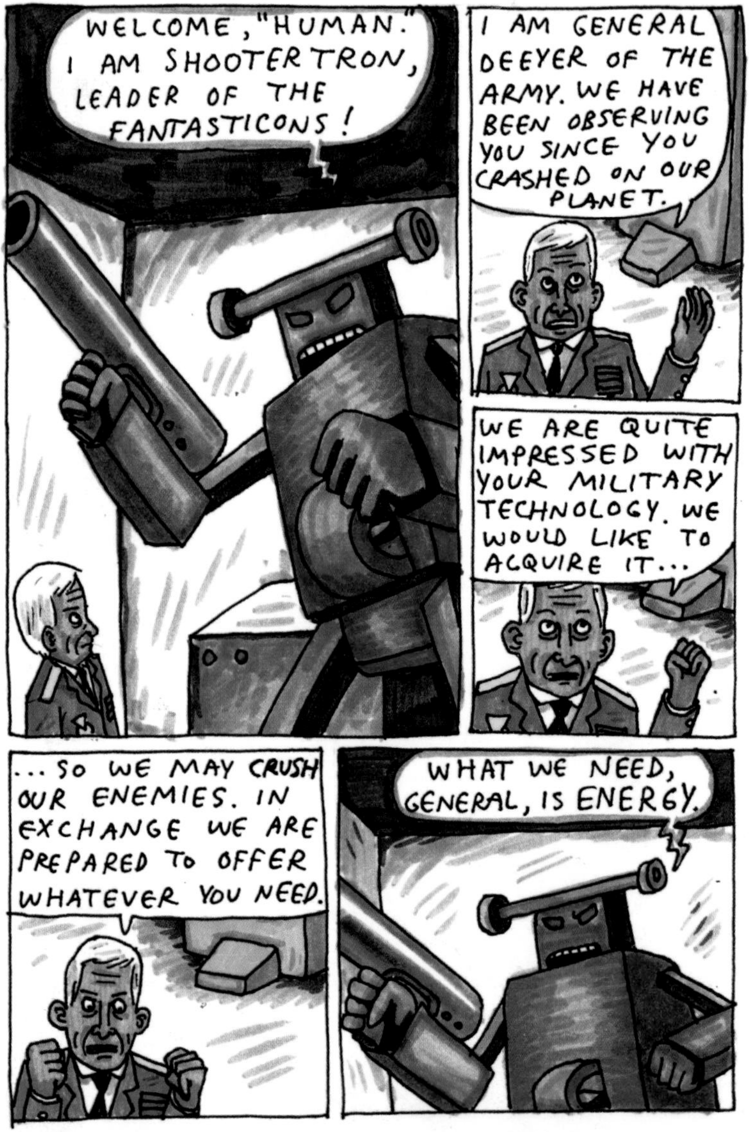
WELCOME, "HUMAN." I AM SHOOTERTRON, LEADER OF THE FANTASTICONS!
I AM GENERAL DEEYER OF THE ARMY. WE HAVE BEEN OBSERVING YOU SINCE YOU CRASHED ON OUR PLANET.
WE ARE QUITE IMPRESSED WITH YOUR MILITARY TECHNOLOGY. WE WOULD LIKE TO ACQUIRE IT...
...SO WE MAY CRUSH OUR ENEMIES. IN EXCHANGE WE ARE PREPARED TO OFFER WHATEVER YOU NEED.
WHAT WE NEED, GENERAL, IS ENERGY.

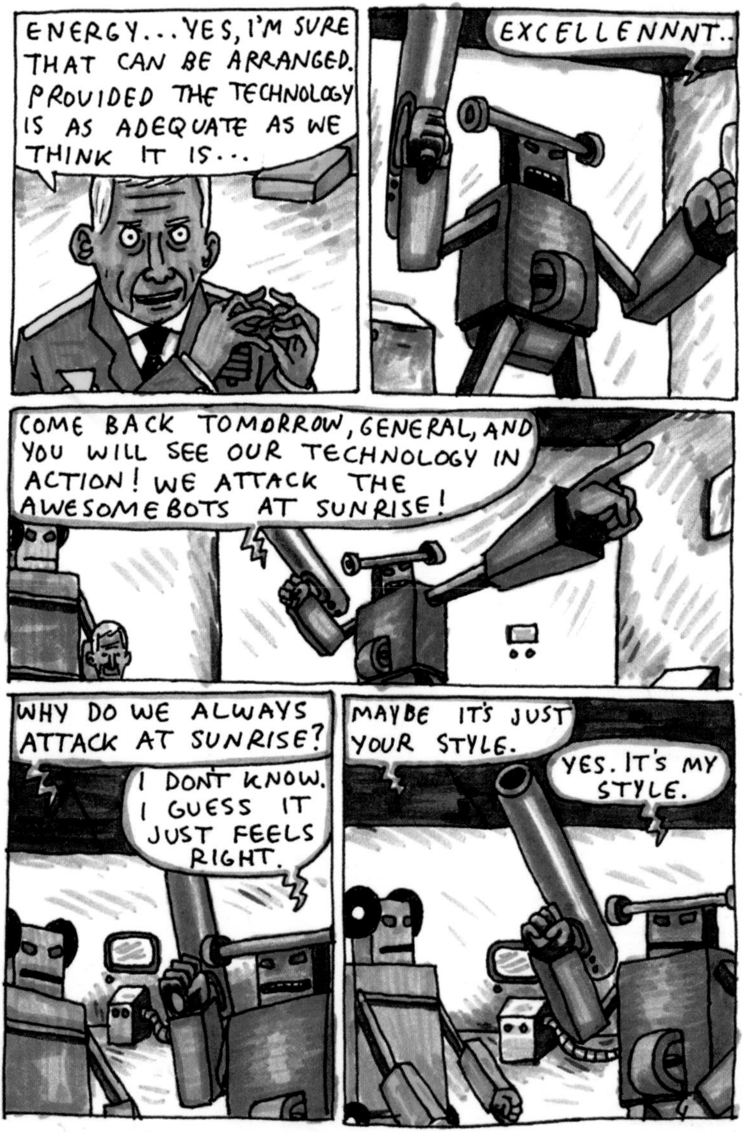
ENERGY... YES, I'M SURE THAT CAN BE ARRANGED. PROVIDED THE TECHNOLOGY IS AS ADEQUATE AS WE THINK IT IS...
EXCELLENNNT..
COME BACK TOMORROW, GENERAL, AND YOU WILL SEE OUR TECHNOLOGY IN ACTION! WE ATTACK THE AWESOMEBOTS AT SUNRISE!
WHY DO WE ALWAYS ATTACK AT SUNRISE?
I DON'T KNOW. I GUESS IT JUST FEELS RIGHT.
MAYBE IT'S JUST YOUR STYLE.
YES. IT'S MY STYLE.

THE NEXT MORNING AT SUNRISE...

INSIDE THE AWESOMEBOT SHIP, IT IS PEACEFUL, UNTIL...

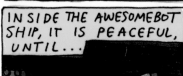

KABOOM!

KABAM KABLOOEY KABOOM

WE'RE UNDER ATTACK!

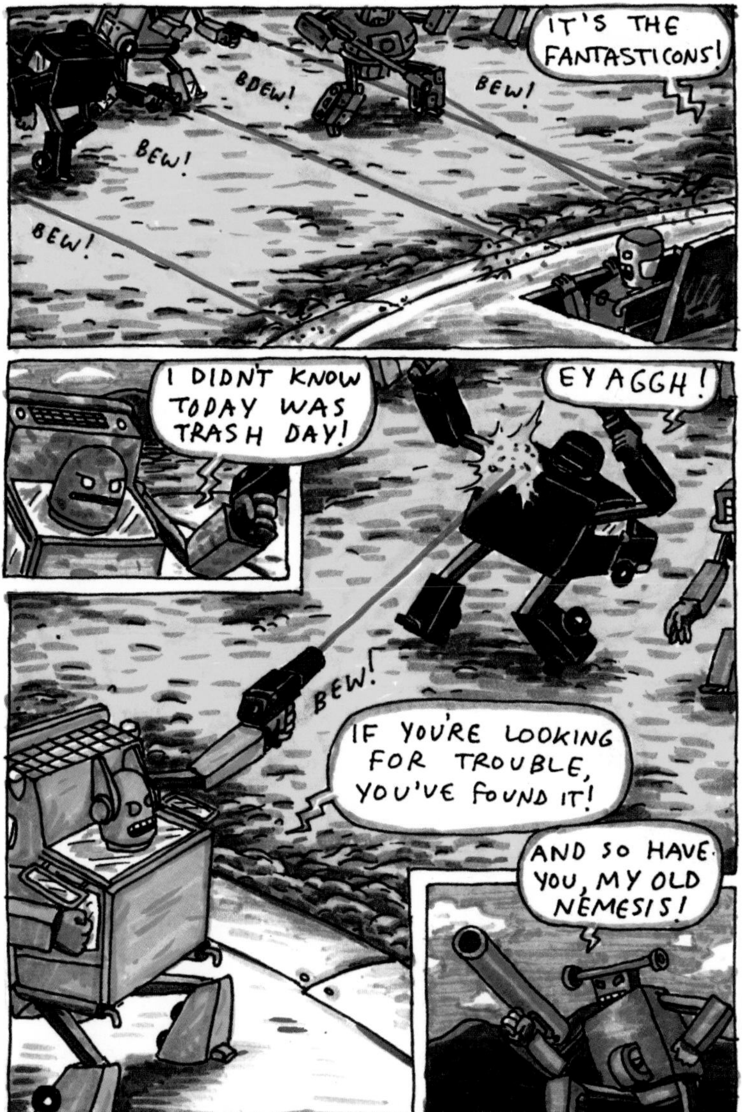
IT'S THE FANTASTICONS!
BDEW!
BEW!
BEW!
BEW!
I DIDN'T KNOW TODAY WAS TRASH DAY!
EYAGGH!
BEW!
IF YOU'RE LOOKING FOR TROUBLE, YOU'VE FOUND IT!
AND SO HAVE YOU, MY OLD NEMESIS!

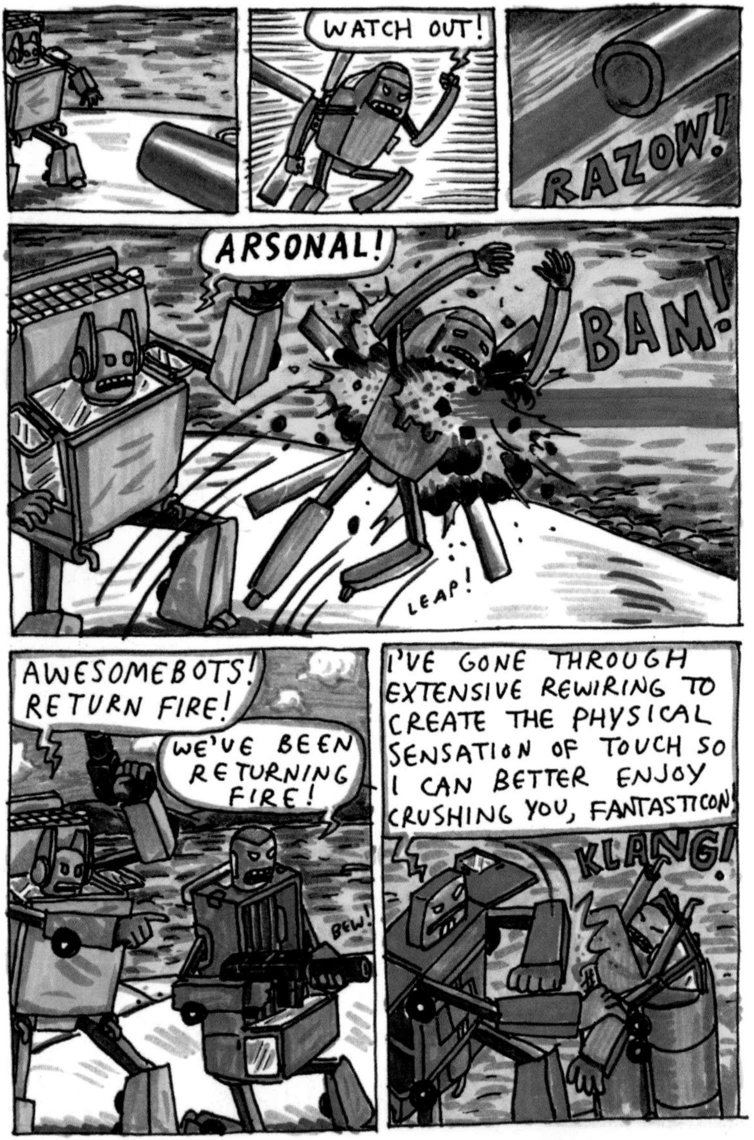
WATCH OUT!
RAZOW!
ARSONAL!
BAM!
LEAP!
AWESOMEBOTS! RETURN FIRE!
WE'VE BEEN RETURNING FIRE!
BEW!
I'VE GONE THROUGH EXTENSIVE REWIRING TO CREATE THE PHYSICAL SENSATION OF TOUCH SO I CAN BETTER ENJOY CRUSHING YOU, FANTASTICON!
KLANG!

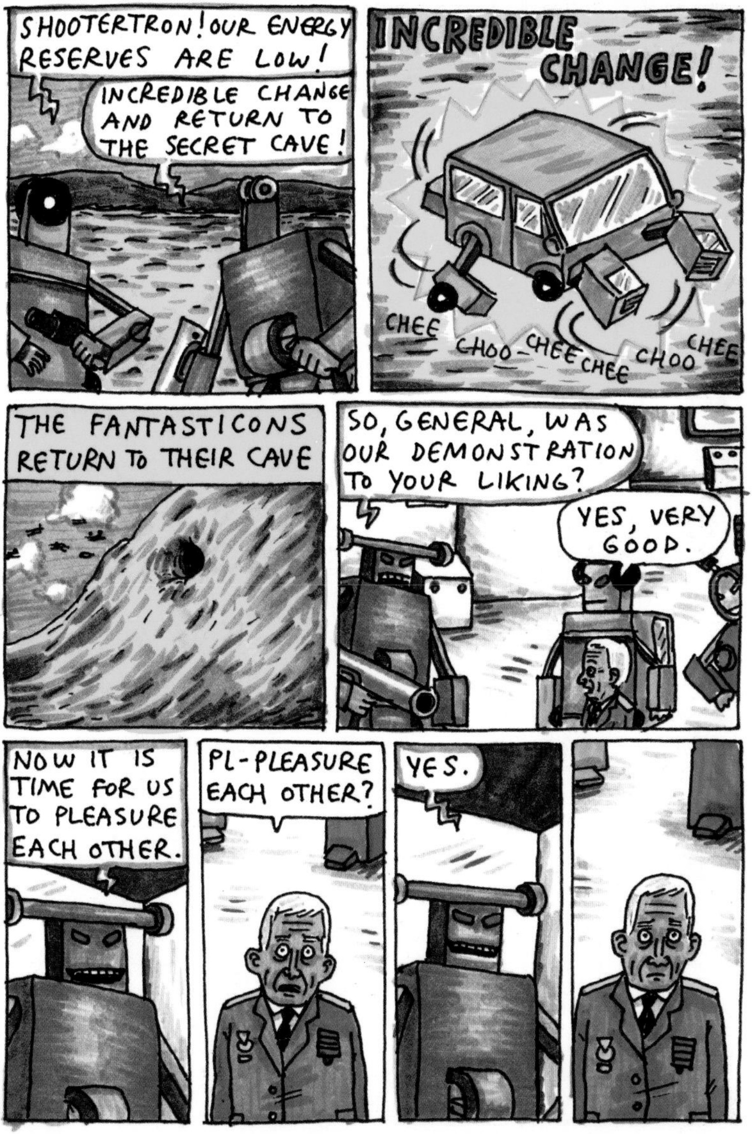
SHOOTERTRON! OUR ENERGY RESERVES ARE LOW!
INCREDIBLE CHANGE AND RETURN TO THE SECRET CAVE!
INCREDIBLE CHANGE!
CHEE CHOO-CHEE CHEE CHOO CHEE
THE FANTASTICONS RETURN TO THEIR CAVE
SO, GENERAL, WAS OUR DEMONSTRATION TO YOUR LIKING?
YES, VERY GOOD.
NOW IT IS TIME FOR US TO PLEASURE EACH OTHER.
PL-PLEASURE EACH OTHER?
YES.

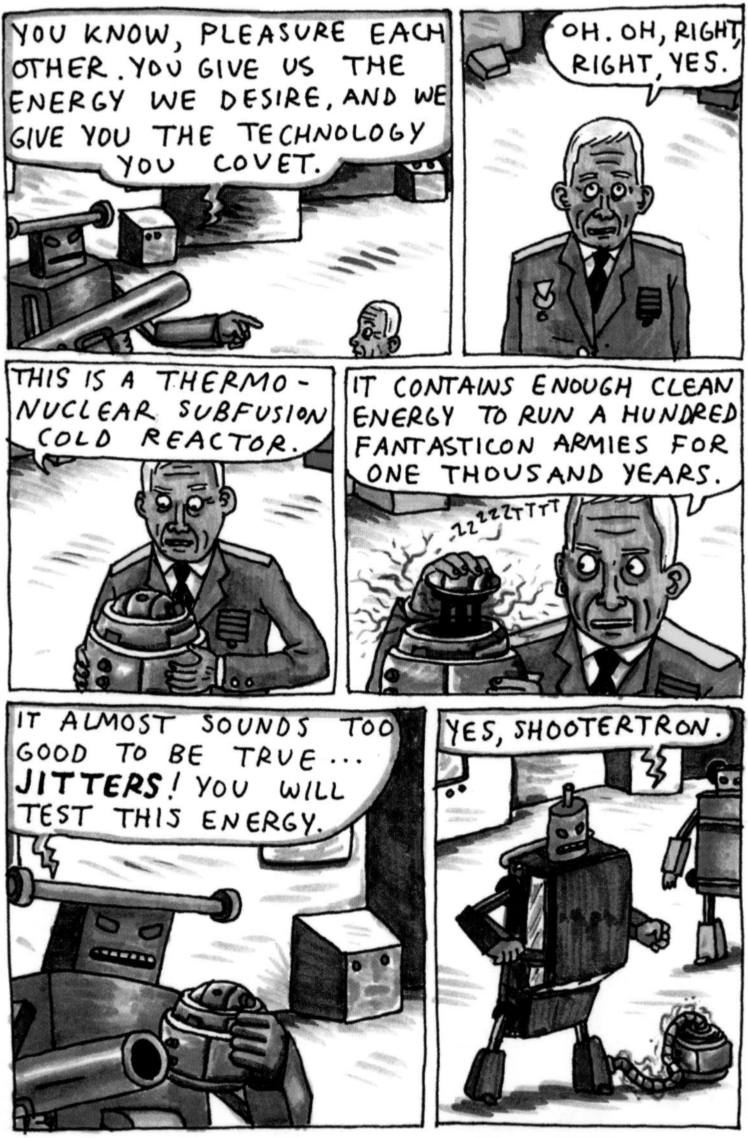
YOU KNOW, PLEASURE EACH OTHER. YOU GIVE US THE ENERGY WE DESIRE, AND WE GIVE YOU THE TECHNOLOGY YOU COVET.
OH. OH, RIGHT, RIGHT, YES.
THIS IS A THERMO-NUCLEAR SUBFUSION COLD REACTOR.
IT CONTAINS ENOUGH CLEAN ENERGY TO RUN A HUNDRED FANTASTICON ARMIES FOR ONE THOUSAND YEARS.
IT ALMOST SOUNDS TOO GOOD TO BE TRUE... **JITTERS!** YOU WILL TEST THIS ENERGY.
YES, SHOOTERTRON.

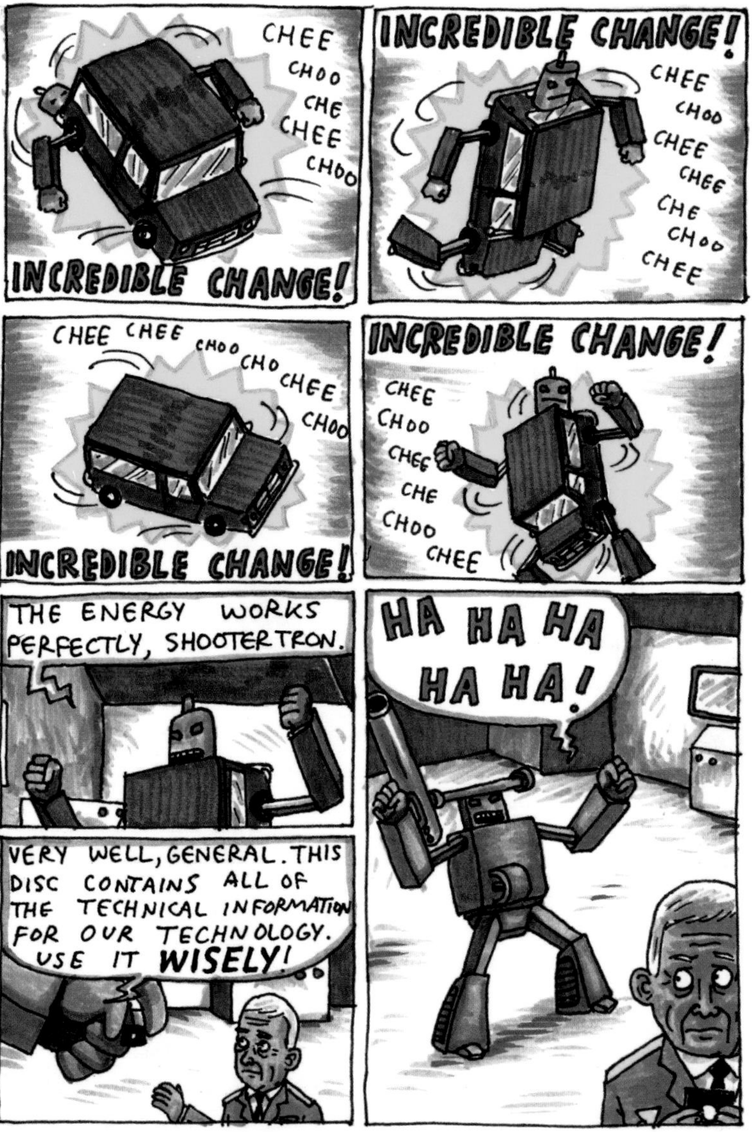
CHEE CHOO CHE CHEE CHOO
INCREDIBLE CHANGE!
INCREDIBLE CHANGE!
CHEE CHOO CHEE CHEE CHE CHOO CHEE
CHEE CHEE CHOO CHO CHEE CHOO
INCREDIBLE CHANGE!
INCREDIBLE CHANGE!
CHEE CHOO CHEE CHE CHOO CHEE
THE ENERGY WORKS PERFECTLY, SHOOTERTRON.
VERY WELL, GENERAL. THIS DISC CONTAINS ALL OF THE TECHNICAL INFORMATION FOR OUR TECHNOLOGY. USE IT WISELY!
HA HA HA HA HA!

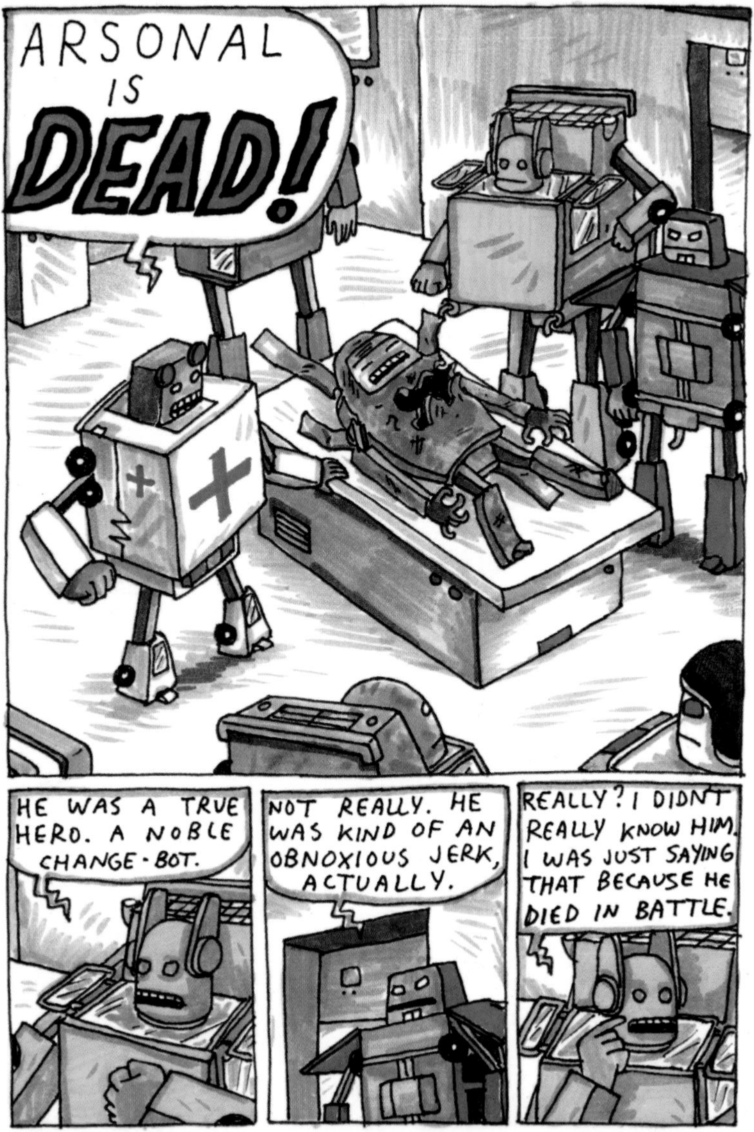
ARSONAL IS DEAD!
HE WAS A TRUE HERO. A NOBLE CHANGE-BOT.
NOT REALLY. HE WAS KIND OF AN OBNOXIOUS JERK, ACTUALLY.
REALLY? I DIDN'T REALLY KNOW HIM. I WAS JUST SAYING THAT BECAUSE HE DIED IN BATTLE.

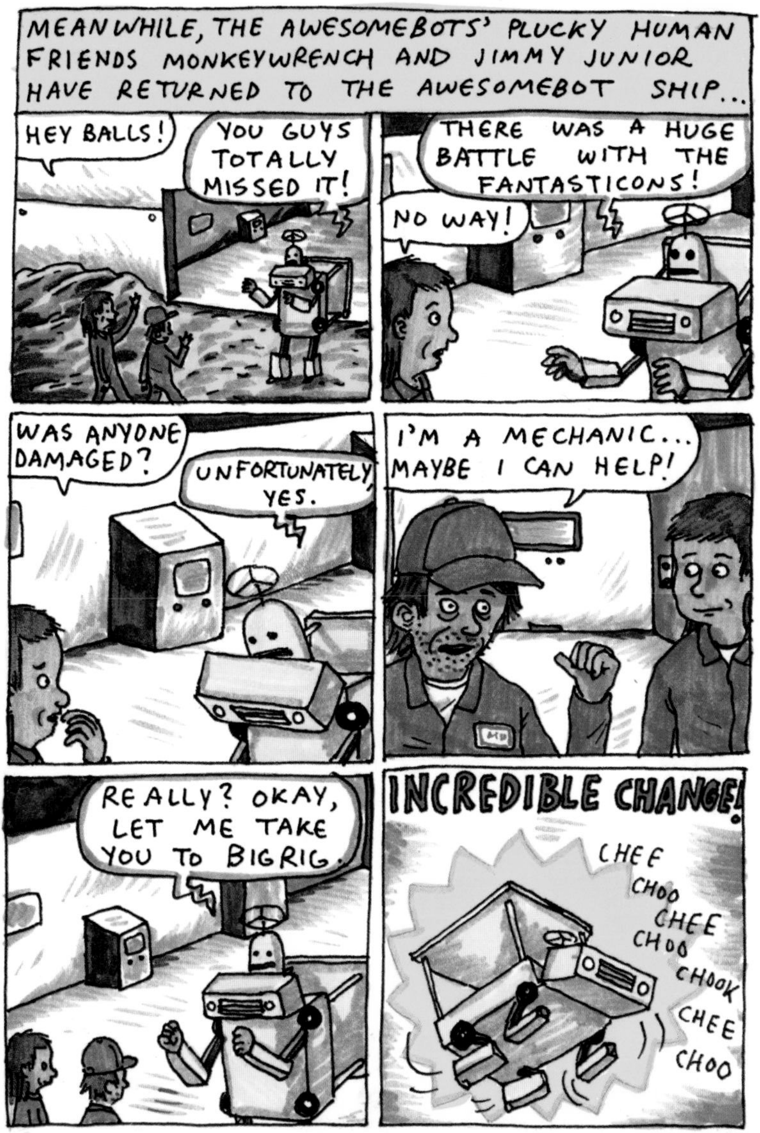
MEANWHILE, THE AWESOMEBOTS' PLUCKY HUMAN FRIENDS MONKEYWRENCH AND JIMMY JUNIOR HAVE RETURNED TO THE AWESOMEBOT SHIP...
HEY BALLS!
YOU GUYS TOTALLY MISSED IT!
THERE WAS A HUGE BATTLE WITH THE FANTASTICONS!
NO WAY!
WAS ANYONE DAMAGED?
UNFORTUNATELY YES.
I'M A MECHANIC... MAYBE I CAN HELP!
REALLY? OKAY, LET ME TAKE YOU TO BIGRIG.
INCREDIBLE CHANGE!
CHEE
CHOO
CHEE
CHOO
CHOOK
CHEE
CHOO

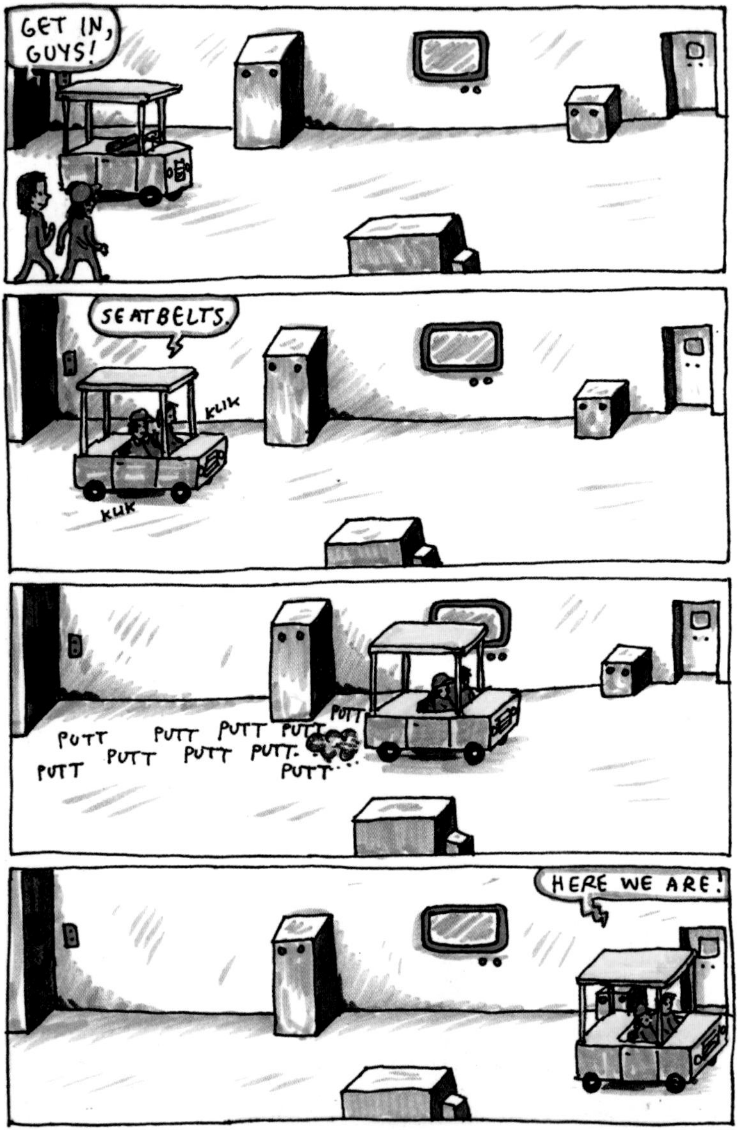
GET IN, GUYS!
SEATBELTS.
KLIK
KLIK
PUTT PUTT PUTT PUTT PUTT PUTT PUTT PUTT PUTT PUTT PUTT...
HERE WE ARE!

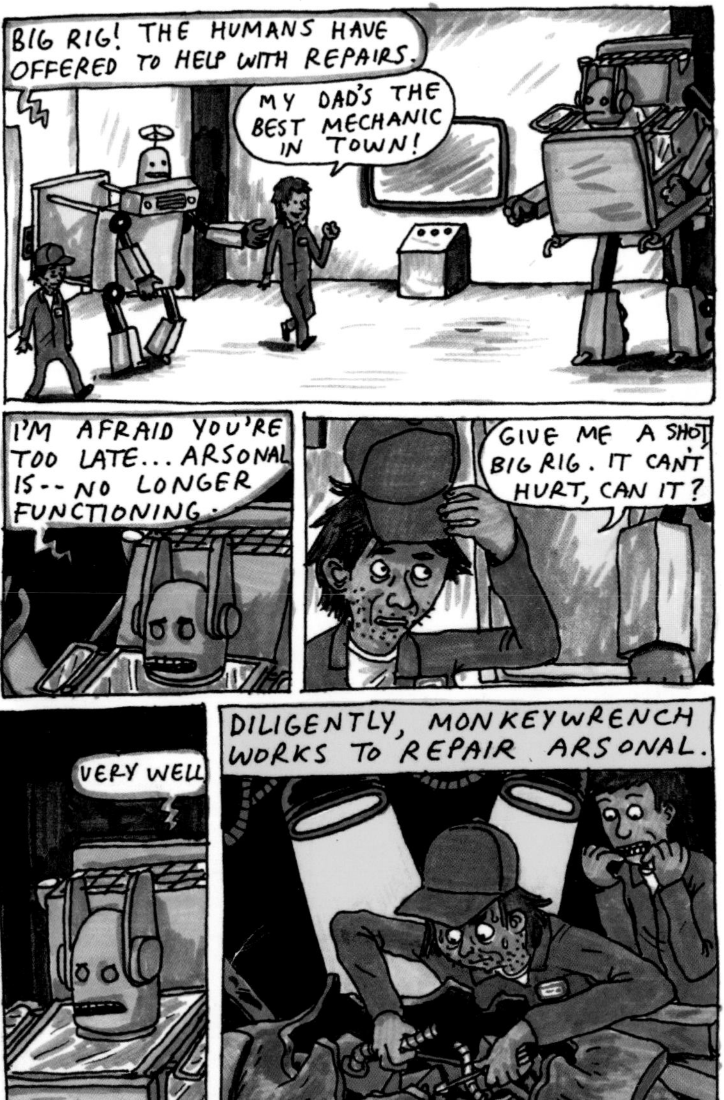
BIG RIG! THE HUMANS HAVE OFFERED TO HELP WITH REPAIRS.
MY DAD'S THE BEST MECHANIC IN TOWN!
I'M AFRAID YOU'RE TOO LATE... ARSONAL IS-- NO LONGER FUNCTIONING.
GIVE ME A SHOT, BIG RIG. IT CAN'T HURT, CAN IT?
VERY WELL
DILIGENTLY, MONKEYWRENCH WORKS TO REPAIR ARSONAL.

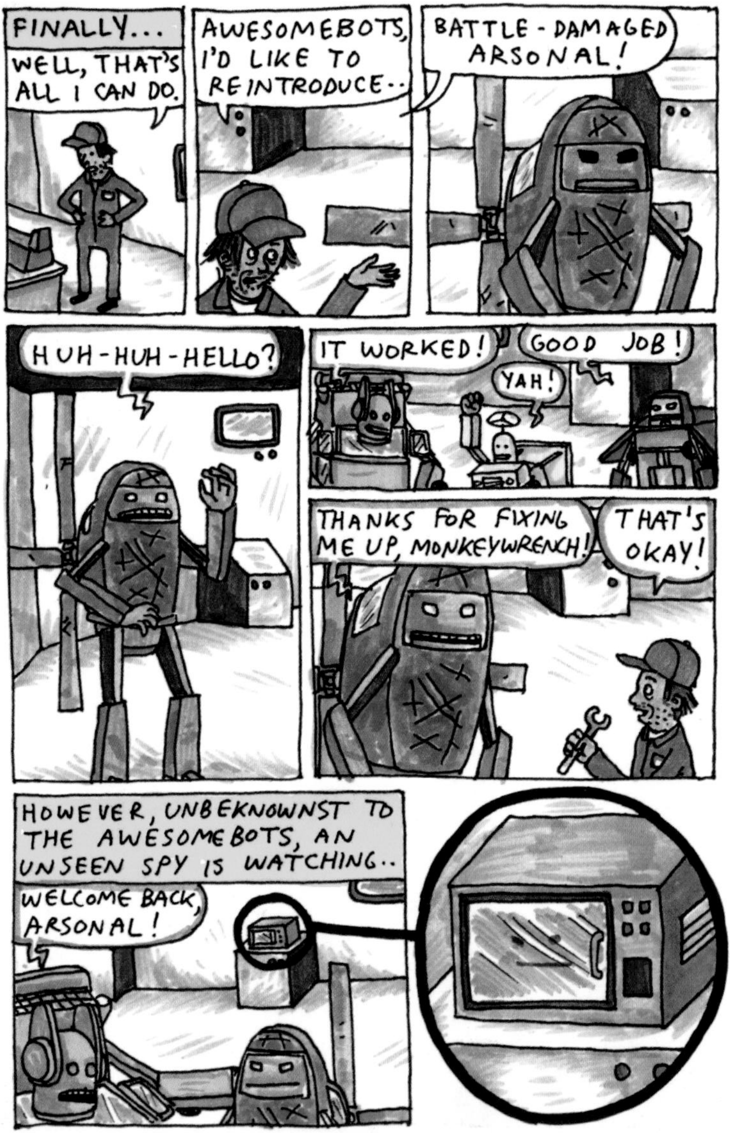
FINALLY...
WELL, THAT'S ALL I CAN DO.
AWESOMEBOTS, I'D LIKE TO REINTRODUCE..
BATTLE-DAMAGED ARSONAL!
HUH-HUH-HELLO?
IT WORKED!
GOOD JOB!
YAH!
THANKS FOR FIXING ME UP, MONKEYWRENCH!
THAT'S OKAY!
HOWEVER, UNBEKNOWNST TO THE AWESOMEBOTS, AN UNSEEN SPY IS WATCHING..
WELCOME BACK, ARSONAL!

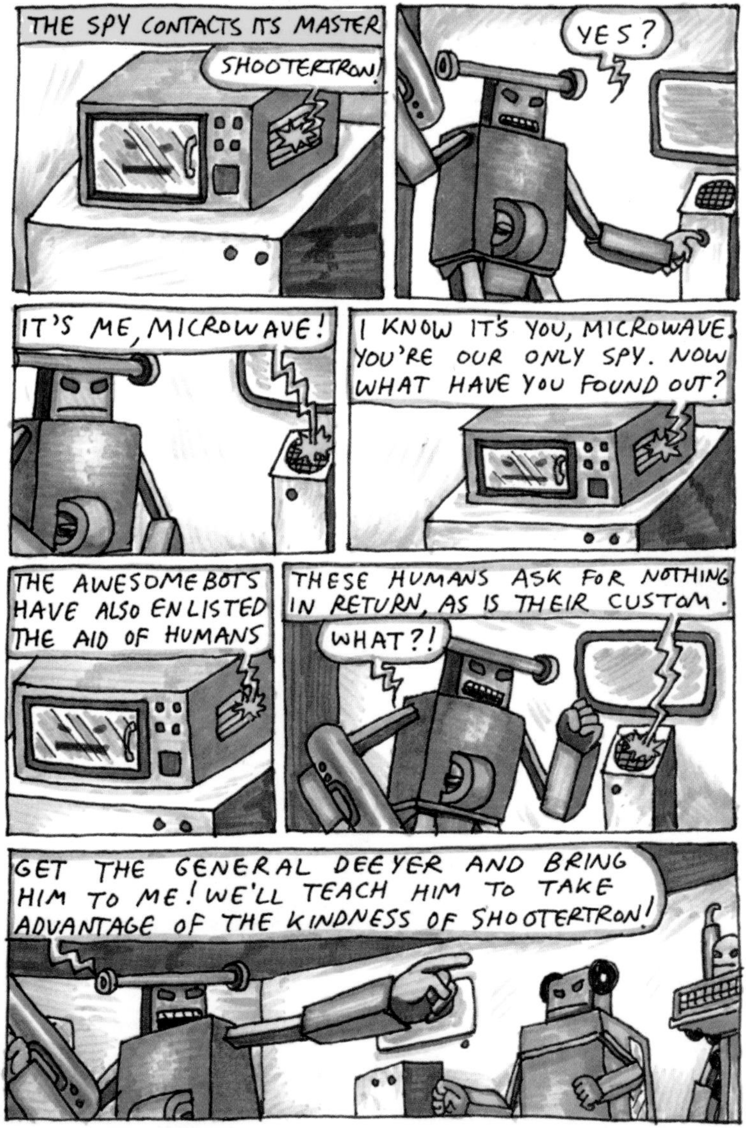

THE SPY CONTACTS ITS MASTER
SHOOTERTRON!
YES?
IT'S ME, MICROWAVE!
I KNOW IT'S YOU, MICROWAVE. YOU'RE OUR ONLY SPY. NOW WHAT HAVE YOU FOUND OUT?
THE AWESOMEBOTS HAVE ALSO ENLISTED THE AID OF HUMANS
THESE HUMANS ASK FOR NOTHING IN RETURN, AS IS THEIR CUSTOM.
WHAT?!
GET THE GENERAL DEEYER AND BRING HIM TO ME! WE'LL TEACH HIM TO TAKE ADVANTAGE OF THE KINDNESS OF SHOOTERTRON!

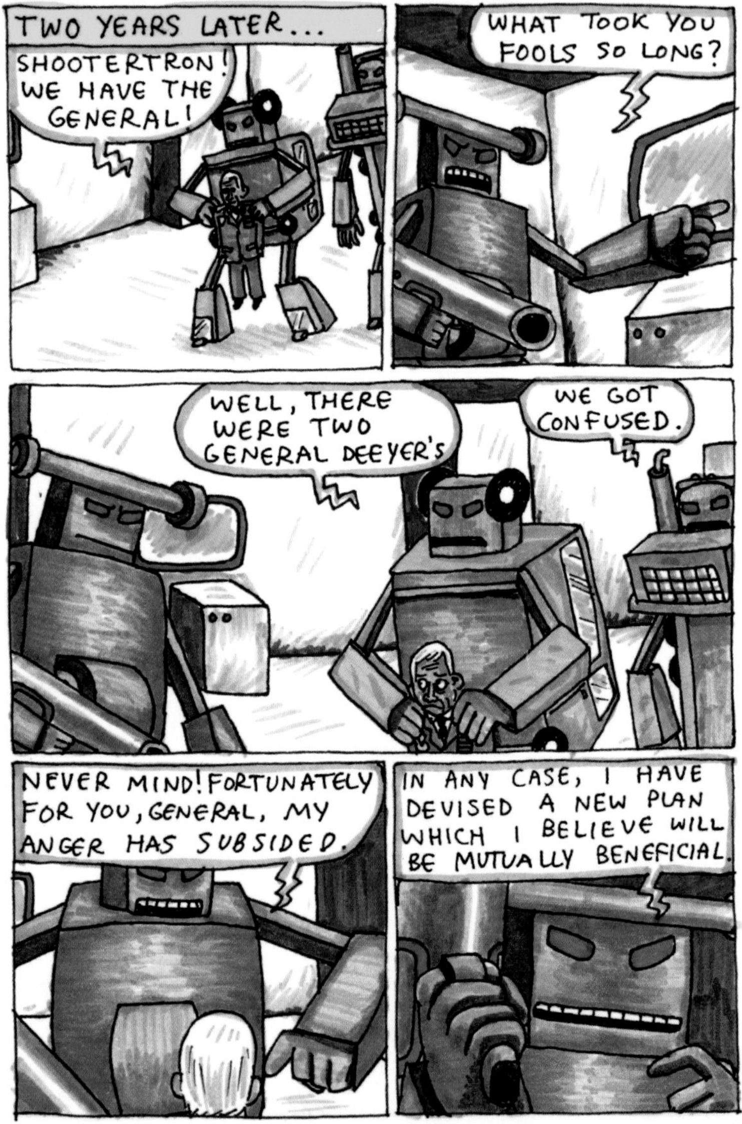
TWO YEARS LATER...
SHOOTERTRON! WE HAVE THE GENERAL!
WHAT TOOK YOU FOOLS SO LONG?
WELL, THERE WERE TWO GENERAL DEEYER'S
WE GOT CONFUSED.
NEVER MIND! FORTUNATELY FOR YOU, GENERAL, MY ANGER HAS SUBSIDED.
IN ANY CASE, I HAVE DEVISED A NEW PLAN WHICH I BELIEVE WILL BE MUTUALLY BENEFICIAL.

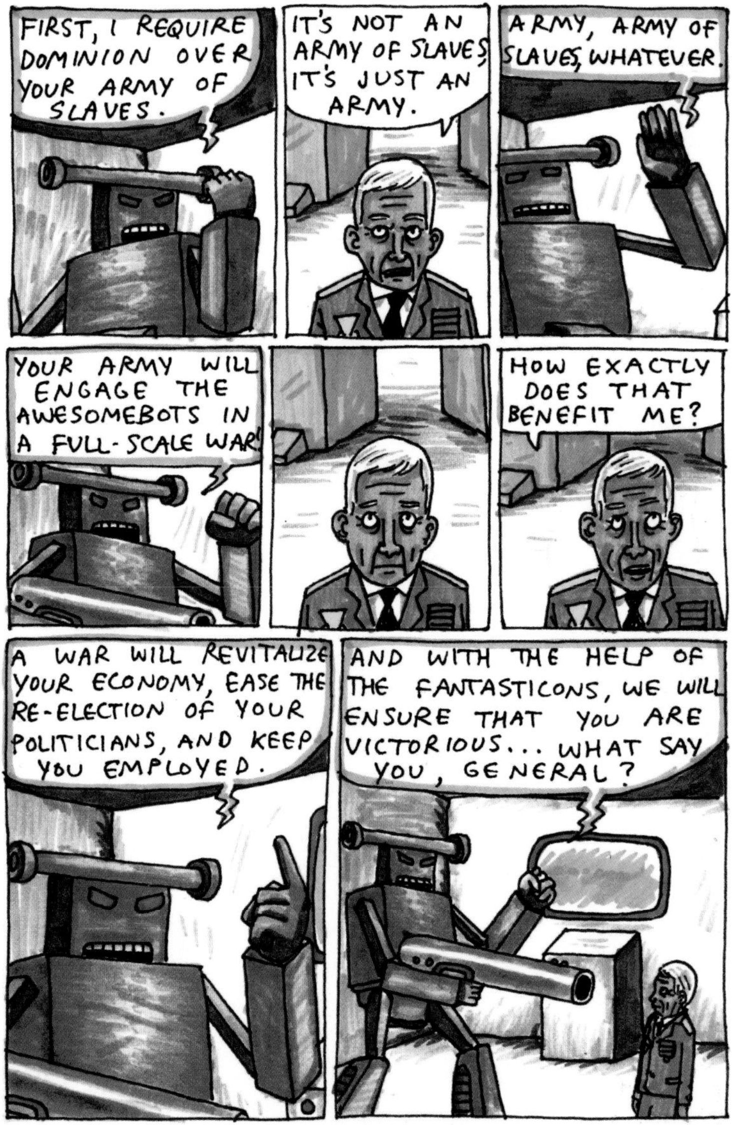
FIRST, I REQUIRE DOMINION OVER YOUR ARMY OF SLAVES.
IT'S NOT AN ARMY OF SLAVES, IT'S JUST AN ARMY.
ARMY, ARMY OF SLAVES, WHATEVER.
YOUR ARMY WILL ENGAGE THE AWESOMEBOTS IN A FULL-SCALE WAR!
HOW EXACTLY DOES THAT BENEFIT ME?
A WAR WILL REVITALIZE YOUR ECONOMY, EASE THE RE-ELECTION OF YOUR POLITICIANS, AND KEEP YOU EMPLOYED.
AND WITH THE HELP OF THE FANTASTICONS, WE WILL ENSURE THAT YOU ARE VICTORIOUS... WHAT SAY YOU, GENERAL?

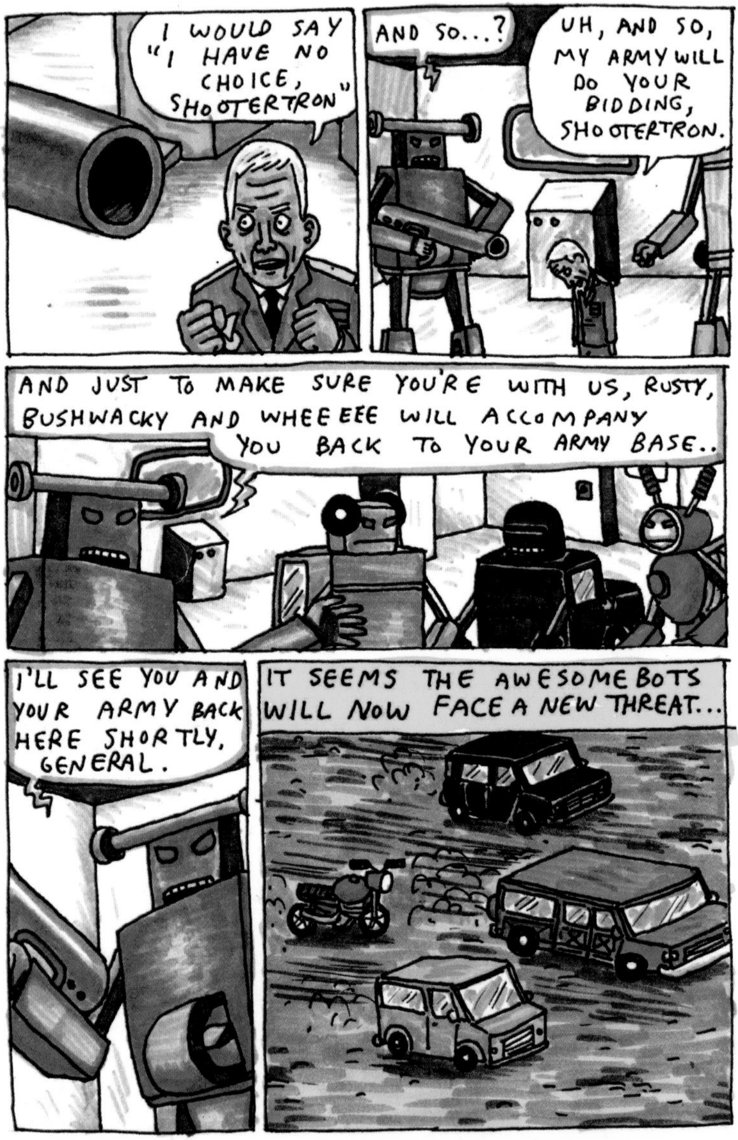
I WOULD SAY "I HAVE NO CHOICE, SHOOTERTRON"
AND SO...?
UH, AND SO, MY ARMY WILL DO YOUR BIDDING, SHOOTERTRON.
AND JUST TO MAKE SURE YOU'RE WITH US, RUSTY, BUSHWACKY AND WHEEEEE WILL ACCOMPANY YOU BACK TO YOUR ARMY BASE..
I'LL SEE YOU AND YOUR ARMY BACK HERE SHORTLY, GENERAL.
IT SEEMS THE AWESOMEBOTS WILL NOW FACE A NEW THREAT...

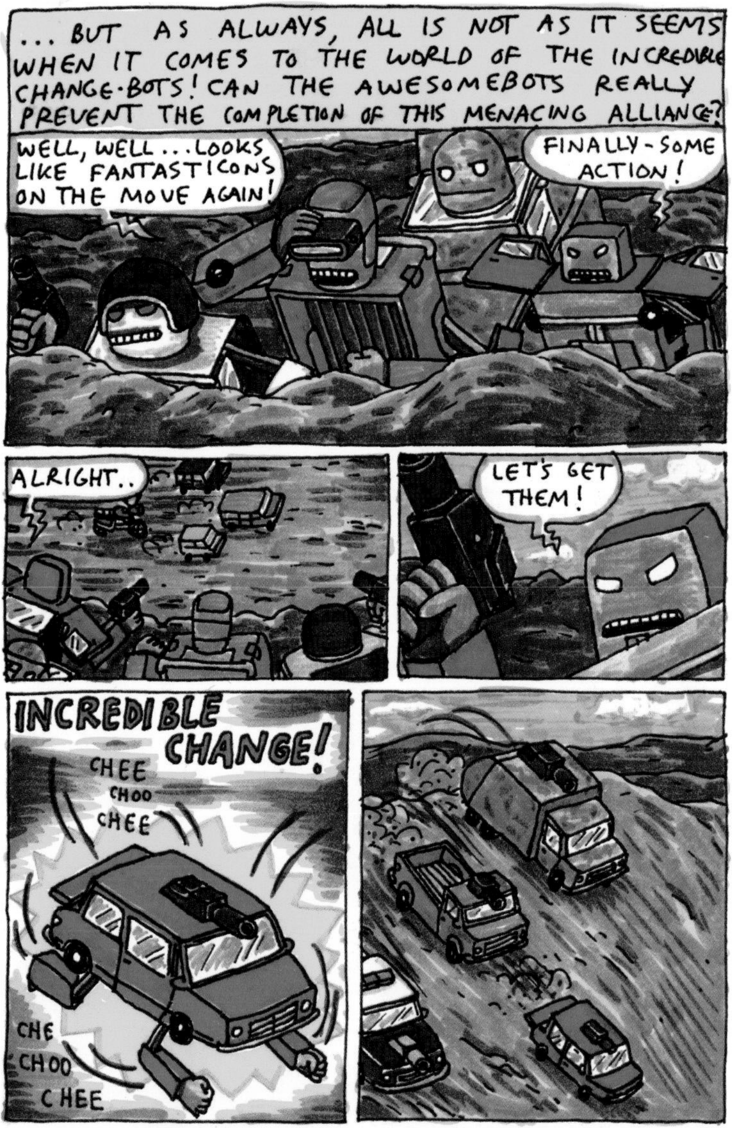
... BUT AS ALWAYS, ALL IS NOT AS IT SEEMS WHEN IT COMES TO THE WORLD OF THE INCREDIBLE CHANGE-BOTS! CAN THE AWESOMEBOTS REALLY PREVENT THE COMPLETION OF THIS MENACING ALLIANCE?
WELL, WELL... LOOKS LIKE FANTASTICONS ON THE MOVE AGAIN!
FINALLY - SOME ACTION!
ALRIGHT..
LET'S GET THEM!
INCREDIBLE CHANGE!
CHEE CHOO CHEE
CHE CHOO CHEE

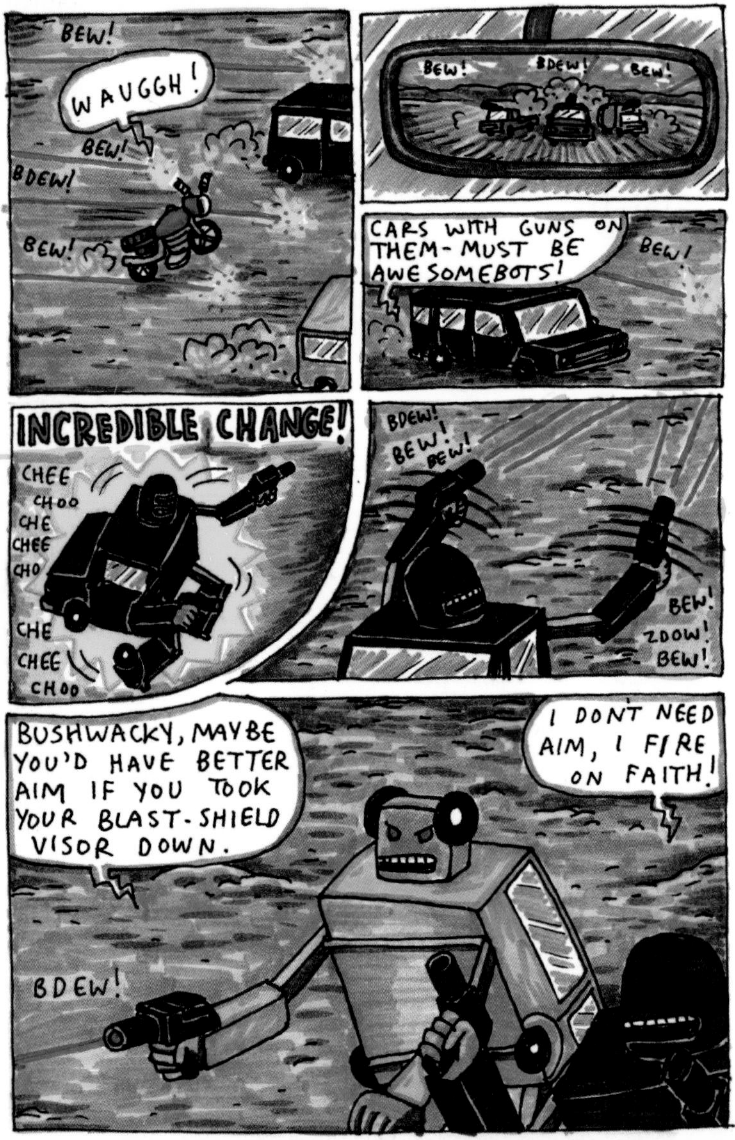
BEW!
WAUGGH!
BEW!
BDEW!
BEW!
BEW!
BDEW!
BEW!
CARS WITH GUNS ON THEM - MUST BE AWESOMEBOTS!
BEW!
INCREDIBLE CHANGE!
CHEE CHOO CHE CHEE CHO
CHE CHEE CHOO
BDEW!
BEW!
BEW!
BEW!
ZDOW!
BEW!
BUSHWACKY, MAYBE YOU'D HAVE BETTER AIM IF YOU TOOK YOUR BLAST-SHIELD VISOR DOWN.
I DON'T NEED AIM, I FIRE ON FAITH!
BDEW!

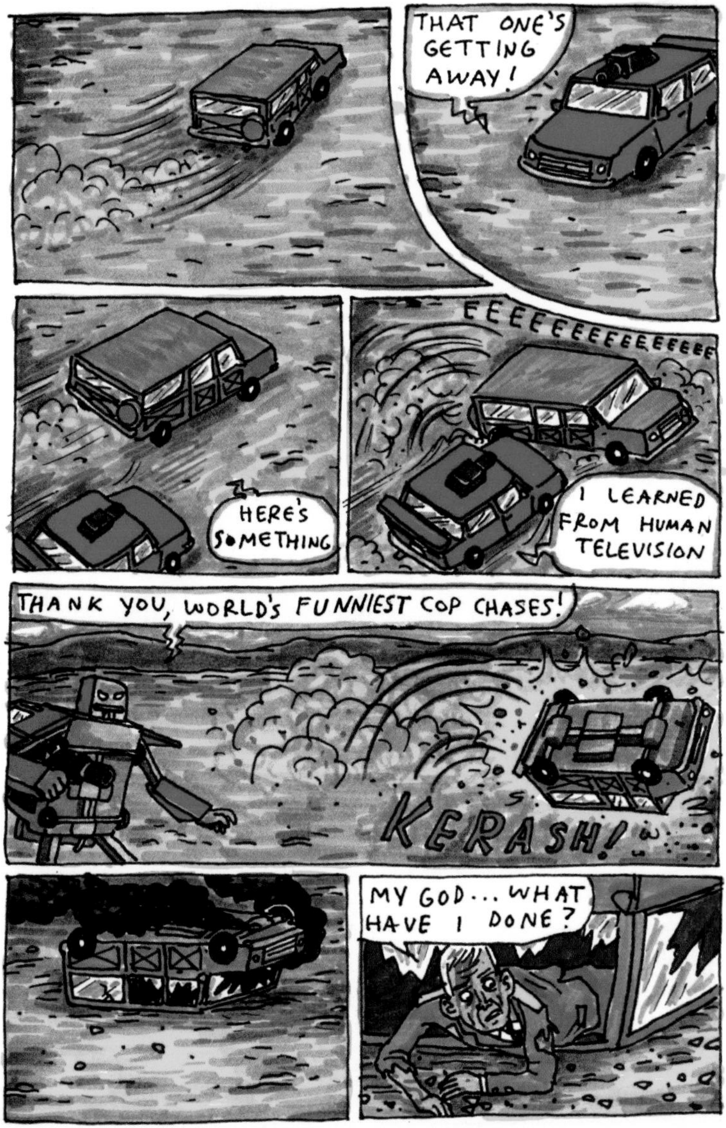
THAT ONE'S GETTING AWAY!
HERE'S SOMETHING
EEEEEEEEEEEEEEEEEE
I LEARNED FROM HUMAN TELEVISION
THANK YOU, WORLD'S FUNNIEST COP CHASES!
KERASH!
MY GOD... WHAT HAVE I DONE?

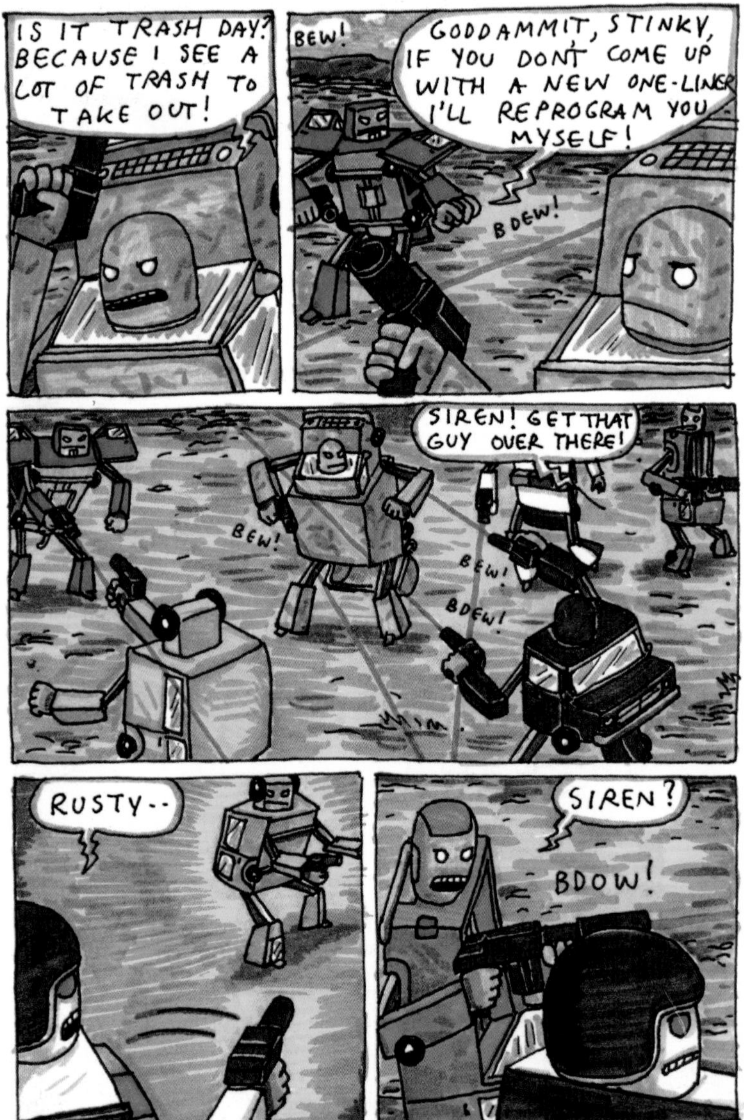
IS IT TRASH DAY? BECAUSE I SEE A LOT OF TRASH TO TAKE OUT!
BEW!
GODDAMMIT, STINKY, IF YOU DON'T COME UP WITH A NEW ONE-LINER I'LL REPROGRAM YOU MYSELF!
BDEW!
SIREN! GET THAT GUY OVER THERE!
BEW!
BEW!
BDEW!
RUSTY--
SIREN?
BDOW!

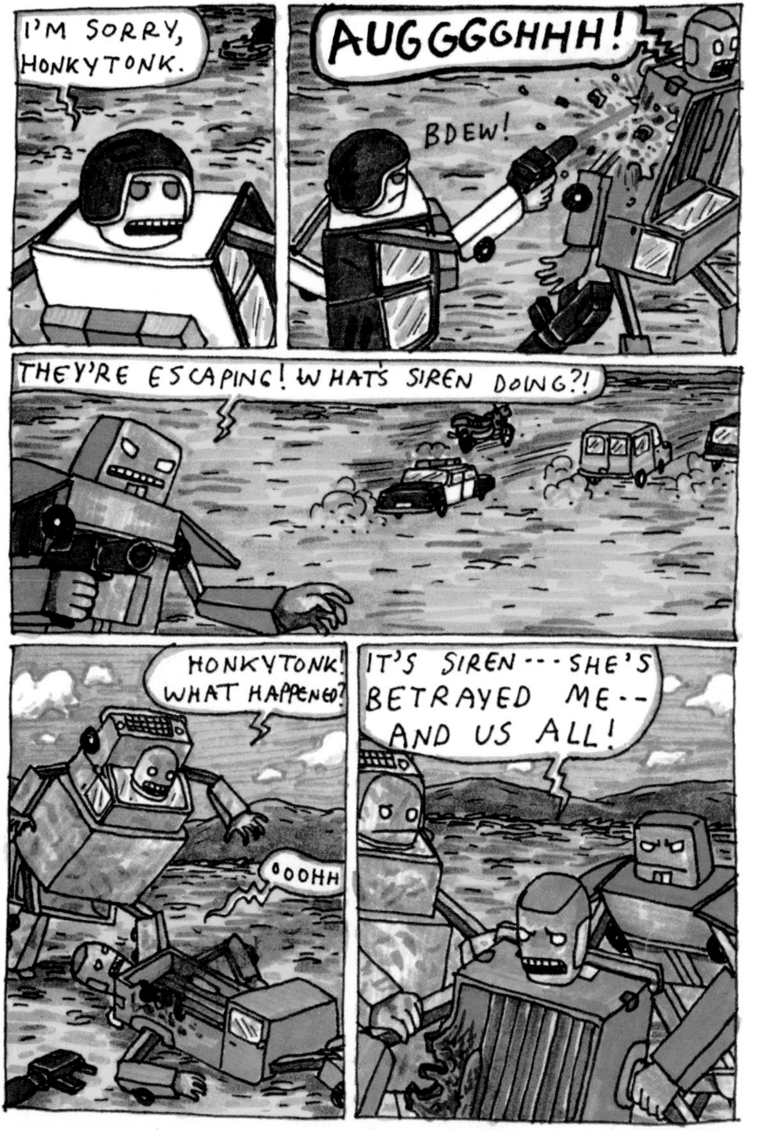
I'M SORRY, HONKYTONK.
AUGGGGHHH!
BDEW!
THEY'RE ESCAPING! WHAT'S SIREN DOING?!
HONKYTONK! WHAT HAPPENED?
OOOHH
IT'S SIREN--- SHE'S BETRAYED ME-- AND US ALL!

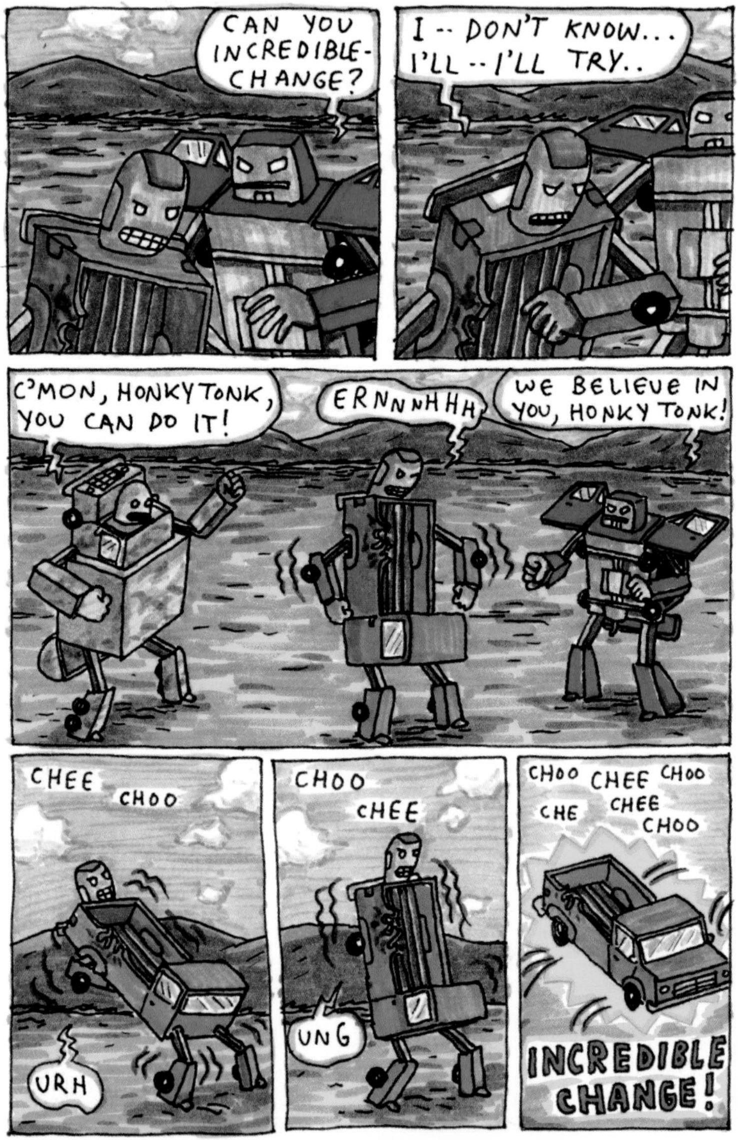
CAN YOU INCREDIBLE-CHANGE?
I -- DON'T KNOW... I'LL -- I'LL TRY..
C'MON, HONKYTONK, YOU CAN DO IT!
ERNNNHHH
WE BELIEVE IN YOU, HONKY TONK!
CHEE
CHOO
URH
CHOO
CHEE
UNG
CHOO CHEE CHOO
CHE CHEE CHOO
INCREDIBLE CHANGE!

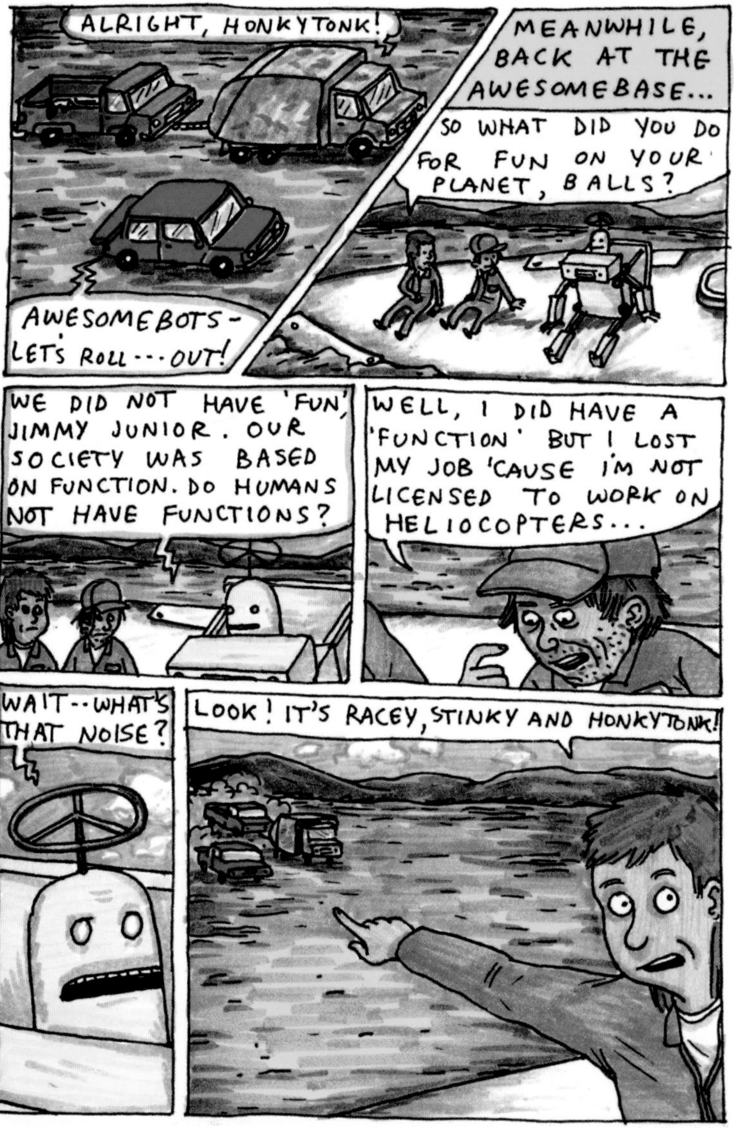
ALRIGHT, HONKYTONK!
AWESOMEBOTS- LET'S ROLL---OUT!
MEANWHILE, BACK AT THE AWESOMEBASE...
SO WHAT DID YOU DO FOR FUN ON YOUR PLANET, BALLS?
WE DID NOT HAVE 'FUN', JIMMY JUNIOR. OUR SOCIETY WAS BASED ON FUNCTION. DO HUMANS NOT HAVE FUNCTIONS?
WELL, I DID HAVE A 'FUNCTION' BUT I LOST MY JOB 'CAUSE I'M NOT LICENSED TO WORK ON HELIOCOPTERS...
WAIT--WHAT'S THAT NOISE?
LOOK! IT'S RACEY, STINKY AND HONKYTONK!

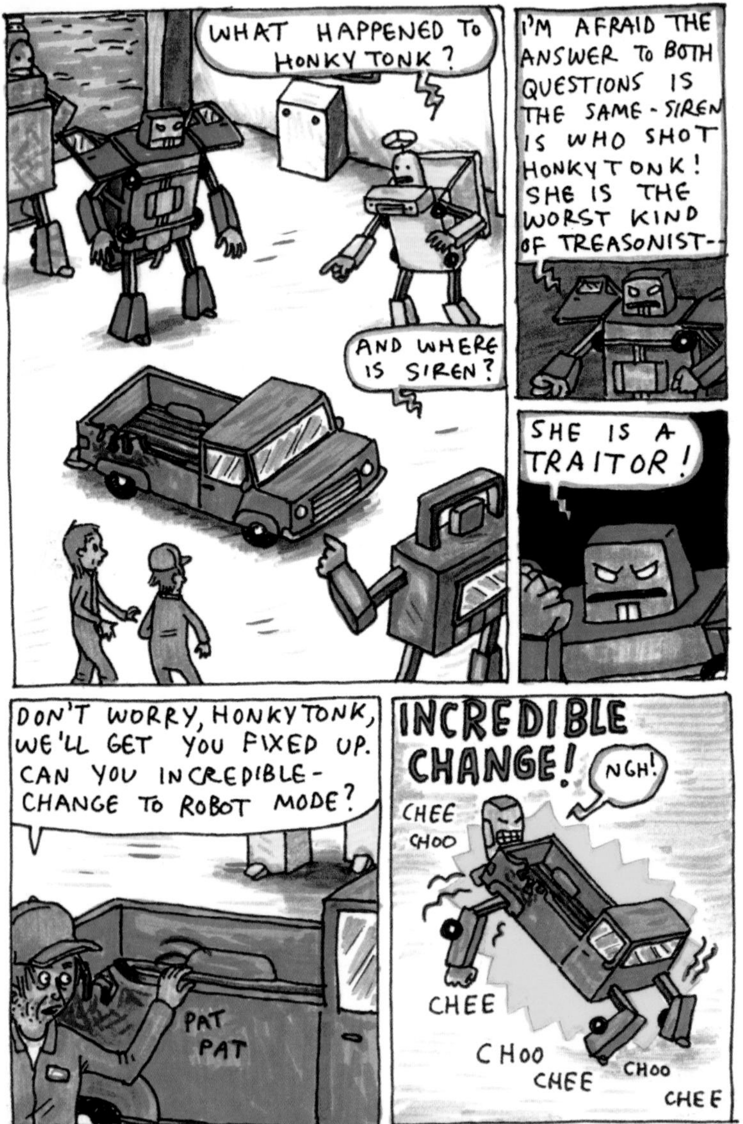
WHAT HAPPENED TO HONKY TONK?
AND WHERE IS SIREN?
I'M AFRAID THE ANSWER TO BOTH QUESTIONS IS THE SAME - SIREN IS WHO SHOT HONKYTONK! SHE IS THE WORST KIND OF TREASONIST--
SHE IS A TRAITOR!
DON'T WORRY, HONKYTONK, WE'LL GET YOU FIXED UP. CAN YOU INCREDIBLE-CHANGE TO ROBOT MODE?
PAT PAT
INCREDIBLE CHANGE!
NGH!
CHEE CHOO
CHEE
CHOO
CHEE
CHOO
CHEE

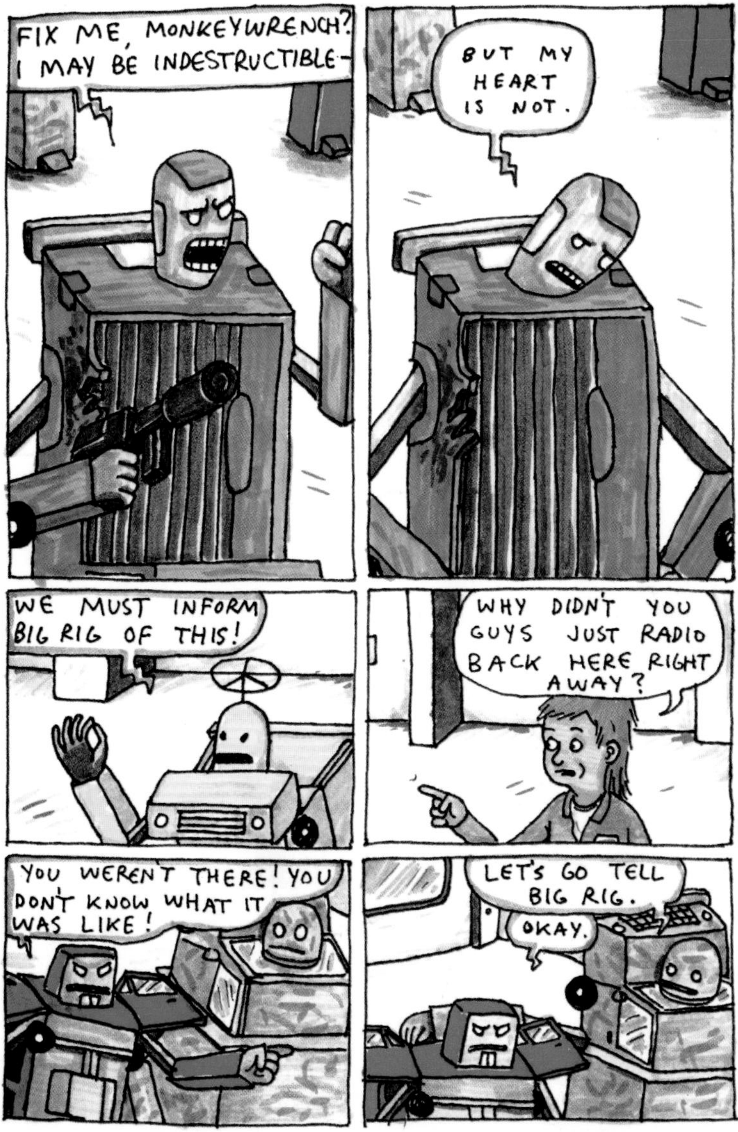
FIX ME, MONKEYWRENCH? I MAY BE INDESTRUCTIBLE-
BUT MY HEART IS NOT.
WE MUST INFORM BIG RIG OF THIS!
WHY DIDN'T YOU GUYS JUST RADIO BACK HERE RIGHT AWAY?
YOU WEREN'T THERE! YOU DON'T KNOW WHAT IT WAS LIKE!
LET'S GO TELL BIG RIG.
OKAY.

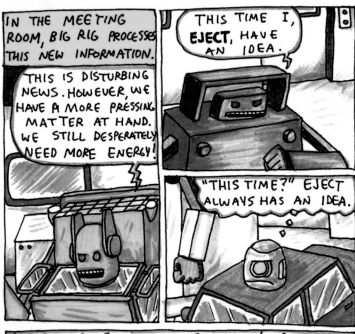

IN THE MEETING ROOM, BIG RIG PROCESSES THIS NEW INFORMATION.

THIS IS DISTURBING NEWS. HOWEVER, WE HAVE A MORE PRESSING MATTER AT HAND. WE STILL DESPERATELY NEED MORE ENERGY!

THIS TIME I, **EJECT**, HAVE AN IDEA.

"THIS TIME?" EJECT ALWAYS HAS AN IDEA.

I'VE STUDIED SOME OF THIS PLANET'S RESOURCES. ONE OF THE GREAT RESOURCES IS THE MIGHTY RAINFORESTS. MY NEW INVENTION WILL ALLOW US TO EXTRACT UNTOLD AMOUNTS OF ENERGY!

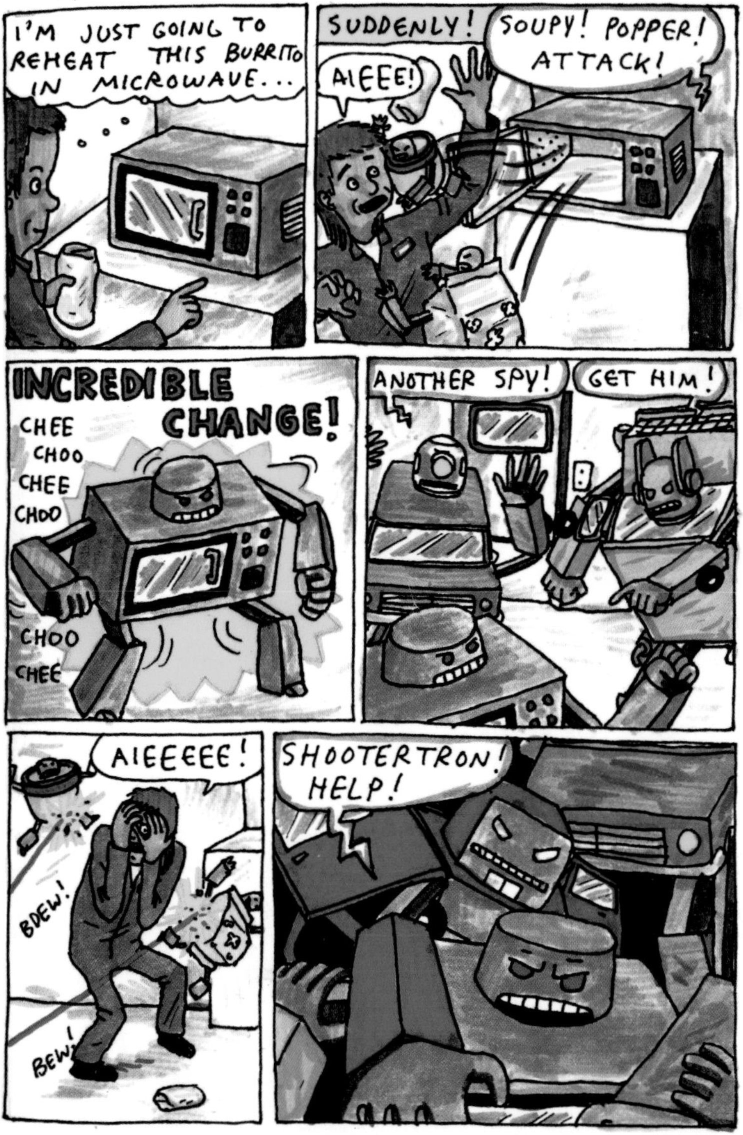
I'M JUST GOING TO REHEAT THIS BURRITO IN MICROWAVE...
SUDDENLY!
SOUPY! POPPER! ATTACK!
AIEEE!
INCREDIBLE CHANGE!
CHEE CHOO CHEE CHOO
CHOO CHEE
ANOTHER SPY!
GET HIM!
AIEEEEE!
BDEW!
BEW!
SHOOTERTRON! HELP!

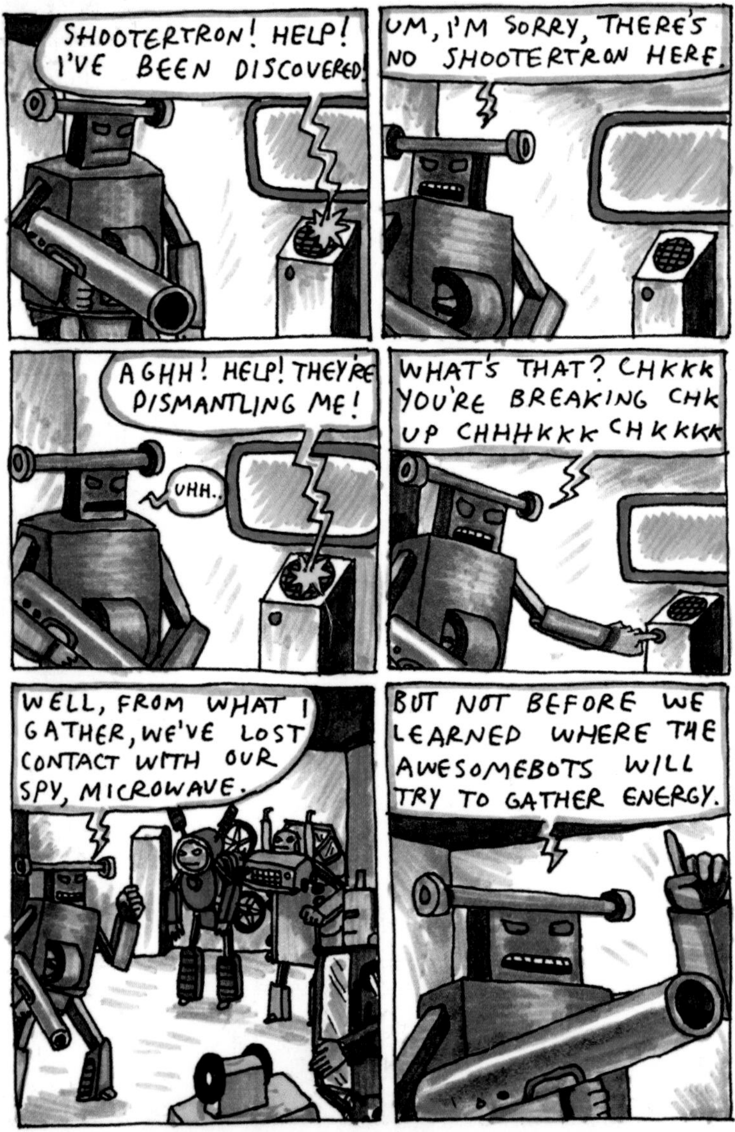
SHOOTERTRON! HELP! I'VE BEEN DISCOVERED!
UM, I'M SORRY, THERE'S NO SHOOTERTRON HERE.
AGHH! HELP! THEY'RE DISMANTLING ME!
UHH..
WHAT'S THAT? CHKKK YOU'RE BREAKING CHK UP CHHHKKK CHKKKK
WELL, FROM WHAT I GATHER, WE'VE LOST CONTACT WITH OUR SPY, MICROWAVE.
BUT NOT BEFORE WE LEARNED WHERE THE AWESOMEBOTS WILL TRY TO GATHER ENERGY.

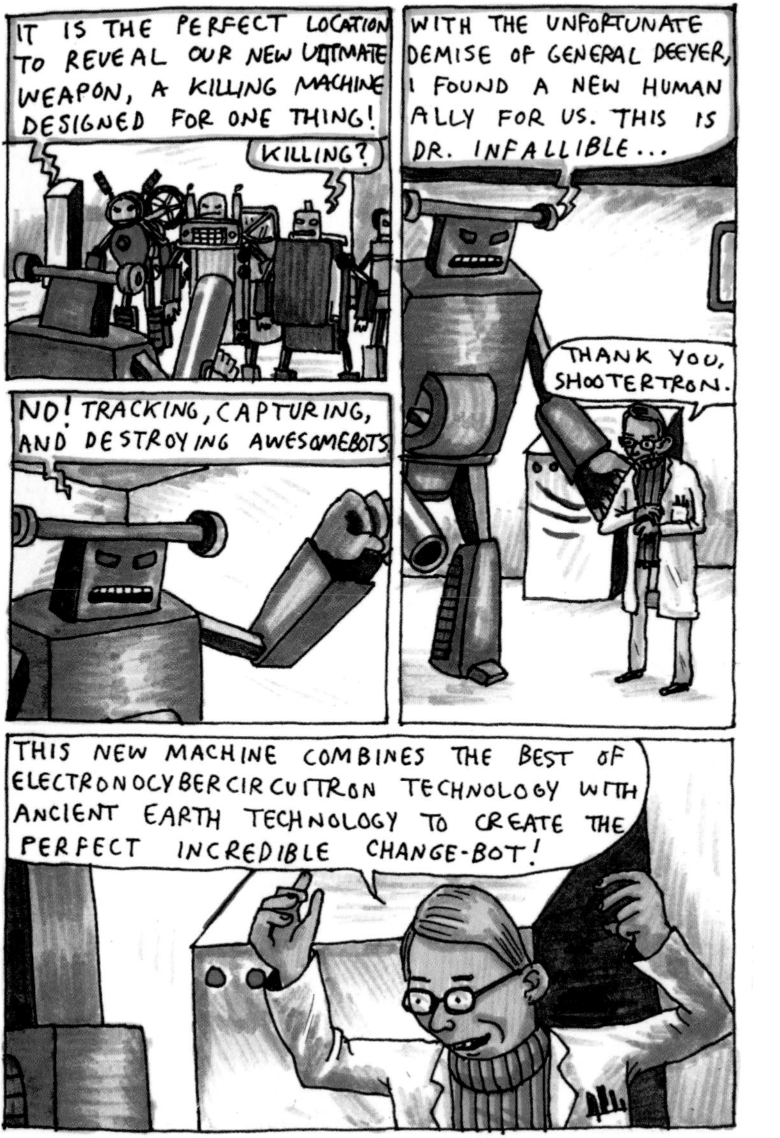
IT IS THE PERFECT LOCATION TO REVEAL OUR NEW ULTIMATE WEAPON, A KILLING MACHINE DESIGNED FOR ONE THING!
KILLING?
WITH THE UNFORTUNATE DEMISE OF GENERAL DEEYER, I FOUND A NEW HUMAN ALLY FOR US. THIS IS DR. INFALLIBLE...
NO! TRACKING, CAPTURING, AND DESTROYING AWESOMEBOTS
THANK YOU, SHOOTERTRON.
THIS NEW MACHINE COMBINES THE BEST OF ELECTRONOCYBERCIRCUITRON TECHNOLOGY WITH ANCIENT EARTH TECHNOLOGY TO CREATE THE PERFECT INCREDIBLE CHANGE-BOT!

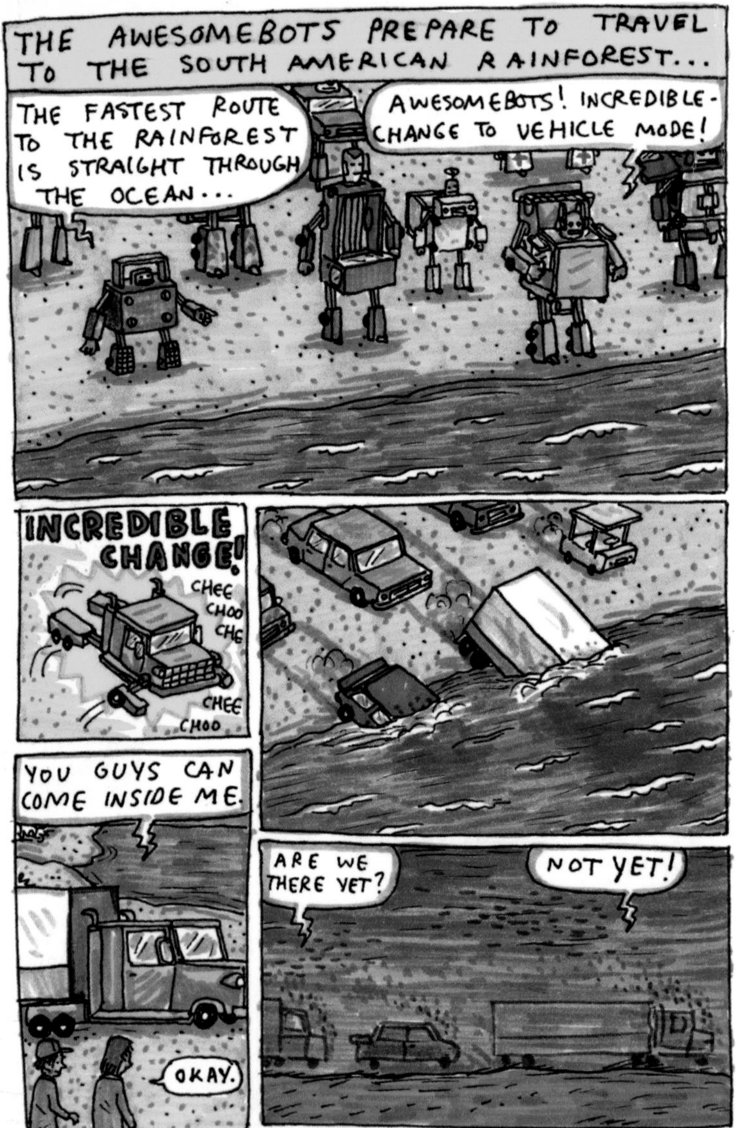
THE AWESOMEBOTS PREPARE TO TRAVEL TO THE SOUTH AMERICAN RAINFOREST...
THE FASTEST ROUTE TO THE RAINFOREST IS STRAIGHT THROUGH THE OCEAN...
AWESOMEBOTS! INCREDIBLE-CHANGE TO VEHICLE MODE!
INCREDIBLE CHANGE!
CHEE CHOO CHE
CHEE CHOO
YOU GUYS CAN COME INSIDE ME.
OKAY.
ARE WE THERE YET?
NOT YET!

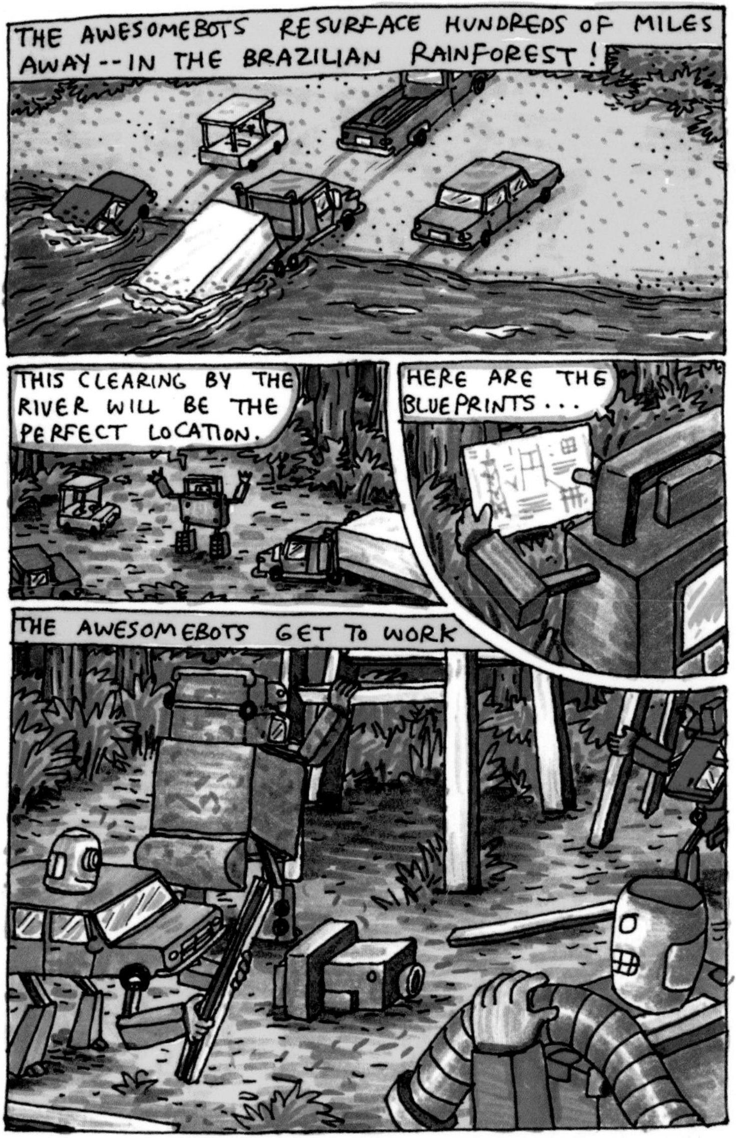
THE AWESOMEBOTS RESURFACE HUNDREDS OF MILES AWAY--IN THE BRAZILIAN RAINFOREST!
THIS CLEARING BY THE RIVER WILL BE THE PERFECT LOCATION.
HERE ARE THE BLUEPRINTS...
THE AWESOMEBOTS GET TO WORK

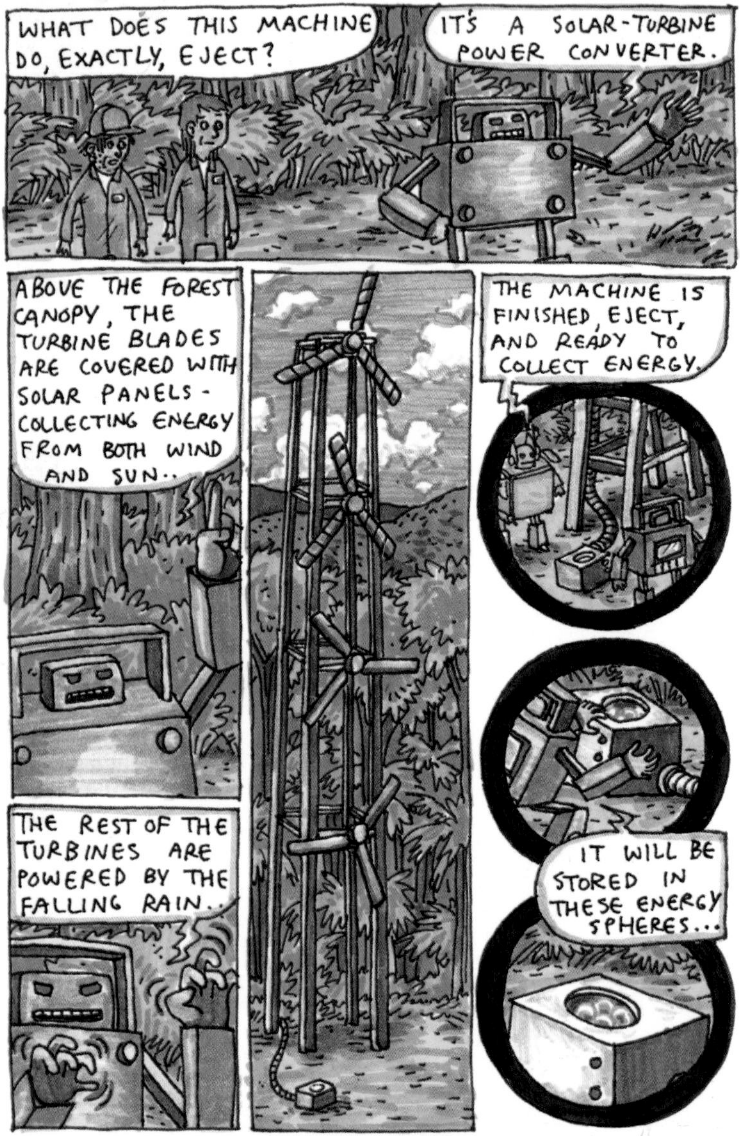
WHAT DOES THIS MACHINE DO, EXACTLY, EJECT?
IT'S A SOLAR-TURBINE POWER CONVERTER.
ABOVE THE FOREST CANOPY, THE TURBINE BLADES ARE COVERED WITH SOLAR PANELS - COLLECTING ENERGY FROM BOTH WIND AND SUN..
THE REST OF THE TURBINES ARE POWERED BY THE FALLING RAIN..
THE MACHINE IS FINISHED, EJECT, AND READY TO COLLECT ENERGY.
IT WILL BE STORED IN THESE ENERGY SPHERES...

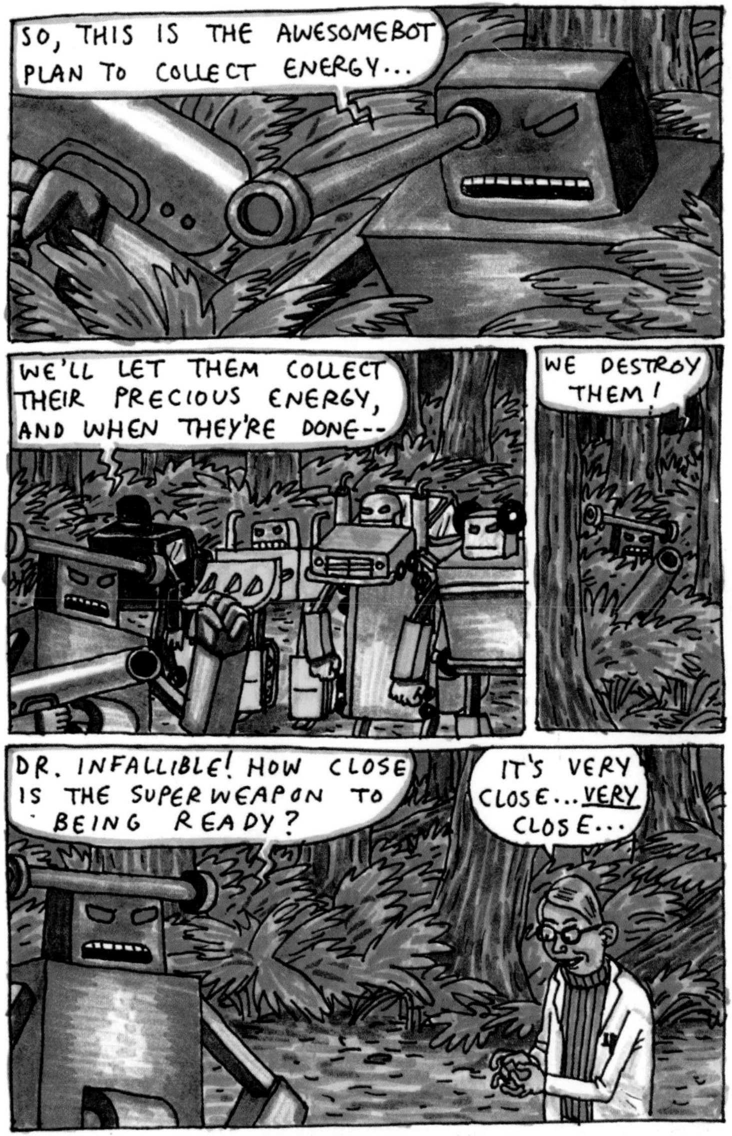
SO, THIS IS THE AWESOMEBOT PLAN TO COLLECT ENERGY...
WE'LL LET THEM COLLECT THEIR PRECIOUS ENERGY, AND WHEN THEY'RE DONE--
WE DESTROY THEM!
DR. INFALLIBLE! HOW CLOSE IS THE SUPERWEAPON TO BEING READY?
IT'S VERY CLOSE... VERY CLOSE...

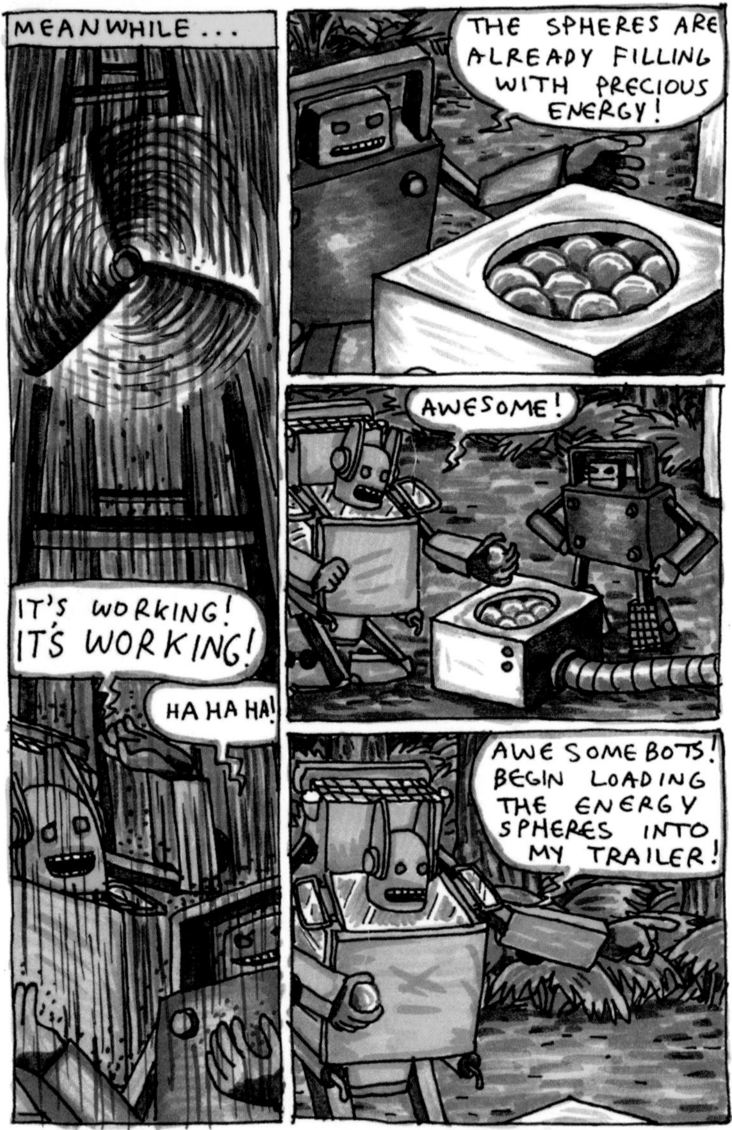
MEANWHILE...
THE SPHERES ARE ALREADY FILLING WITH PRECIOUS ENERGY!
IT'S WORKING! IT'S WORKING!
HA HA HA!
AWESOME!
AWESOMEBOTS! BEGIN LOADING THE ENERGY SPHERES INTO MY TRAILER!

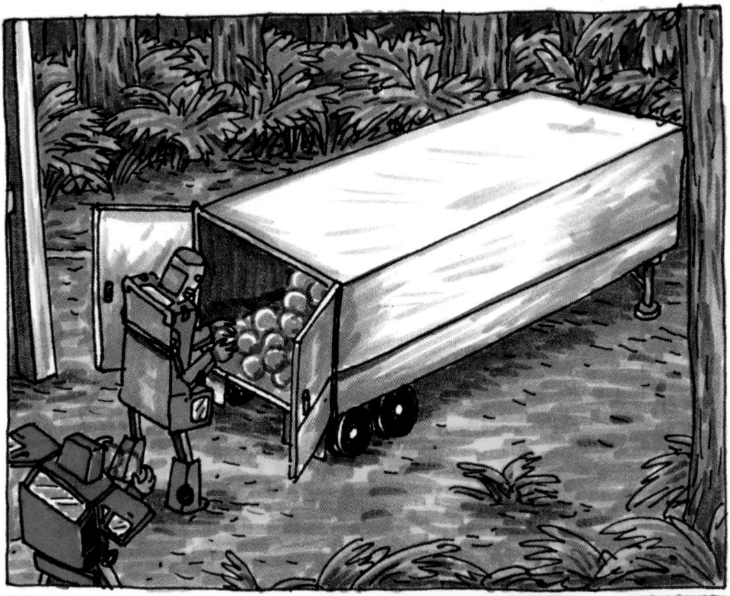

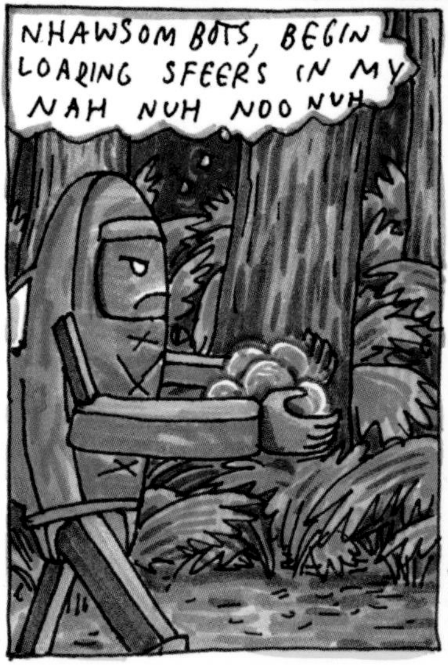
NHAWSOM BOTS, BEGIN LOADING SFEERS IN MY NAH NUH NOO NUH

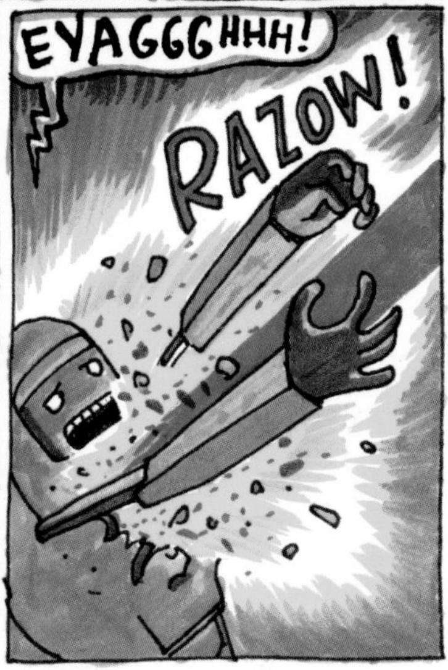
EYAGGGHHH!
RAZOW!

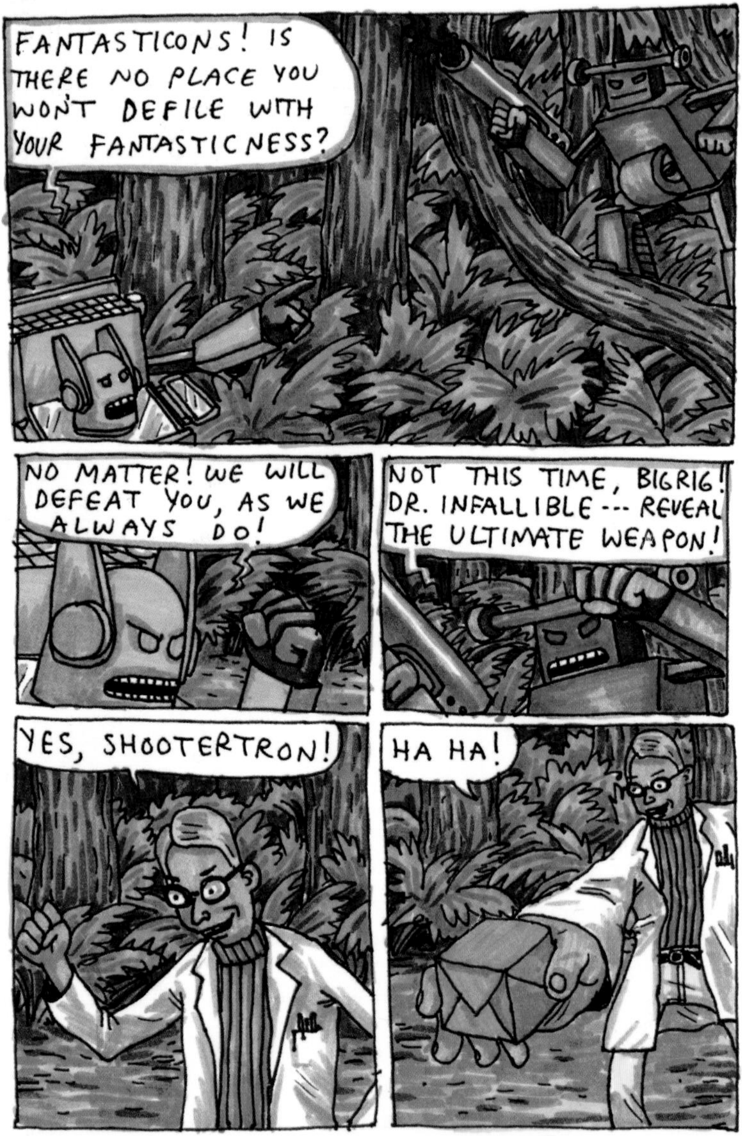
FANTASTICONS! IS THERE NO PLACE YOU WON'T DEFILE WITH YOUR FANTASTICNESS?
NO MATTER! WE WILL DEFEAT YOU, AS WE ALWAYS DO!
NOT THIS TIME, BIGRIG! DR. INFALLIBLE --- REVEAL THE ULTIMATE WEAPON!
YES, SHOOTERTRON!
HA HA!

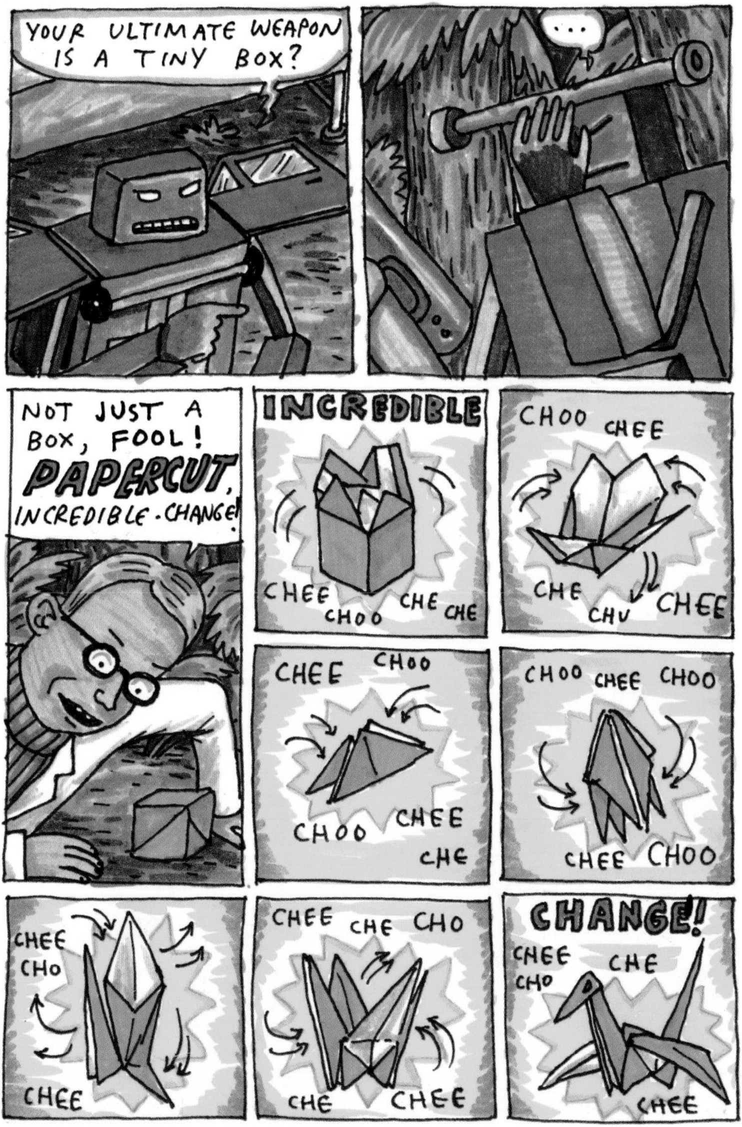
YOUR ULTIMATE WEAPON IS A TINY BOX?
...
NOT JUST A BOX, FOOL! PAPERCUT, INCREDIBLE-CHANGE!
INCREDIBLE
CHEE CHOO CHE CHE
CHOO CHEE
CHE CHU CHEE
CHEE CHOO
CHOO CHEE CHE
CHOO CHEE CHOO
CHEE CHOO
CHEE CHO
CHEE
CHEE CHE CHO
CHE CHEE
CHANGE!
CHEE CHO CHE
CHEE

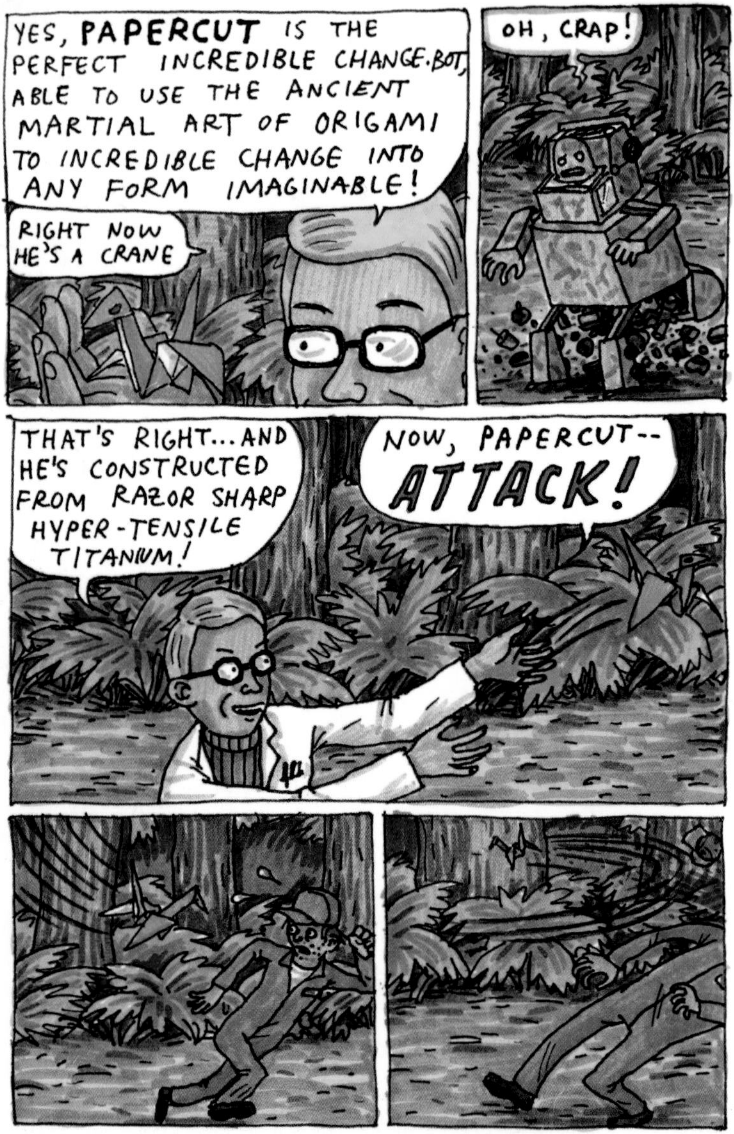
YES, PAPERCUT IS THE PERFECT INCREDIBLE CHANGE.BOT, ABLE TO USE THE ANCIENT MARTIAL ART OF ORIGAMI TO INCREDIBLE CHANGE INTO ANY FORM IMAGINABLE!
RIGHT NOW HE'S A CRANE
OH, CRAP!
THAT'S RIGHT... AND HE'S CONSTRUCTED FROM RAZOR SHARP HYPER-TENSILE TITANIUM!
NOW, PAPERCUT-- ATTACK!

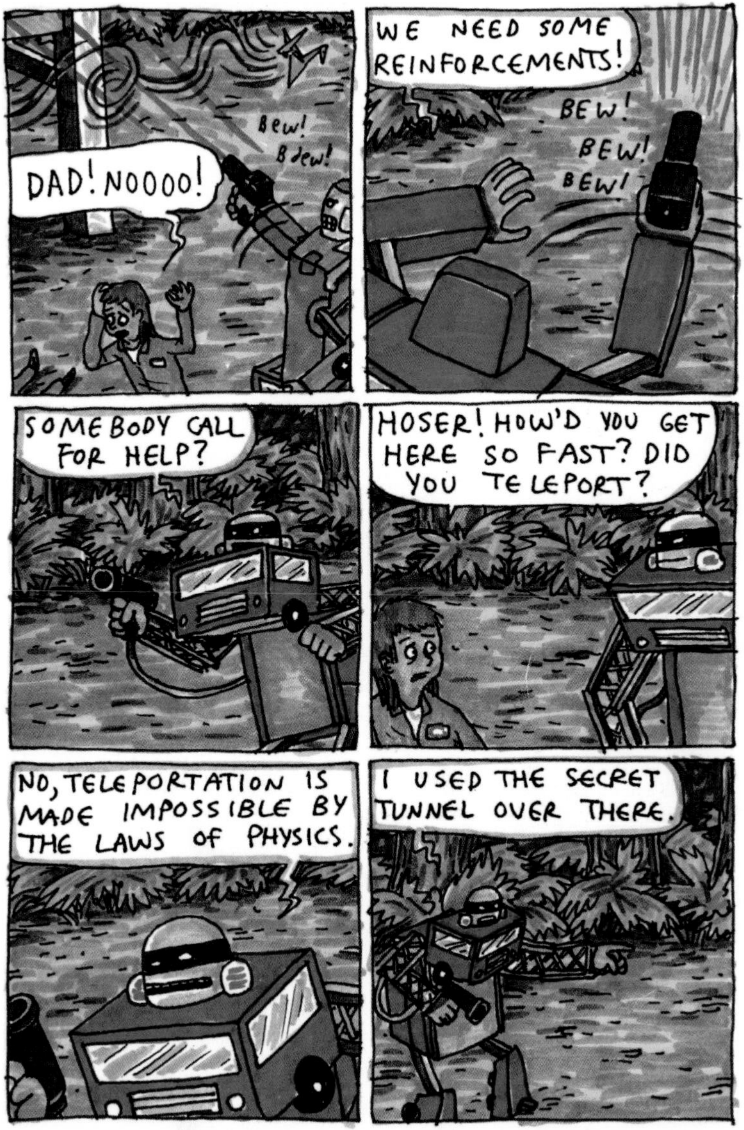
Bew!
Bdew!
DAD! NOOOO!
WE NEED SOME REINFORCEMENTS!
BEW!
BEW!
BEW!
SOMEBODY CALL FOR HELP?
HOSER! HOW'D YOU GET HERE SO FAST? DID YOU TELEPORT?
NO, TELEPORTATION IS MADE IMPOSSIBLE BY THE LAWS OF PHYSICS.
I USED THE SECRET TUNNEL OVER THERE.

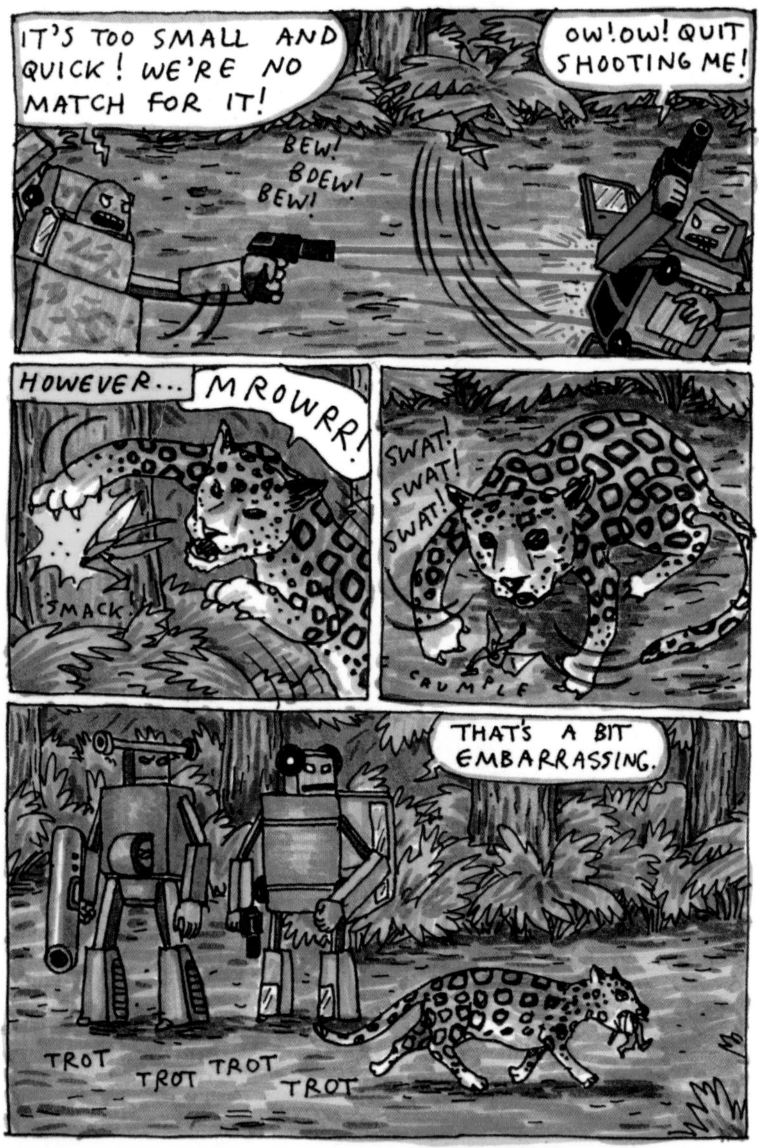
IT'S TOO SMALL AND QUICK! WE'RE NO MATCH FOR IT!
OW! OW! QUIT SHOOTING ME!
BEW! BDEW! BEW!
HOWEVER...
MROWRR!
SMACK!
SWAT! SWAT! SWAT!
CRUMPLE
THAT'S A BIT EMBARRASSING.
TROT TROT TROT TROT

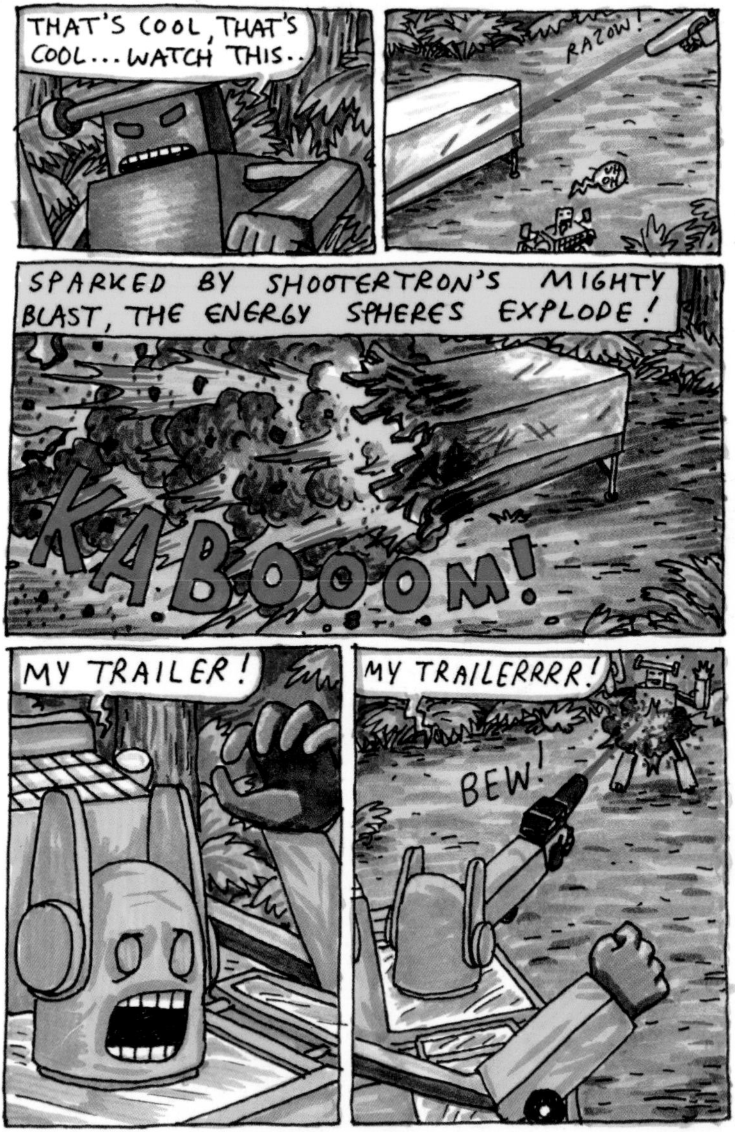
THAT'S COOL, THAT'S COOL... WATCH THIS..
RAZOW!
UH OH
SPARKED BY SHOOTERTRON'S MIGHTY BLAST, THE ENERGY SPHERES EXPLODE!
KABOOOM!
MY TRAILER!
MY TRAILERRRR!
BEW!

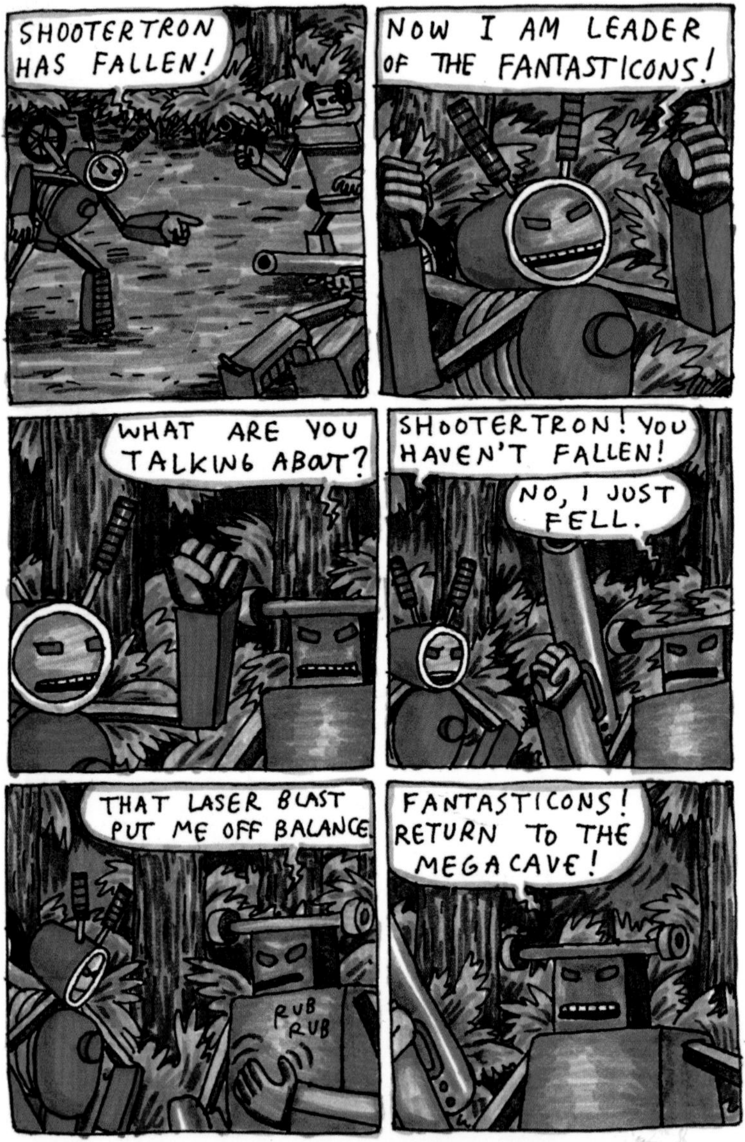
SHOOTERTRON HAS FALLEN!
NOW I AM LEADER OF THE FANTASTICONS!
WHAT ARE YOU TALKING ABOUT?
SHOOTERTRON! YOU HAVEN'T FALLEN!
NO, I JUST FELL.
THAT LASER BLAST PUT ME OFF BALANCE.
RUB RUB
FANTASTICONS! RETURN TO THE MEGACAVE!

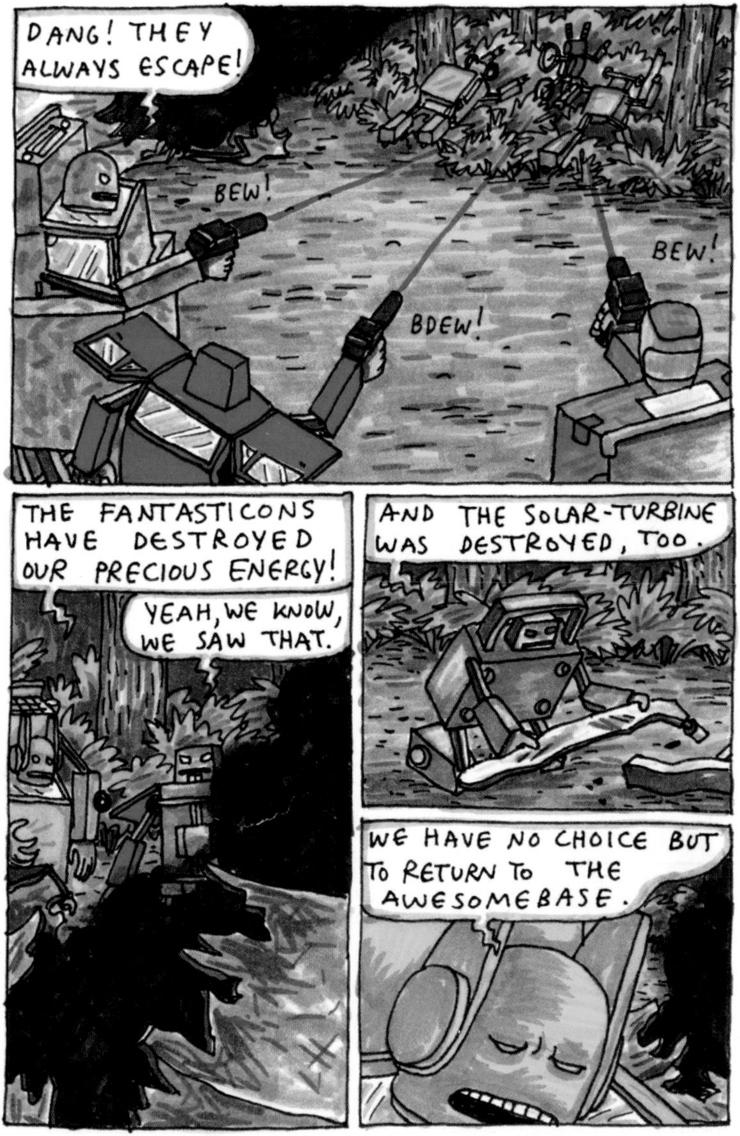
DANG! THEY ALWAYS ESCAPE!
BEW!
BDEW!
BEW!
THE FANTASTICONS HAVE DESTROYED OUR PRECIOUS ENERGY!
YEAH, WE KNOW, WE SAW THAT.
AND THE SOLAR-TURBINE WAS DESTROYED, TOO.
WE HAVE NO CHOICE BUT TO RETURN TO THE AWESOMEBASE.

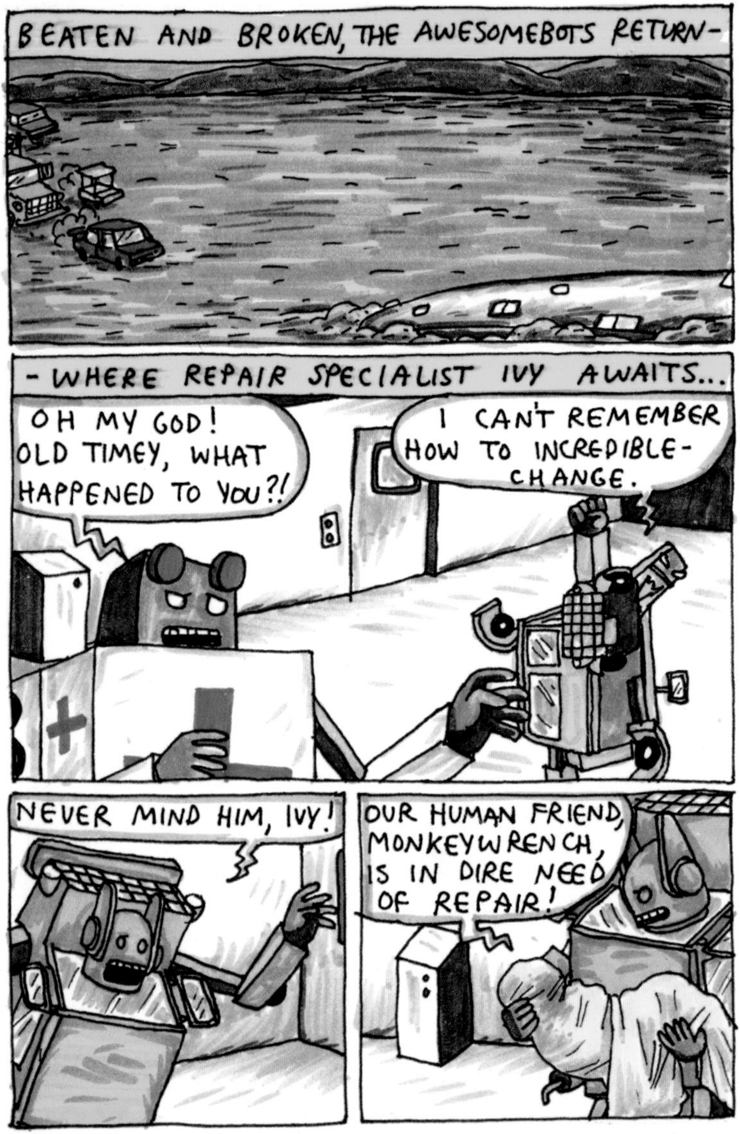
BEATEN AND BROKEN, THE AWESOMEBOTS RETURN-
-WHERE REPAIR SPECIALIST IVY AWAITS...
OH MY GOD! OLD TIMEY, WHAT HAPPENED TO YOU?!
I CAN'T REMEMBER HOW TO INCREDIBLE-CHANGE.
NEVER MIND HIM, IVY!
OUR HUMAN FRIEND, MONKEYWRENCH, IS IN DIRE NEED OF REPAIR!

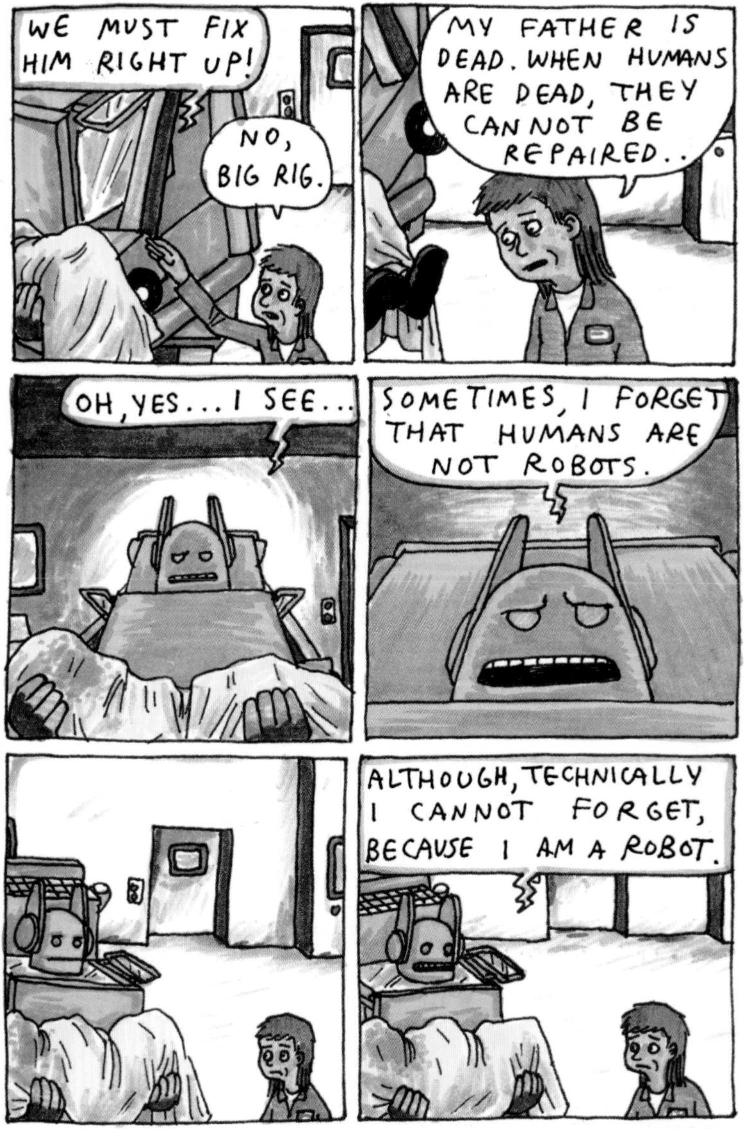
WE MUST FIX HIM RIGHT UP!
NO, BIG RIG.
MY FATHER IS DEAD. WHEN HUMANS ARE DEAD, THEY CANNOT BE REPAIRED..
OH, YES... I SEE...
SOMETIMES, I FORGET THAT HUMANS ARE NOT ROBOTS.
ALTHOUGH, TECHNICALLY I CANNOT FORGET, BECAUSE I AM A ROBOT.

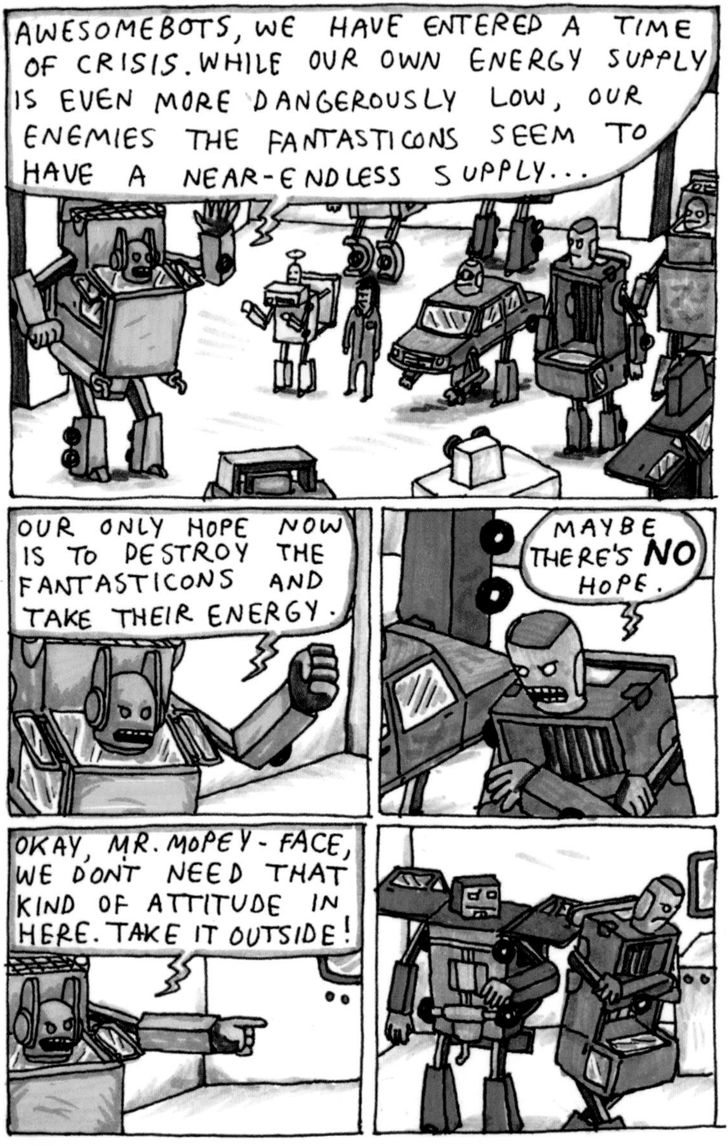
AWESOMEBOTS, WE HAVE ENTERED A TIME OF CRISIS. WHILE OUR OWN ENERGY SUPPLY IS EVEN MORE DANGEROUSLY LOW, OUR ENEMIES THE FANTASTICONS SEEM TO HAVE A NEAR-ENDLESS SUPPLY...
OUR ONLY HOPE NOW IS TO DESTROY THE FANTASTICONS AND TAKE THEIR ENERGY.
MAYBE THERE'S **NO** HOPE.
OKAY, MR. MOPEY-FACE, WE DON'T NEED THAT KIND OF ATTITUDE IN HERE. TAKE IT OUTSIDE!

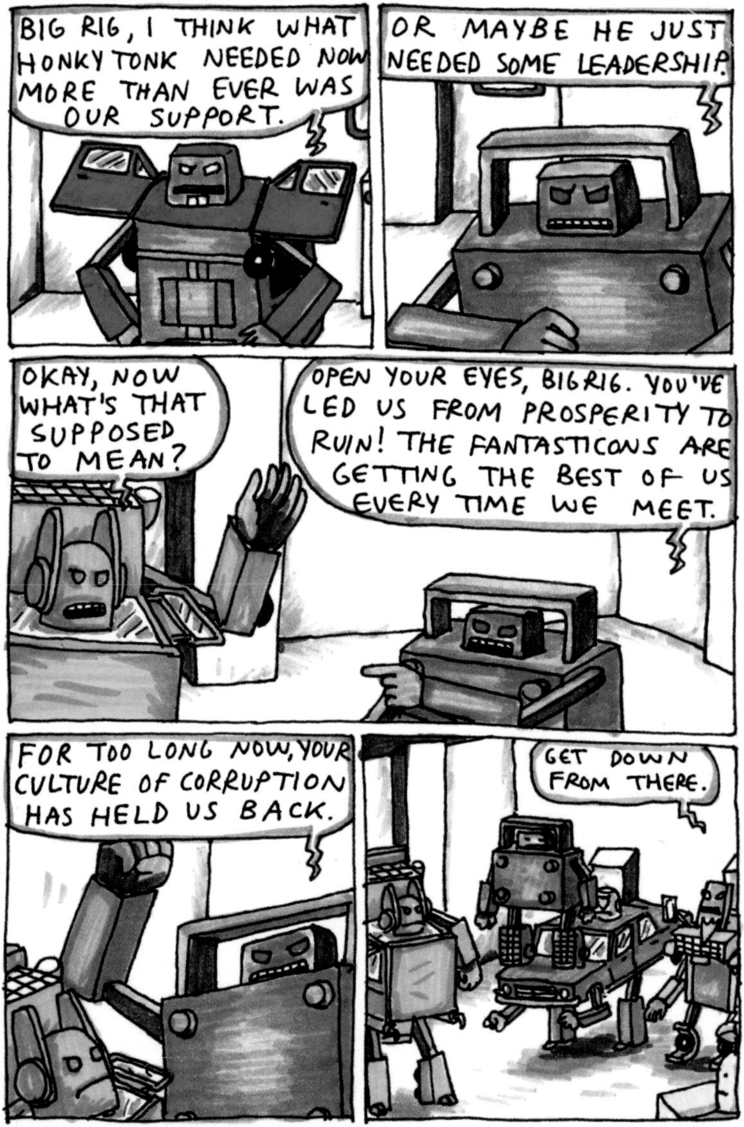
BIG RIG, I THINK WHAT HONKYTONK NEEDED NOW MORE THAN EVER WAS OUR SUPPORT.
OR MAYBE HE JUST NEEDED SOME LEADERSHIP.
OKAY, NOW WHAT'S THAT SUPPOSED TO MEAN?
OPEN YOUR EYES, BIGRIG. YOU'VE LED US FROM PROSPERITY TO RUIN! THE FANTASTICONS ARE GETTING THE BEST OF US EVERY TIME WE MEET.
FOR TOO LONG NOW, YOUR CULTURE OF CORRUPTION HAS HELD US BACK.
GET DOWN FROM THERE.

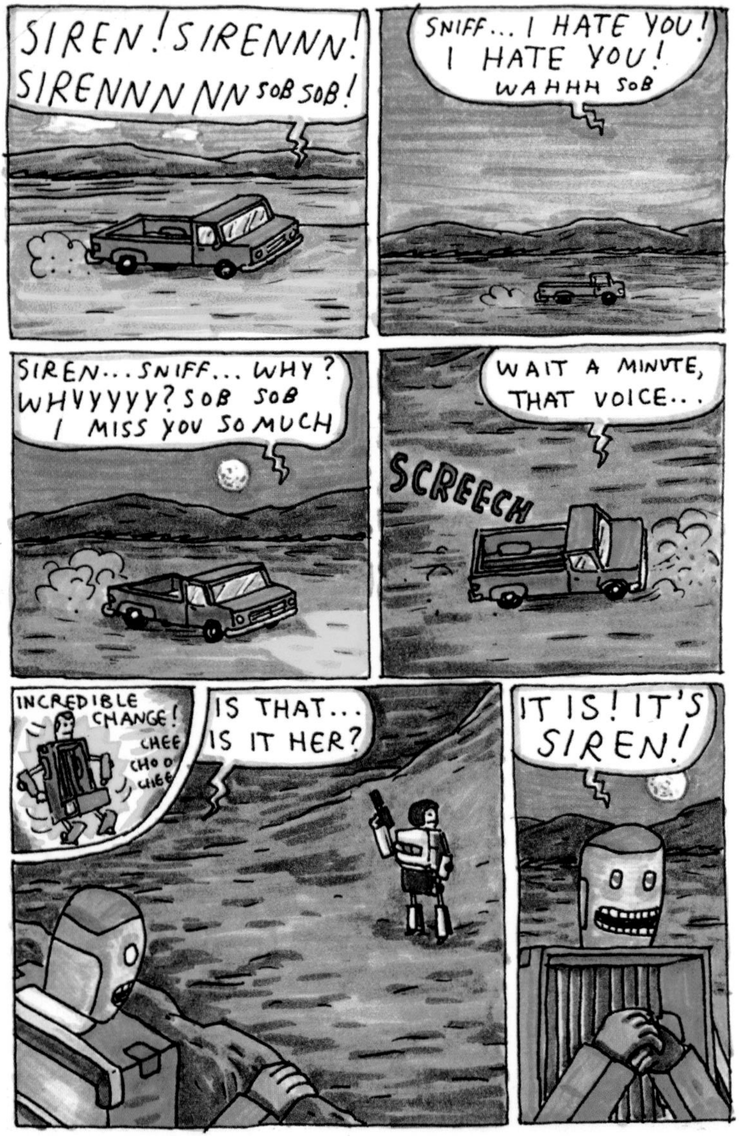
SIREN! SIRENNN! SIRENNNNNN SOB SOB!
SNIFF... I HATE YOU! I HATE YOU! WAHHH SOB
SIREN... SNIFF... WHY? WHYYYYY? SOB SOB I MISS YOU SO MUCH
WAIT A MINUTE, THAT VOICE...
SCREECH
INCREDIBLE CHANGE!
CHEE CHO CHEE
IS THAT... IS IT HER?
IT IS! IT'S SIREN!

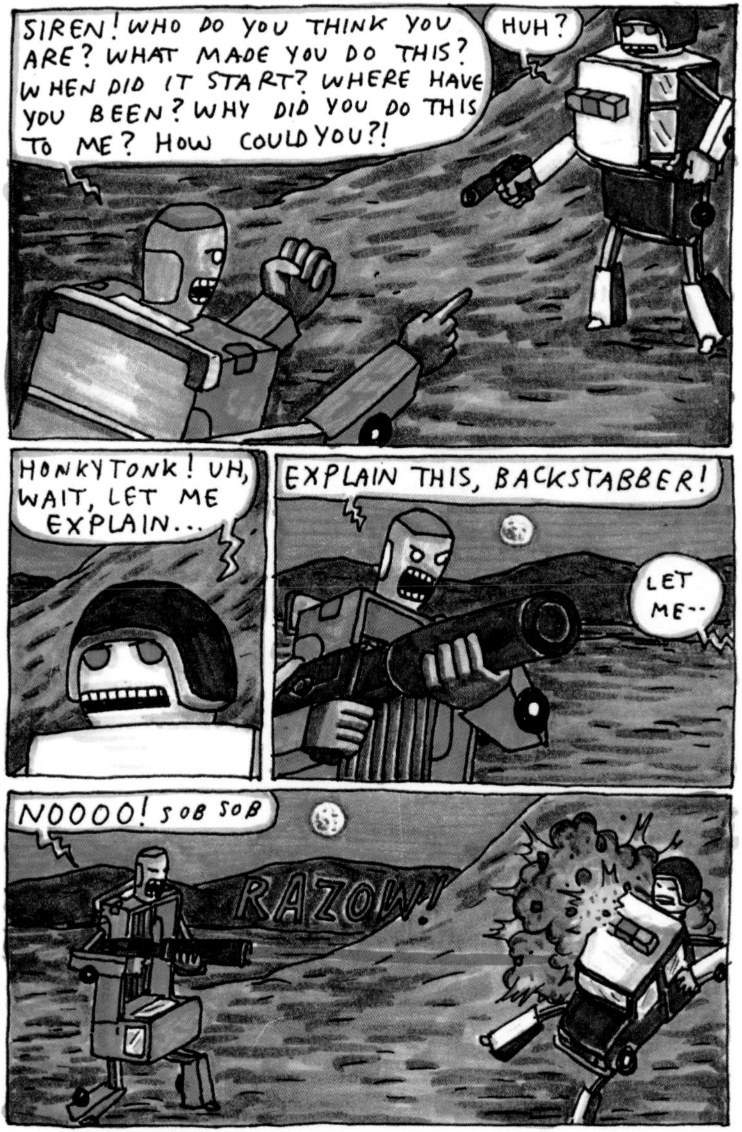
SIREN! WHO DO YOU THINK YOU ARE? WHAT MADE YOU DO THIS? WHEN DID IT START? WHERE HAVE YOU BEEN? WHY DID YOU DO THIS TO ME? HOW COULD YOU?!
HUH?
HONKYTONK! UH, WAIT, LET ME EXPLAIN...
EXPLAIN THIS, BACKSTABBER!
LET ME--
NOOOO! SOB SOB
RAZOW!

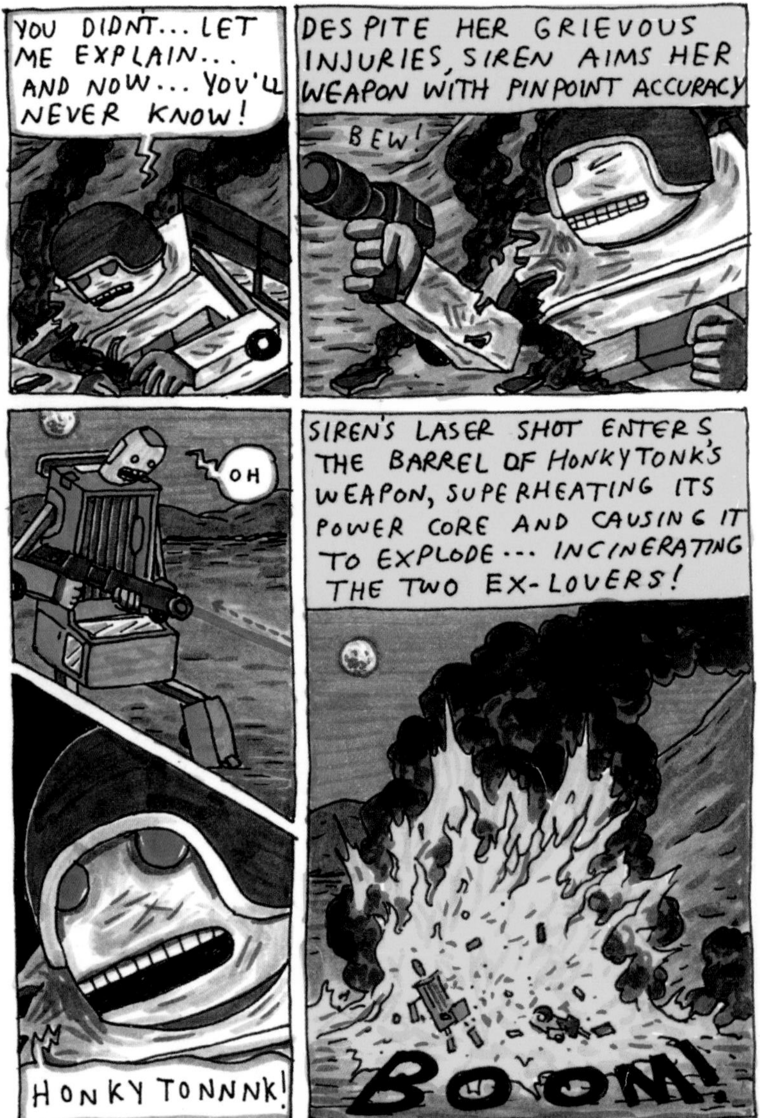
YOU DIDN'T... LET ME EXPLAIN... AND NOW... YOU'LL NEVER KNOW!
DESPITE HER GRIEVOUS INJURIES, SIREN AIMS HER WEAPON WITH PINPOINT ACCURACY
BEW!
OH
HONKY TONNNK!
SIREN'S LASER SHOT ENTERS THE BARREL OF HONKYTONK'S WEAPON, SUPERHEATING ITS POWER CORE AND CAUSING IT TO EXPLODE... INCINERATING THE TWO EX-LOVERS!
BOOM!

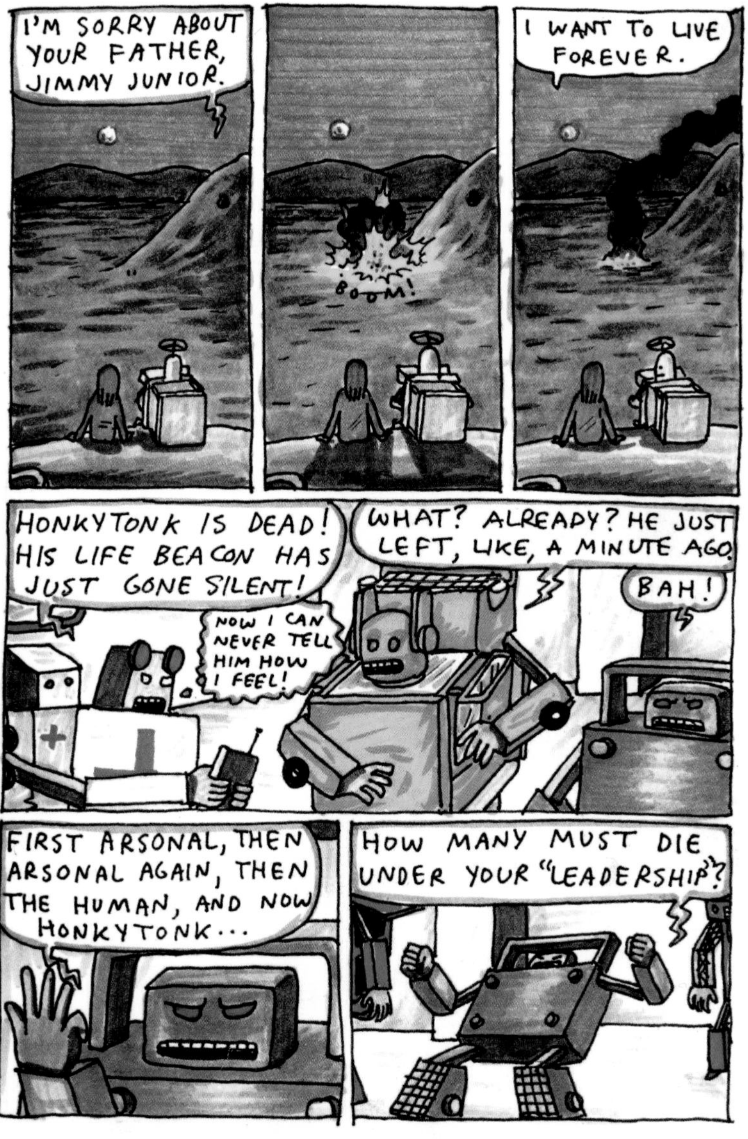
I'M SORRY ABOUT YOUR FATHER, JIMMY JUNIOR.
BOOM!
I WANT TO LIVE FOREVER.
HONKYTONK IS DEAD! HIS LIFE BEACON HAS JUST GONE SILENT!
WHAT? ALREADY? HE JUST LEFT, LIKE, A MINUTE AGO.
NOW I CAN NEVER TELL HIM HOW I FEEL!
BAH!
FIRST ARSONAL, THEN ARSONAL AGAIN, THEN THE HUMAN, AND NOW HONKYTONK...
HOW MANY MUST DIE UNDER YOUR "LEADERSHIP"?

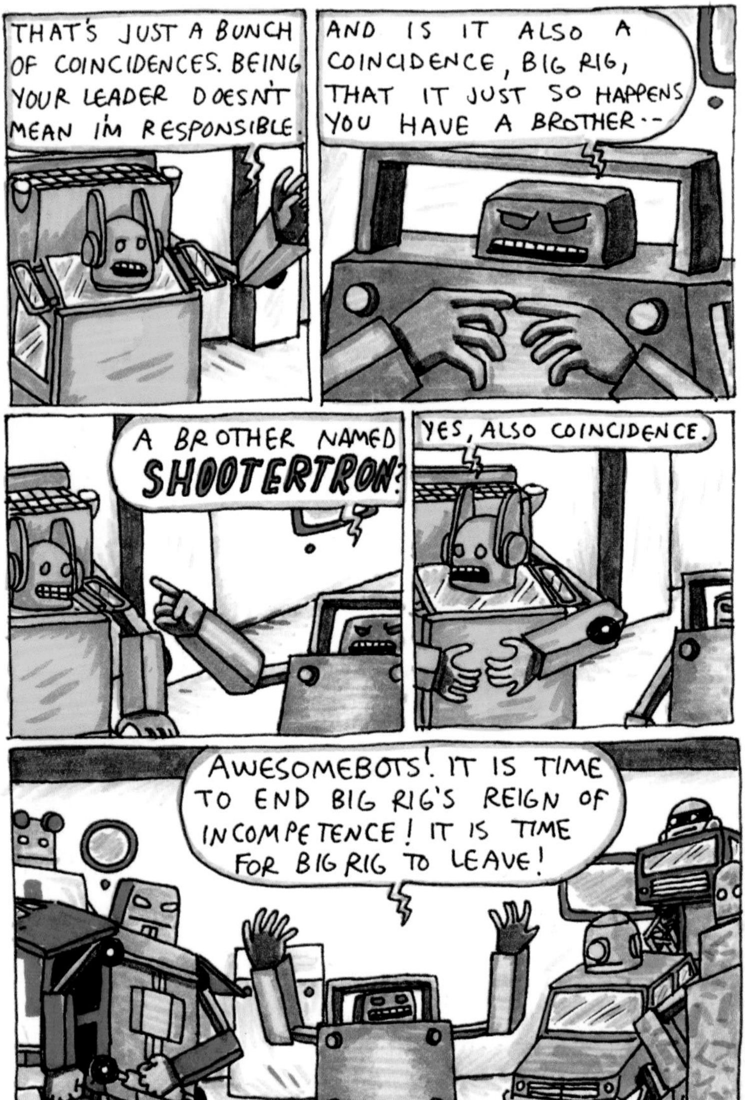
THAT'S JUST A BUNCH OF COINCIDENCES. BEING YOUR LEADER DOESN'T MEAN I'M RESPONSIBLE.
AND IS IT ALSO A COINCIDENCE, BIG RIG, THAT IT JUST SO HAPPENS YOU HAVE A BROTHER--
A BROTHER NAMED SHOOTERTRON?
YES, ALSO COINCIDENCE.
AWESOMEBOTS! IT IS TIME TO END BIG RIG'S REIGN OF INCOMPETENCE! IT IS TIME FOR BIG RIG TO LEAVE!

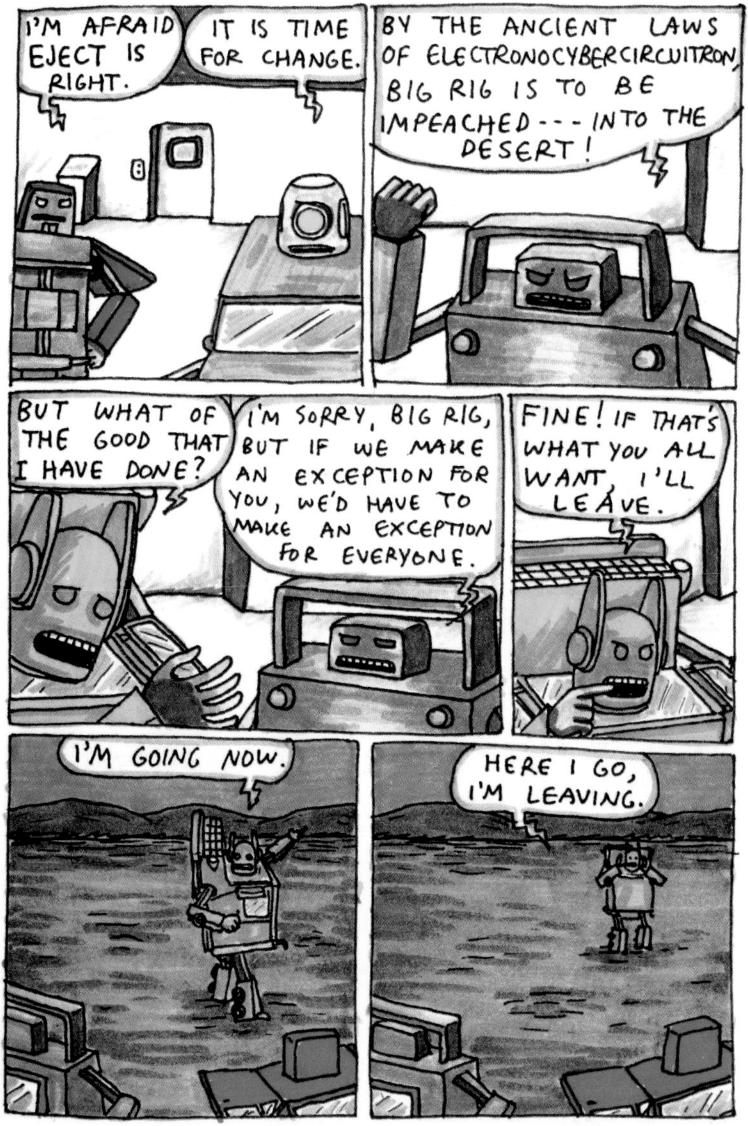
I'M AFRAID EJECT IS RIGHT.
IT IS TIME FOR CHANGE.
BY THE ANCIENT LAWS OF ELECTRONOCYBERCIRCUITRON, BIG RIG IS TO BE IMPEACHED--- INTO THE DESERT!
BUT WHAT OF THE GOOD THAT I HAVE DONE?
I'M SORRY, BIG RIG, BUT IF WE MAKE AN EXCEPTION FOR YOU, WE'D HAVE TO MAKE AN EXCEPTION FOR EVERYONE.
FINE! IF THAT'S WHAT YOU ALL WANT, I'LL LEAVE.
I'M GOING NOW.
HERE I GO, I'M LEAVING.

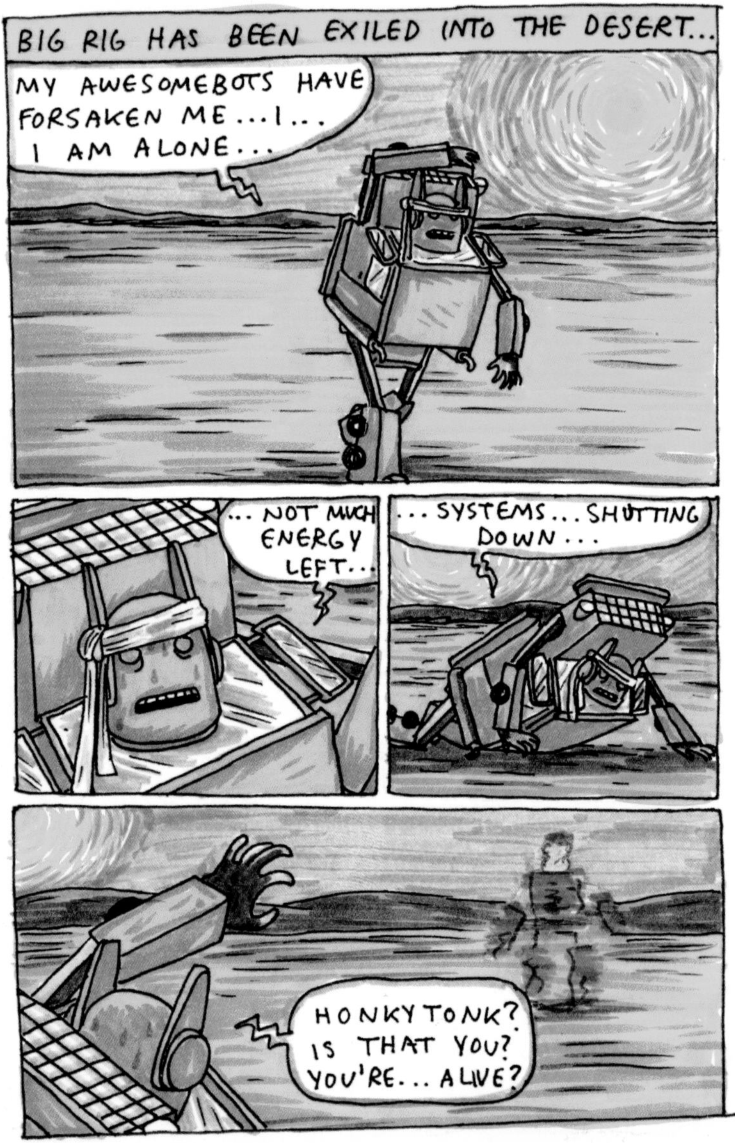
BIG RIG HAS BEEN EXILED INTO THE DESERT...
MY AWESOMEBOTS HAVE FORSAKEN ME...I... I AM ALONE...
...NOT MUCH ENERGY LEFT...
...SYSTEMS...SHUTTING DOWN...
HONKYTONK? IS THAT YOU? YOU'RE... ALIVE?

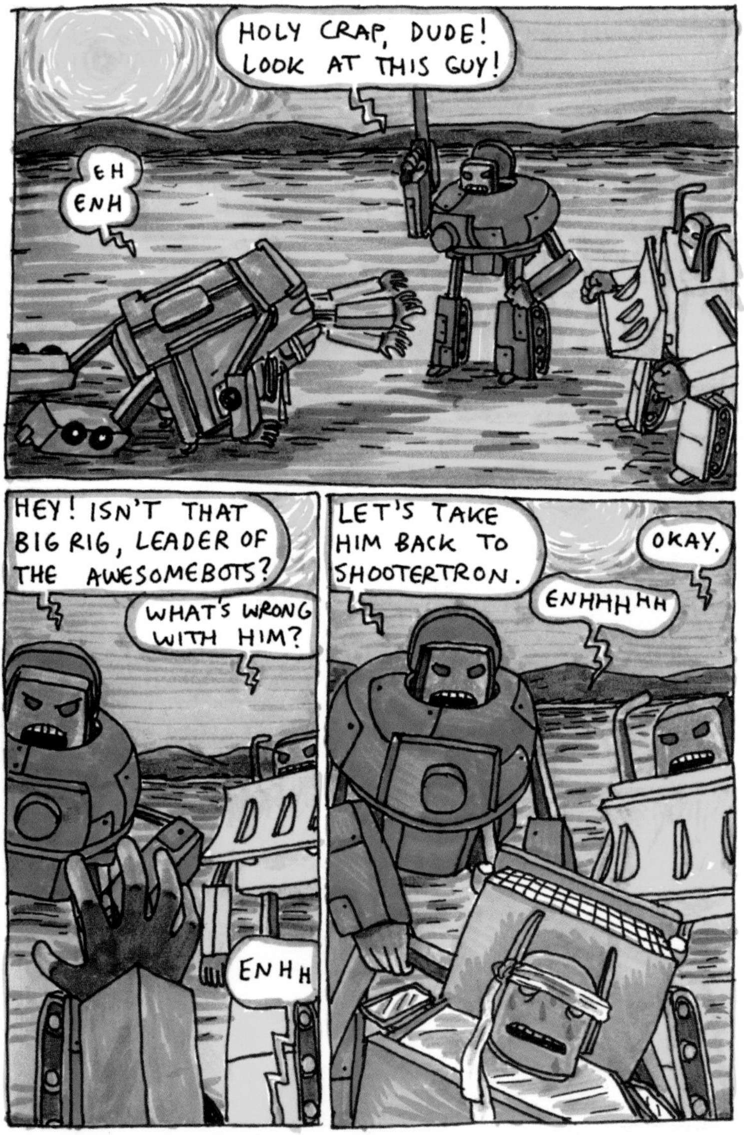
HOLY CRAP, DUDE! LOOK AT THIS GUY!
EH ENH
HEY! ISN'T THAT BIG RIG, LEADER OF THE AWESOMEBOTS?
WHAT'S WRONG WITH HIM?
ENHH
LET'S TAKE HIM BACK TO SHOOTERTRON.
OKAY.
ENHHHHH

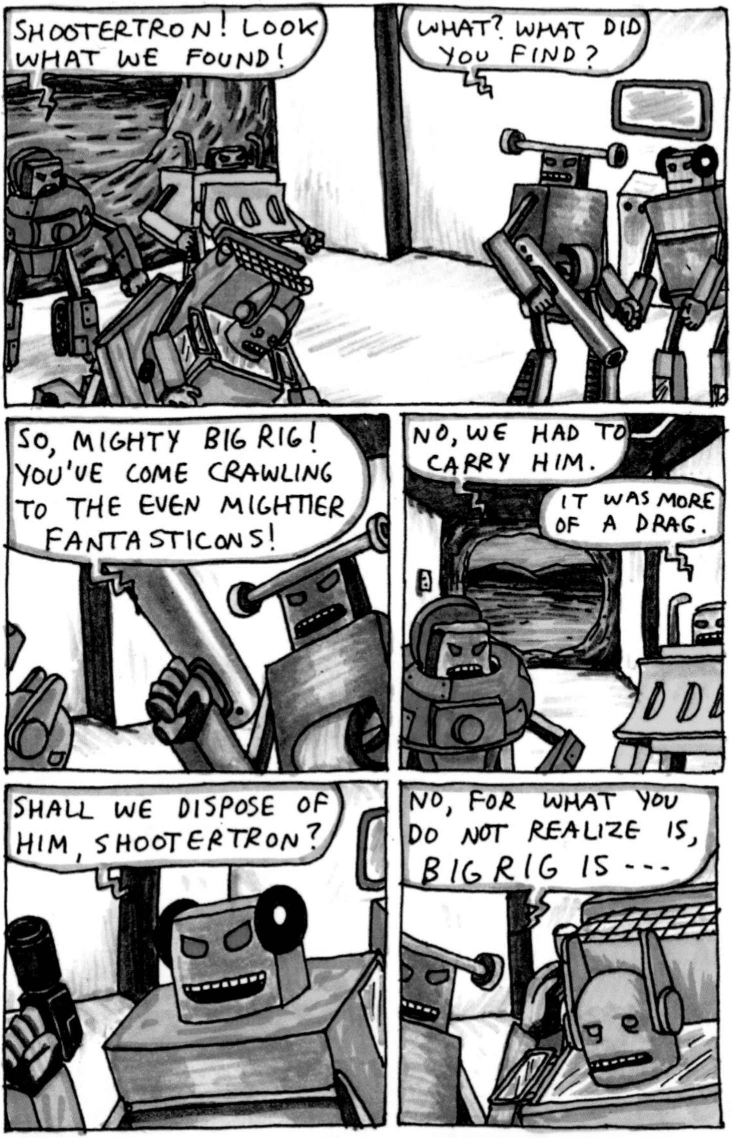
SHOOTERTRON! LOOK WHAT WE FOUND!
WHAT? WHAT DID YOU FIND?
SO, MIGHTY BIG RIG! YOU'VE COME CRAWLING TO THE EVEN MIGHTIER FANTASTICONS!
NO, WE HAD TO CARRY HIM.
IT WAS MORE OF A DRAG.
SHALL WE DISPOSE OF HIM, SHOOTERTRON?
NO, FOR WHAT YOU DO NOT REALIZE IS, BIGRIG IS---

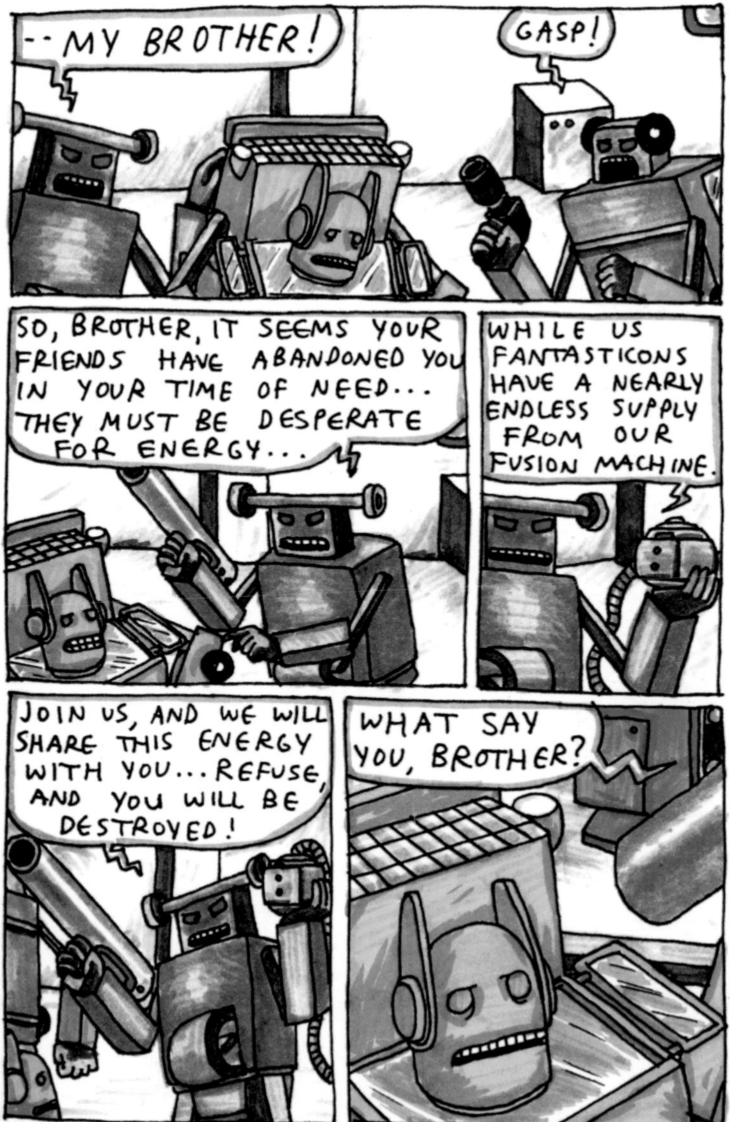
--MY BROTHER!
GASP!
SO, BROTHER, IT SEEMS YOUR FRIENDS HAVE ABANDONED YOU IN YOUR TIME OF NEED... THEY MUST BE DESPERATE FOR ENERGY...
WHILE US FANTASTICONS HAVE A NEARLY ENDLESS SUPPLY FROM OUR FUSION MACHINE.
JOIN US, AND WE WILL SHARE THIS ENERGY WITH YOU... REFUSE, AND YOU WILL BE DESTROYED!
WHAT SAY YOU, BROTHER?

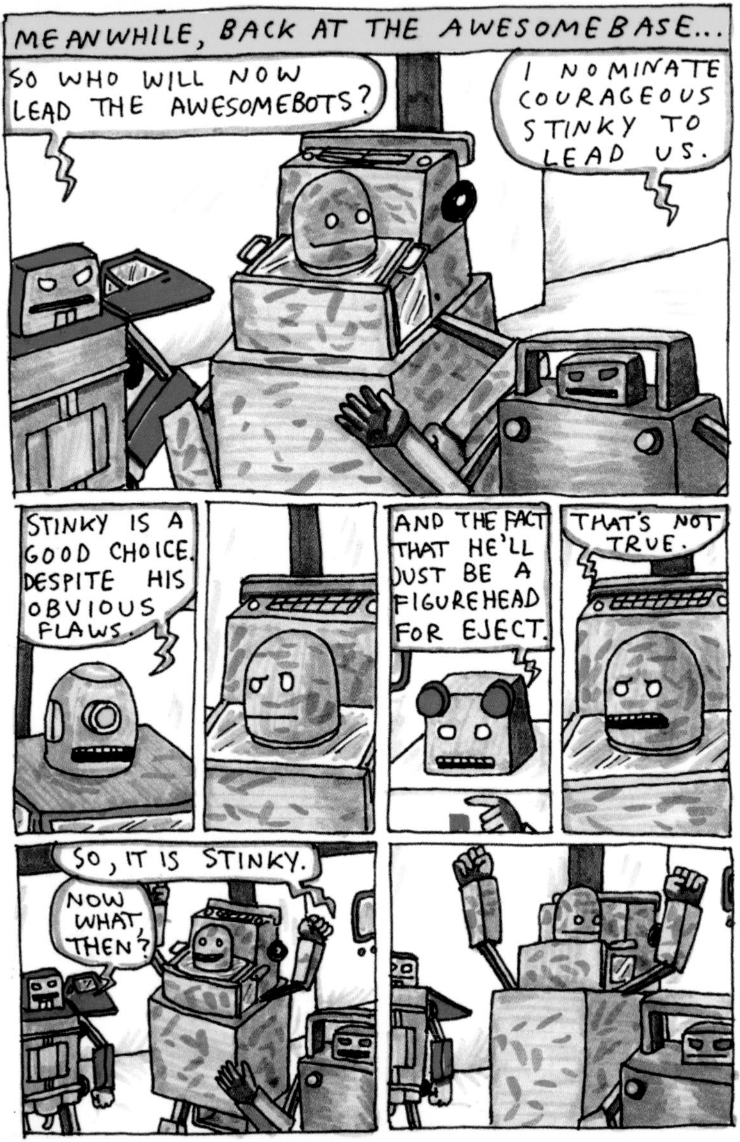
MEANWHILE, BACK AT THE AWESOMEBASE...
SO WHO WILL NOW LEAD THE AWESOMEBOTS?
I NOMINATE COURAGEOUS STINKY TO LEAD US.
STINKY IS A GOOD CHOICE. DESPITE HIS OBVIOUS FLAWS.
AND THE FACT THAT HE'LL JUST BE A FIGUREHEAD FOR EJECT.
THAT'S NOT TRUE.
SO, IT IS STINKY.
NOW WHAT, THEN?

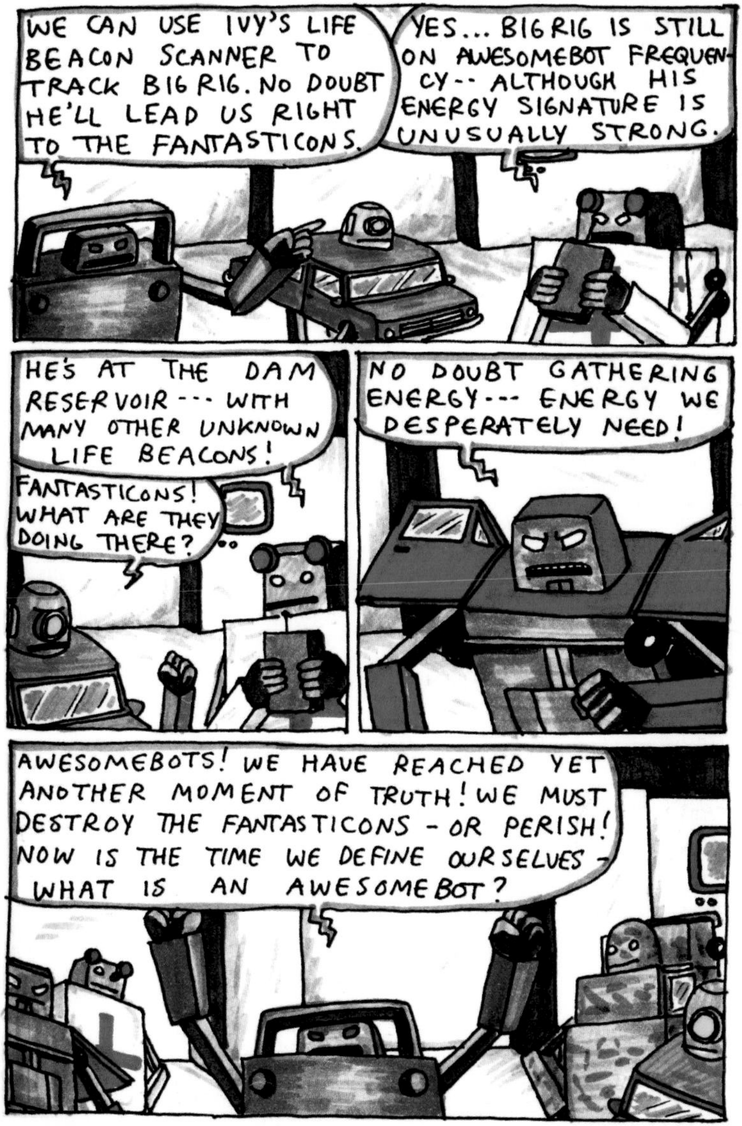
WE CAN USE IVY'S LIFE BEACON SCANNER TO TRACK BIG RIG. NO DOUBT HE'LL LEAD US RIGHT TO THE FANTASTICONS.
YES... BIG RIG IS STILL ON AWESOMEBOT FREQUENCY-- ALTHOUGH HIS ENERGY SIGNATURE IS UNUSUALLY STRONG.
HE'S AT THE DAM RESERVOIR--- WITH MANY OTHER UNKNOWN LIFE BEACONS!
FANTASTICONS! WHAT ARE THEY DOING THERE?
NO DOUBT GATHERING ENERGY--- ENERGY WE DESPERATELY NEED!
AWESOMEBOTS! WE HAVE REACHED YET ANOTHER MOMENT OF TRUTH! WE MUST DESTROY THE FANTASTICONS - OR PERISH! NOW IS THE TIME WE DEFINE OURSELVES - WHAT IS AN AWESOMEBOT?

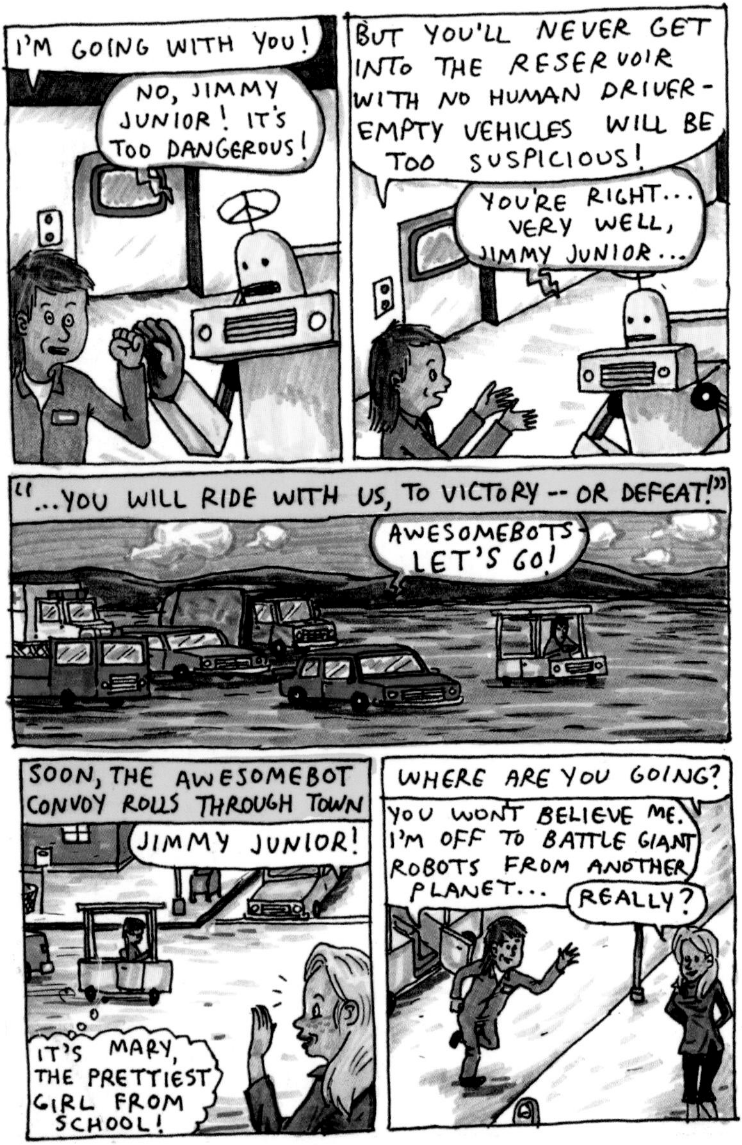
I'M GOING WITH YOU!
NO, JIMMY JUNIOR! IT'S TOO DANGEROUS!
BUT YOU'LL NEVER GET INTO THE RESERVOIR WITH NO HUMAN DRIVER - EMPTY VEHICLES WILL BE TOO SUSPICIOUS!
YOU'RE RIGHT... VERY WELL, JIMMY JUNIOR...
"...YOU WILL RIDE WITH US, TO VICTORY -- OR DEFEAT!"
AWESOMEBOTS - LET'S GO!
SOON, THE AWESOMEBOT CONVOY ROLLS THROUGH TOWN
JIMMY JUNIOR!
IT'S MARY, THE PRETTIEST GIRL FROM SCHOOL!
WHERE ARE YOU GOING?
YOU WONT BELIEVE ME. I'M OFF TO BATTLE GIANT ROBOTS FROM ANOTHER PLANET...
REALLY?

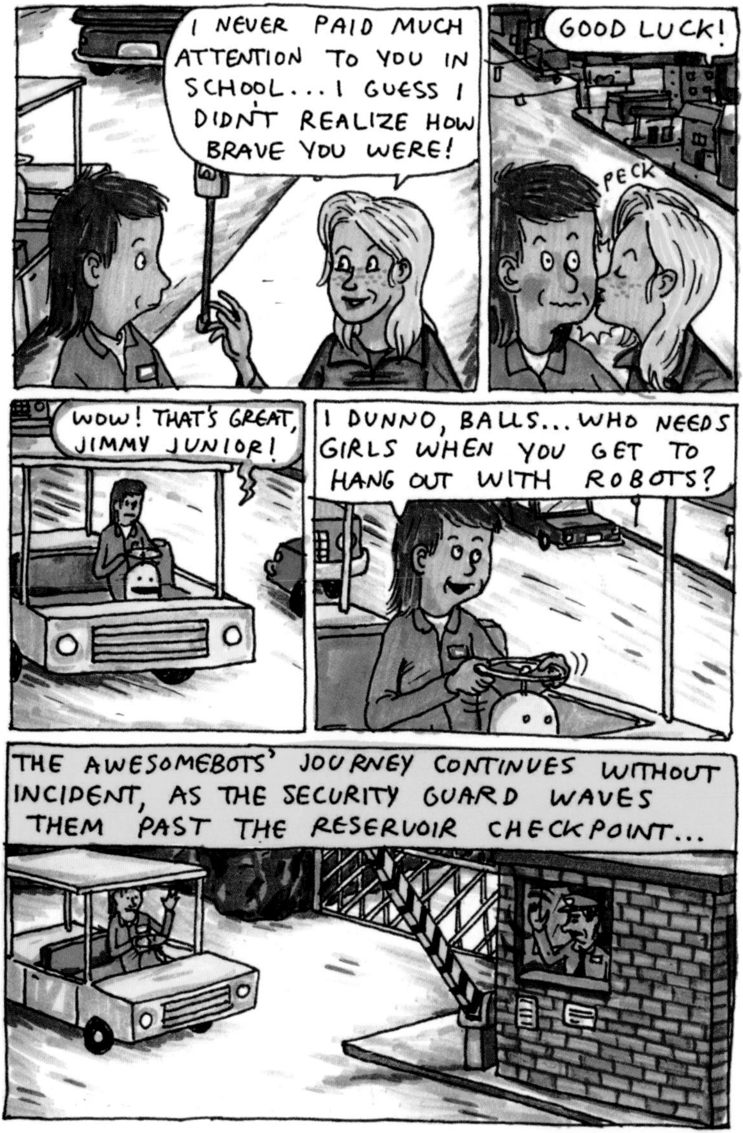
I NEVER PAID MUCH ATTENTION TO YOU IN SCHOOL... I GUESS I DIDN'T REALIZE HOW BRAVE YOU WERE!
GOOD LUCK!
PECK
WOW! THAT'S GREAT, JIMMY JUNIOR!
I DUNNO, BALLS... WHO NEEDS GIRLS WHEN YOU GET TO HANG OUT WITH ROBOTS?
THE AWESOMEBOTS' JOURNEY CONTINUES WITHOUT INCIDENT, AS THE SECURITY GUARD WAVES THEM PAST THE RESERVOIR CHECKPOINT...

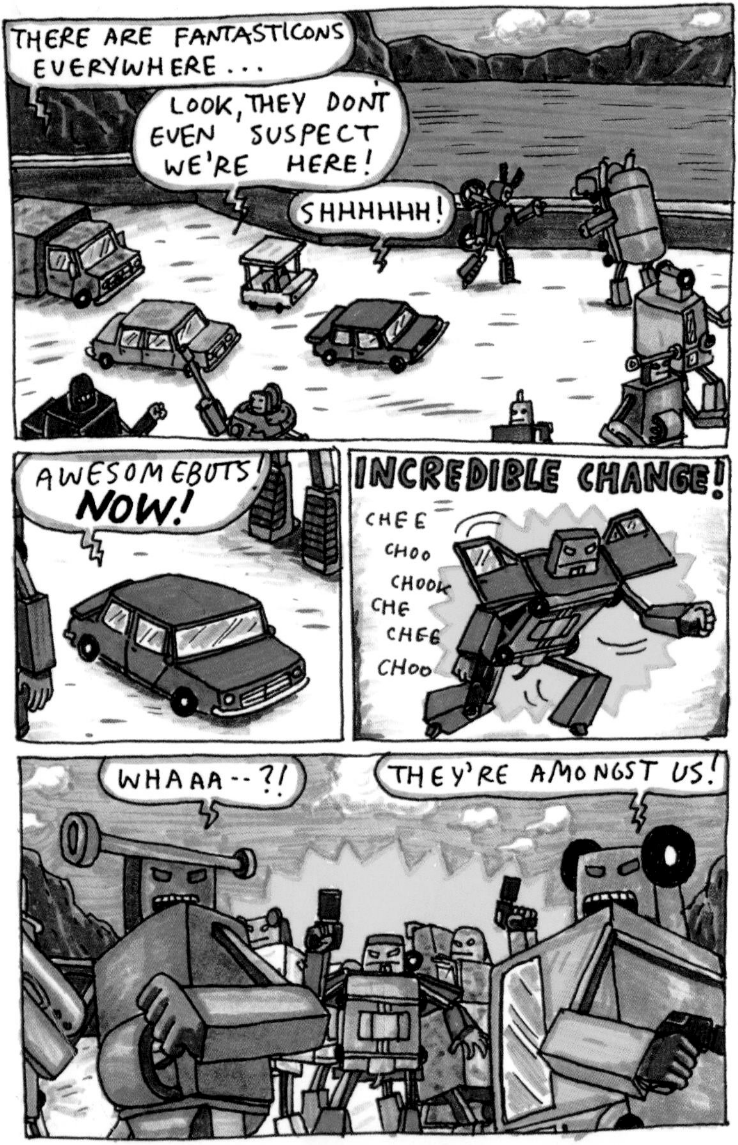
THERE ARE FANTASTICONS EVERYWHERE...
LOOK, THEY DON'T EVEN SUSPECT WE'RE HERE!
SHHHHHH!
AWESOMEBUTS! NOW!
INCREDIBLE CHANGE!
CHEE
CHOO
CHOOK
CHE
CHEE
CHOO
WHAAA--?!
THEY'RE AMONGST US!

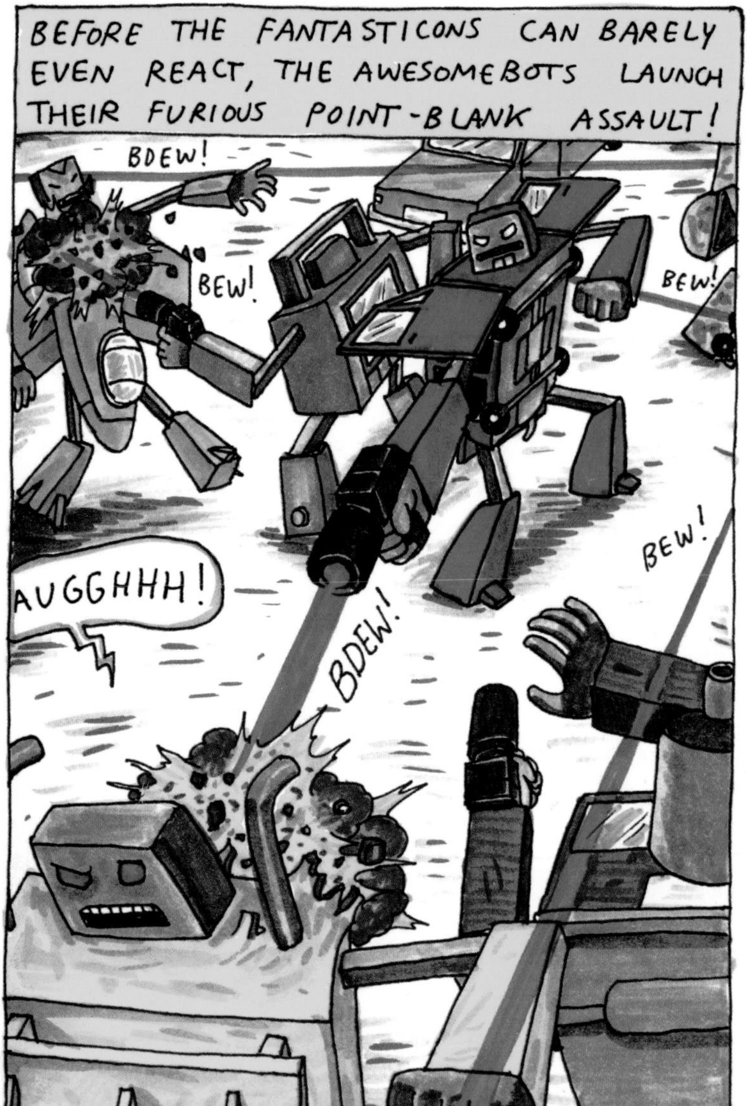
BEFORE THE FANTASTICONS CAN BARELY EVEN REACT, THE AWESOMEBOTS LAUNCH THEIR FURIOUS POINT-BLANK ASSAULT!
BDEW!
BEW!
BEW!
AUGGHHH!
BEW!
BDEW!

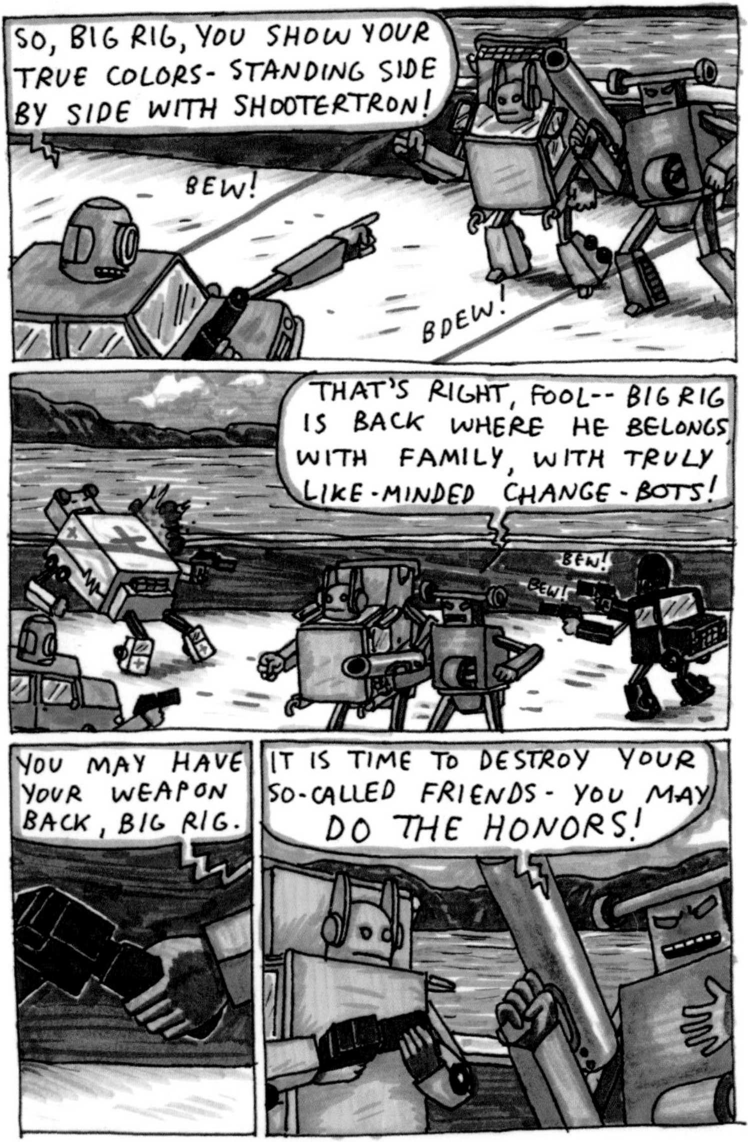
SO, BIG RIG, YOU SHOW YOUR TRUE COLORS- STANDING SIDE BY SIDE WITH SHOOTERTRON!
BEW!
BDEW!
THAT'S RIGHT, FOOL-- BIG RIG IS BACK WHERE HE BELONGS, WITH FAMILY, WITH TRULY LIKE-MINDED CHANGE-BOTS!
BEW!
BEW!
YOU MAY HAVE YOUR WEAPON BACK, BIG RIG.
IT IS TIME TO DESTROY YOUR SO-CALLED FRIENDS- YOU MAY DO THE HONORS!

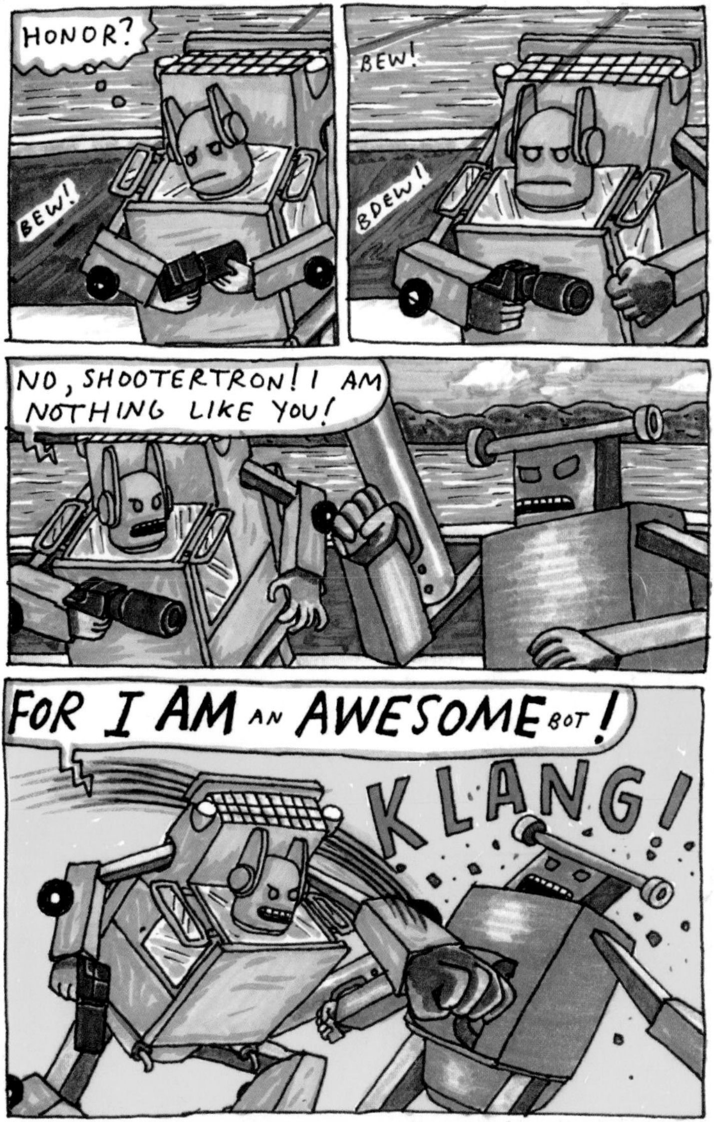
HONOR?
BEW!
BEW!
BDEW!
NO, SHOOTERTRON! I AM NOTHING LIKE YOU!
FOR I AM AN AWESOME BOT!
KLANG!

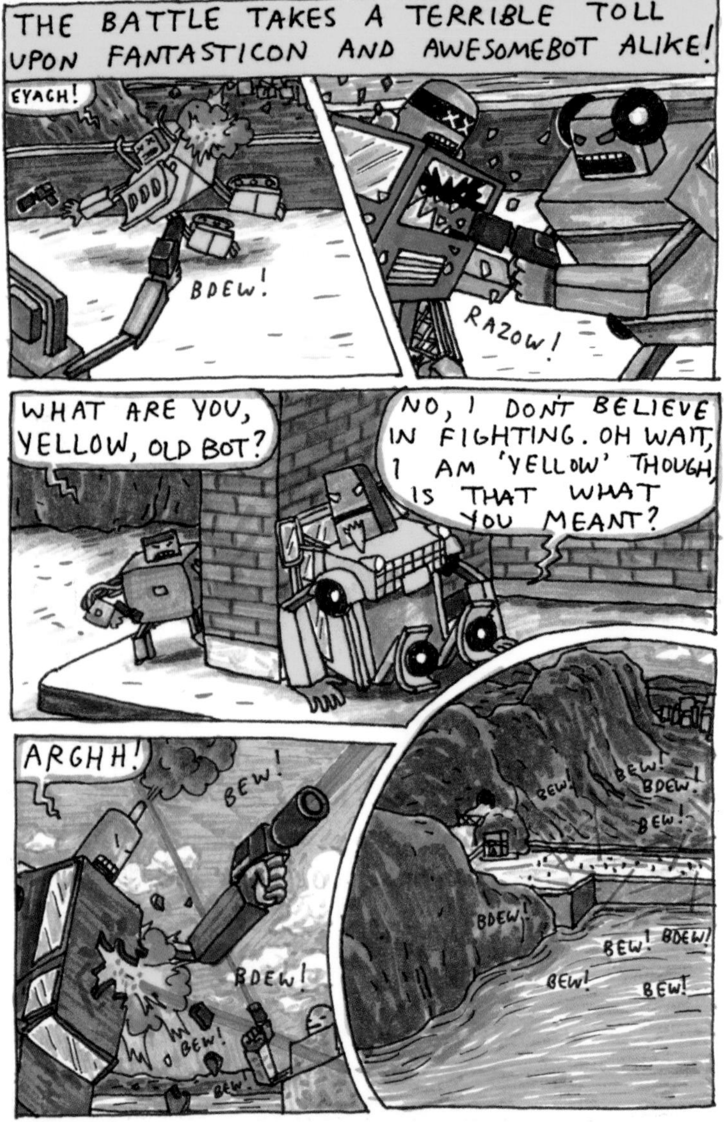

THE BATTLE TAKES A TERRIBLE TOLL UPON FANTASTICON AND AWESOMEBOT ALIKE!
EYACH!
BDEW!
RAZOW!
WHAT ARE YOU, YELLOW, OLD BOT?
NO, I DON'T BELIEVE IN FIGHTING. OH WAIT, I AM 'YELLOW' THOUGH, IS THAT WHAT YOU MEANT?
ARGHH!
BEW!
BDEW!
BEW!
BEW!
BEW!
BEW!
BDEW!
BEW!
BDEW!
BEW!
BDEW!
BEW!
BEW!

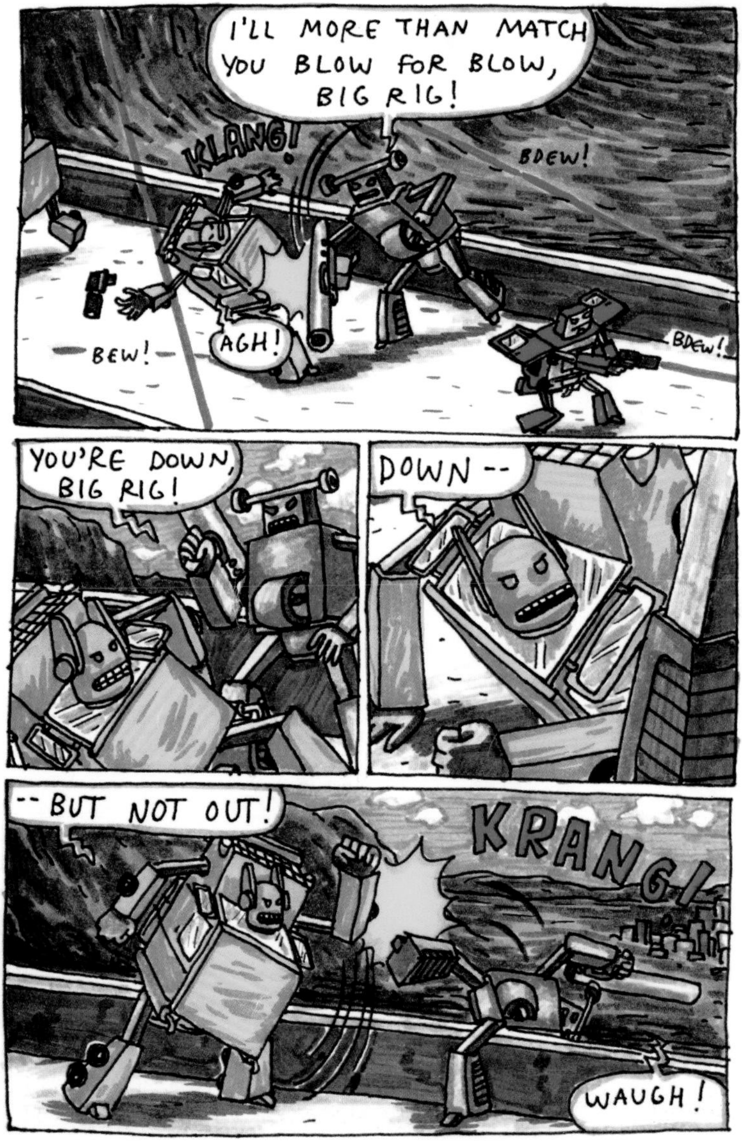
I'LL MORE THAN MATCH YOU BLOW FOR BLOW, BIG RIG!
KLANG!
BDEW!
AGH!
BEW!
BDEW!
YOU'RE DOWN, BIG RIG!
DOWN --
-- BUT NOT OUT!
KRANG!
WAUGH!

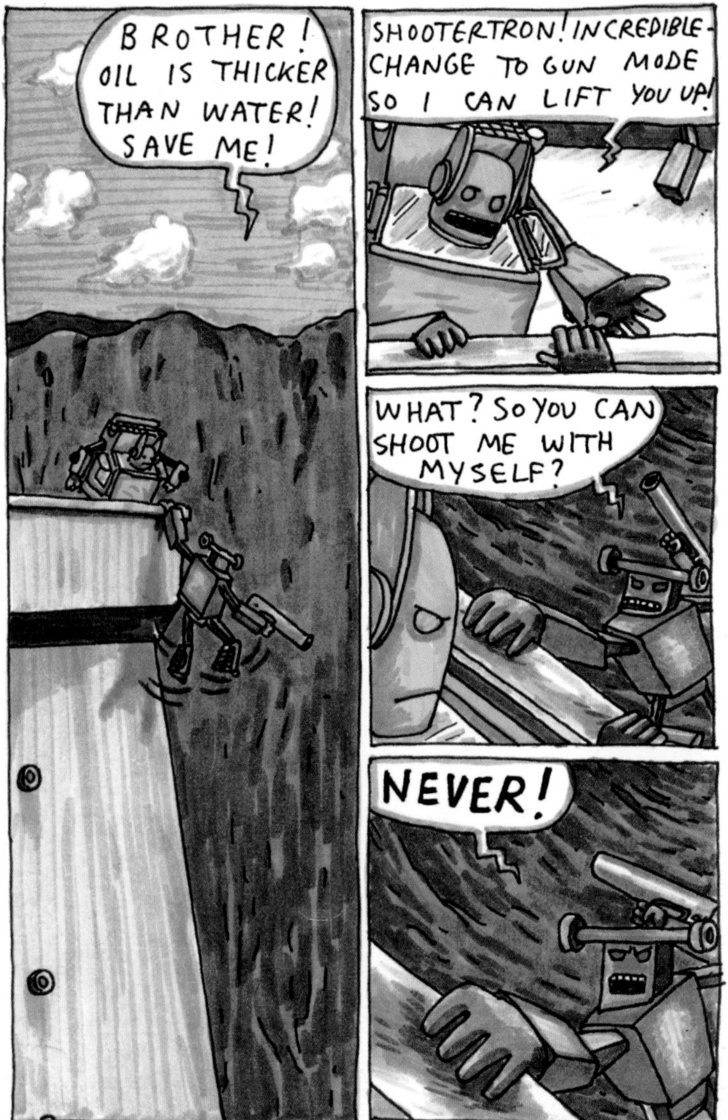
BROTHER! OIL IS THICKER THAN WATER! SAVE ME!
SHOOTERTRON! INCREDIBLE-CHANGE TO GUN MODE SO I CAN LIFT YOU UP!
WHAT? SO YOU CAN SHOOT ME WITH MYSELF?
NEVER!

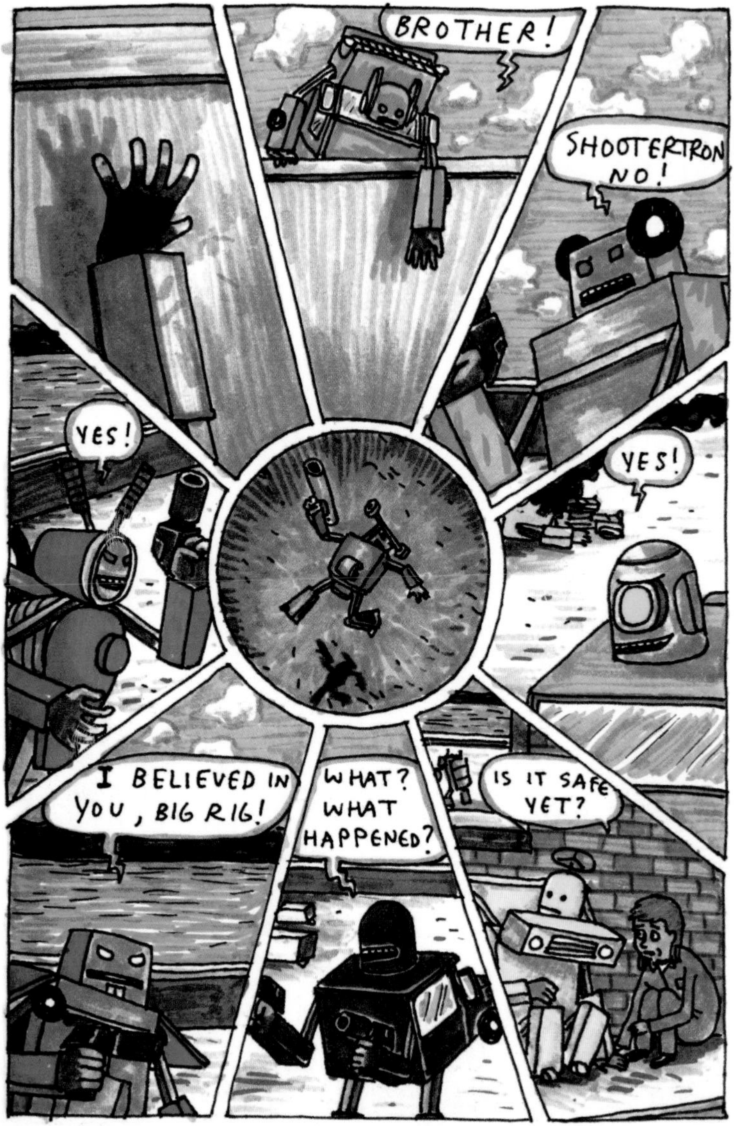
BROTHER!
SHOOTERTRON NO!
YES!
YES!
I BELIEVED IN YOU, BIG RIG!
WHAT? WHAT HAPPENED?
IS IT SAFE YET?

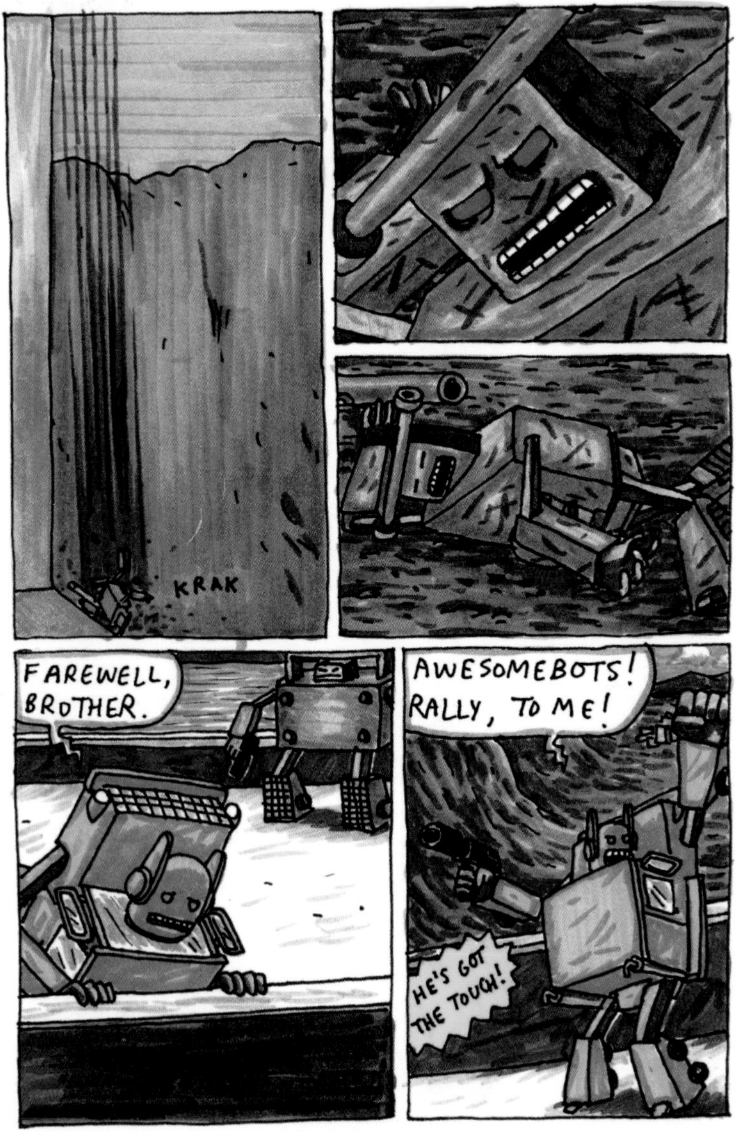
KRAK
FAREWELL, BROTHER.
AWESOMEBOTS! RALLY, TO ME!
HE'S GOT THE TOUCH!

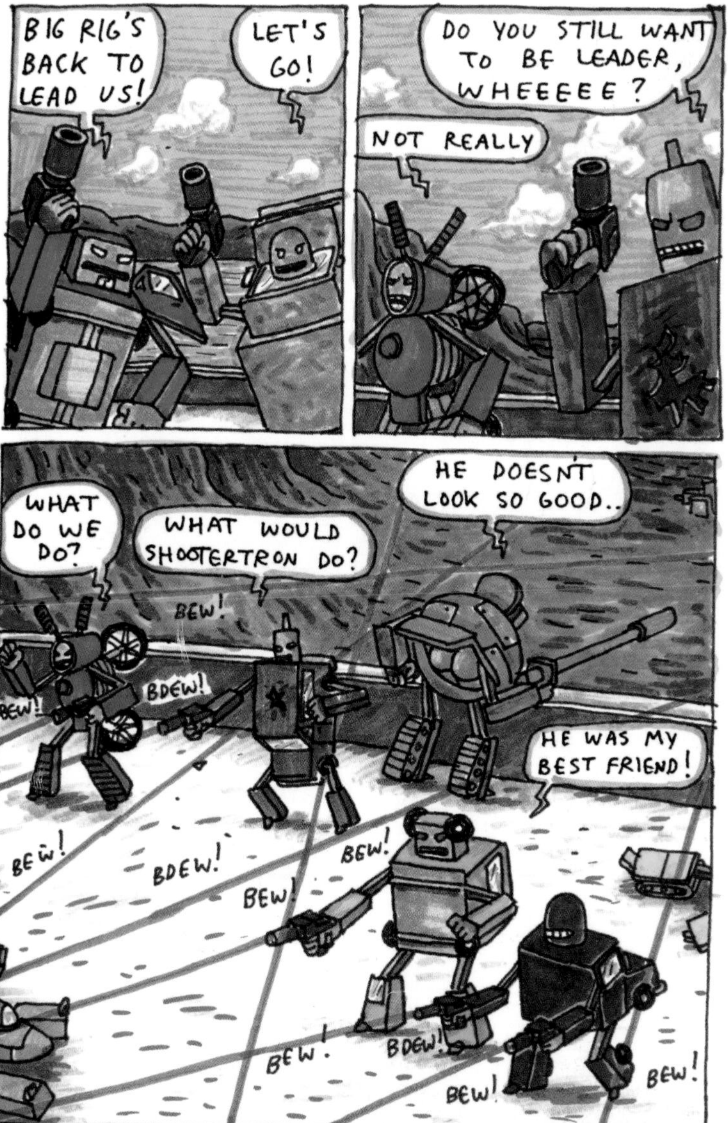
BIG RIG'S BACK TO LEAD US!
LET'S GO!
DO YOU STILL WANT TO BE LEADER, WHEEEEEE?
NOT REALLY
WHAT DO WE DO?
WHAT WOULD SHOOTERTRON DO?
HE DOESN'T LOOK SO GOOD..
BEW!
BDEW!
BEW!
HE WAS MY BEST FRIEND!
BEW!
BDEW!
BEW!
BEW!
BEW!
BDEW!
BEW!
BEW!

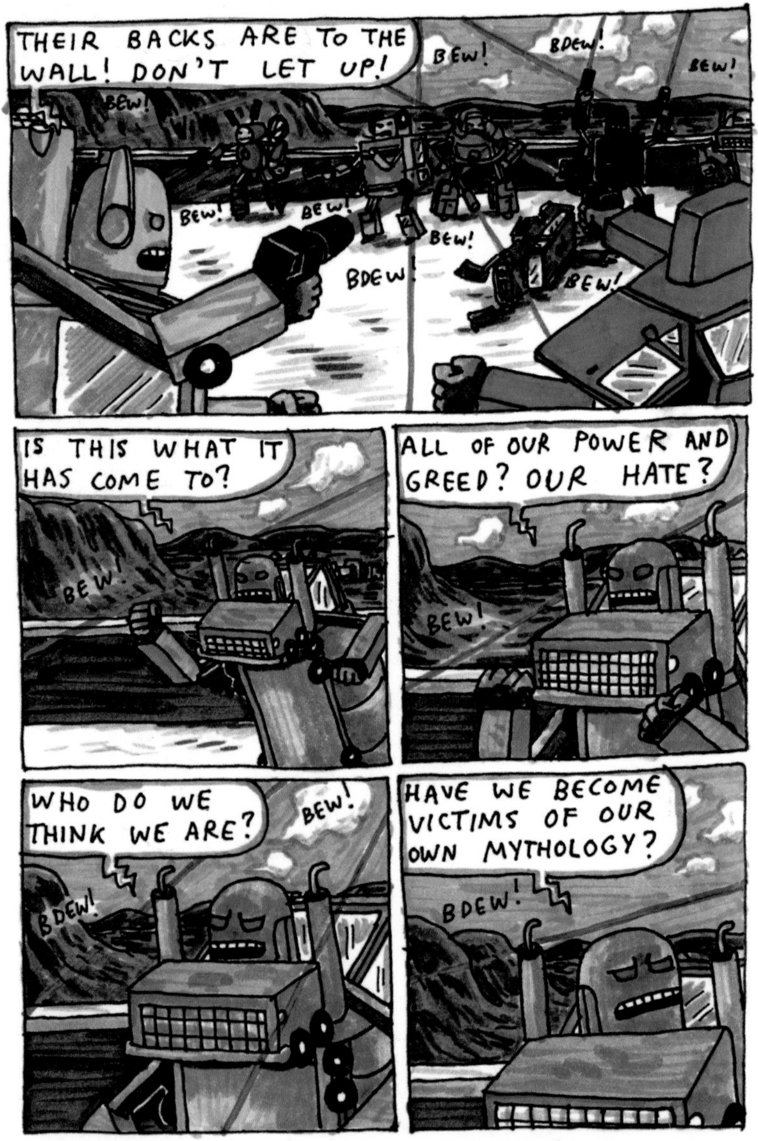
THEIR BACKS ARE TO THE WALL! DON'T LET UP!
BEW!
BEW!
BDEW!
BEW!
BEW!
BEW!
BEW!
BDEW!
BEW!
IS THIS WHAT IT HAS COME TO?
BEW!
ALL OF OUR POWER AND GREED? OUR HATE?
BEW!
WHO DO WE THINK WE ARE?
BEW!
BDEW!
HAVE WE BECOME VICTIMS OF OUR OWN MYTHOLOGY?
BDEW!

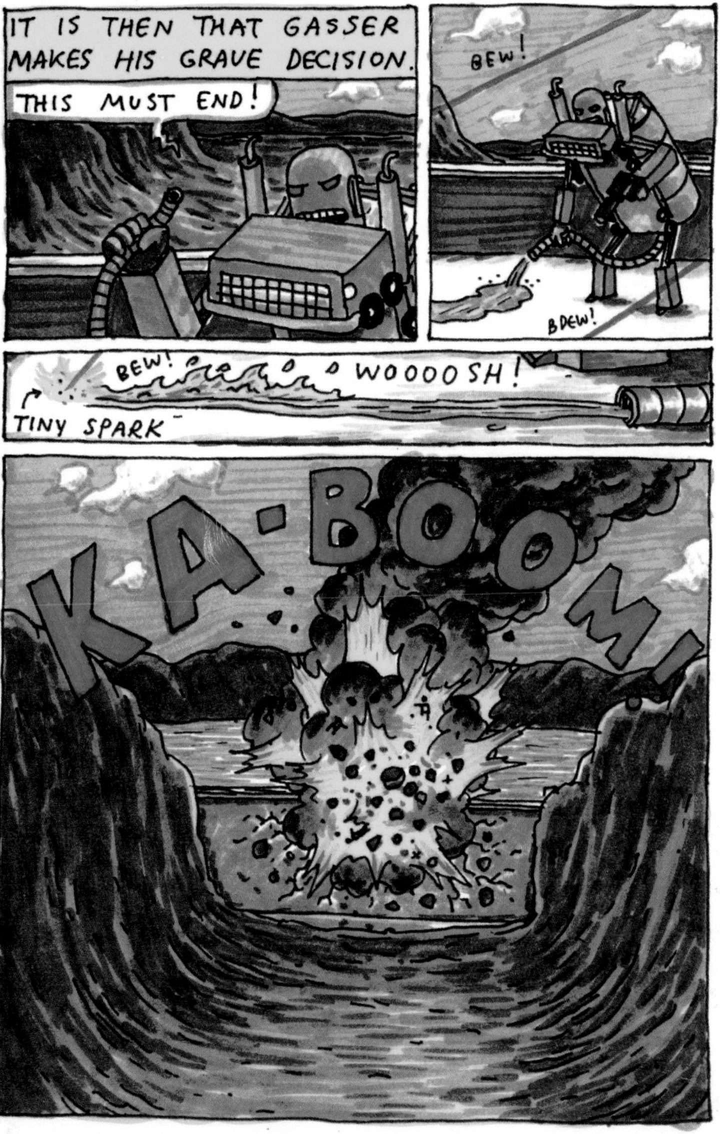

IT IS THEN THAT GASSER MAKES HIS GRAVE DECISION.
THIS MUST END!
BEW!
BDEW!
BEW!
WOOOOSH!
TINY SPARK
KA-BOOM!

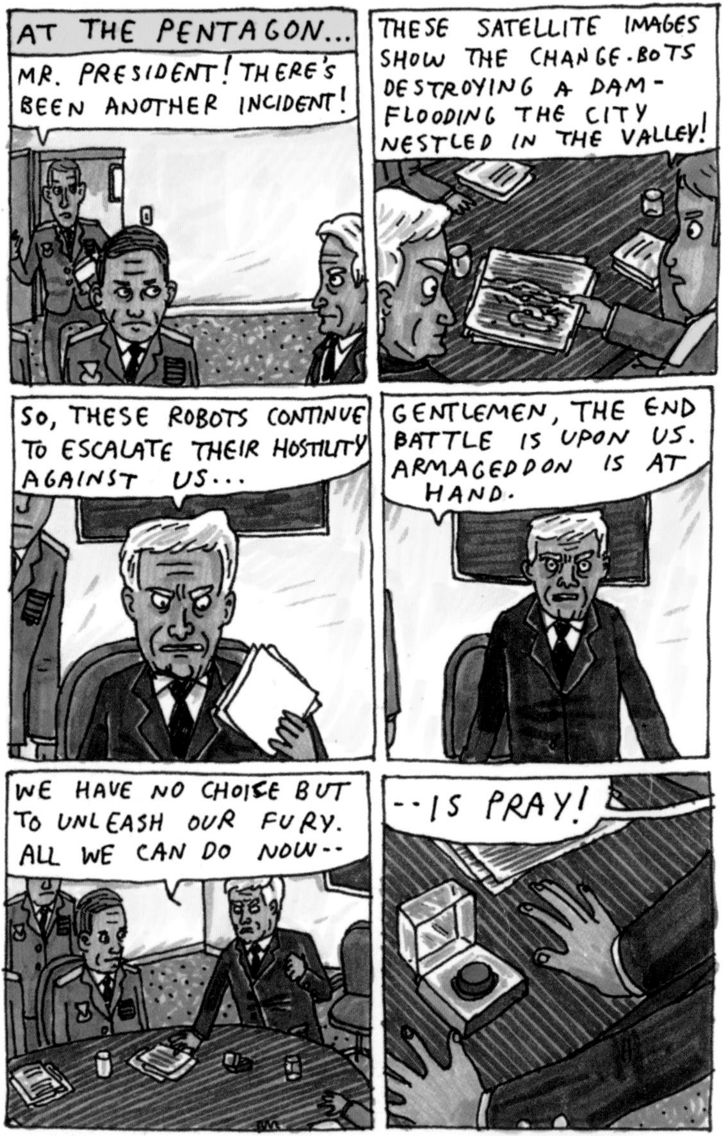

AT THE PENTAGON...
MR. PRESIDENT! THERE'S BEEN ANOTHER INCIDENT!
THESE SATELLITE IMAGES SHOW THE CHANGE-BOTS DESTROYING A DAM-FLOODING THE CITY NESTLED IN THE VALLEY!
SO, THESE ROBOTS CONTINUE TO ESCALATE THEIR HOSTILITY AGAINST US...
GENTLEMEN, THE END BATTLE IS UPON US. ARMAGEDDON IS AT HAND.
WE HAVE NO CHOISE BUT TO UNLEASH OUR FURY. ALL WE CAN DO NOW--
--IS PRAY!

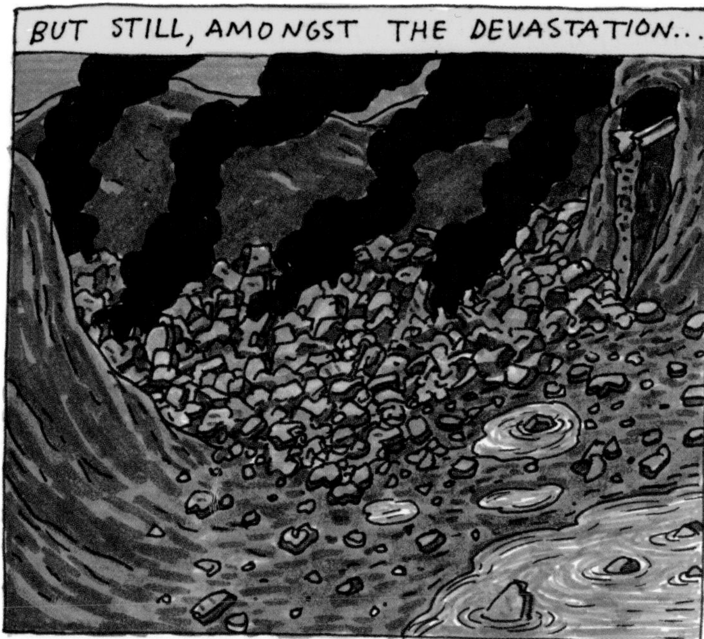
BUT STILL, AMONGST THE DEVASTATION...

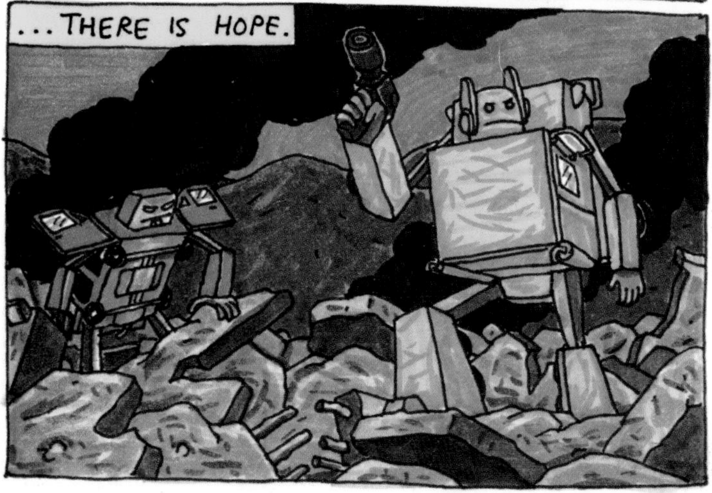
...THERE IS HOPE.

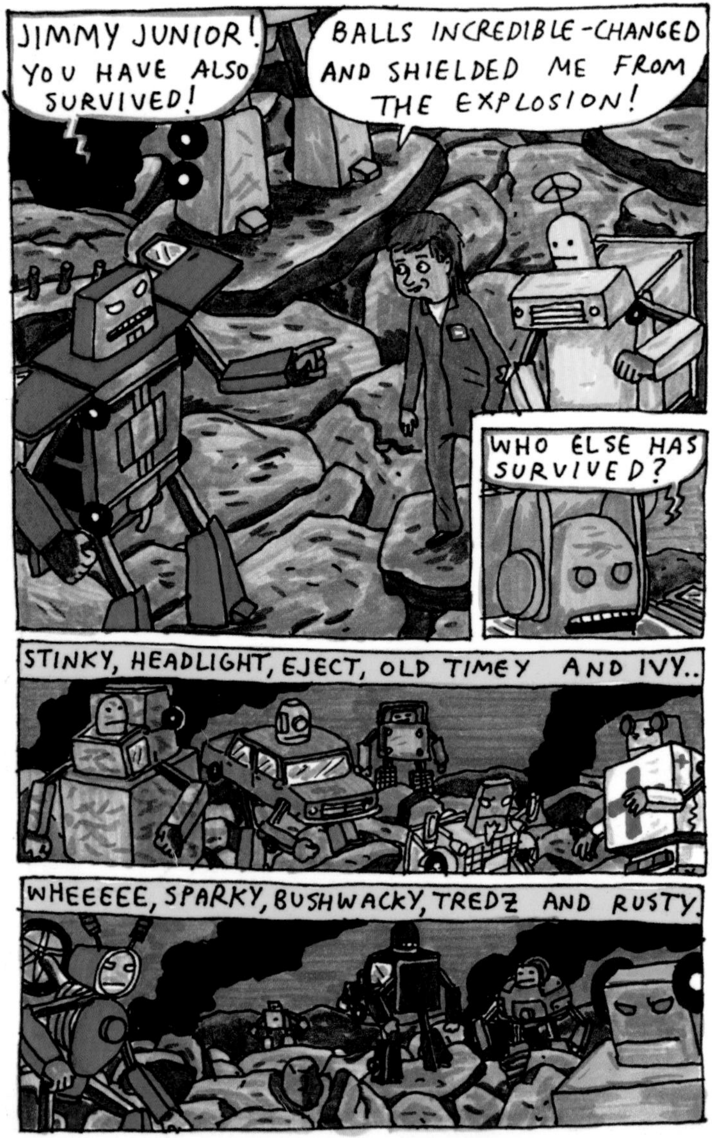
JIMMY JUNIOR! YOU HAVE ALSO SURVIVED!
BALLS INCREDIBLE-CHANGED AND SHIELDED ME FROM THE EXPLOSION!
WHO ELSE HAS SURVIVED?
STINKY, HEADLIGHT, EJECT, OLD TIMEY AND IVY..
WHEEEEE, SPARKY, BUSHWACKY, TREDZ AND RUSTY.

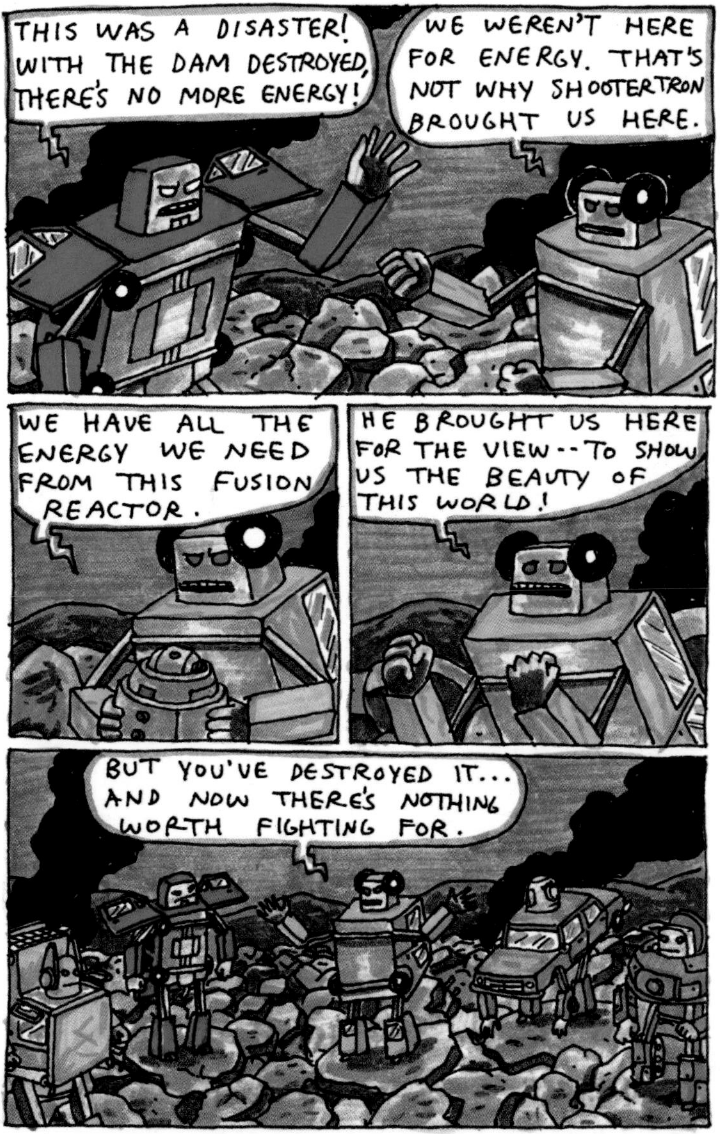
THIS WAS A DISASTER! WITH THE DAM DESTROYED, THERE'S NO MORE ENERGY!
WE WEREN'T HERE FOR ENERGY. THAT'S NOT WHY SHOOTERTRON BROUGHT US HERE.
WE HAVE ALL THE ENERGY WE NEED FROM THIS FUSION REACTOR.
HE BROUGHT US HERE FOR THE VIEW--TO SHOW US THE BEAUTY OF THIS WORLD!
BUT YOU'VE DESTROYED IT... AND NOW THERE'S NOTHING WORTH FIGHTING FOR.

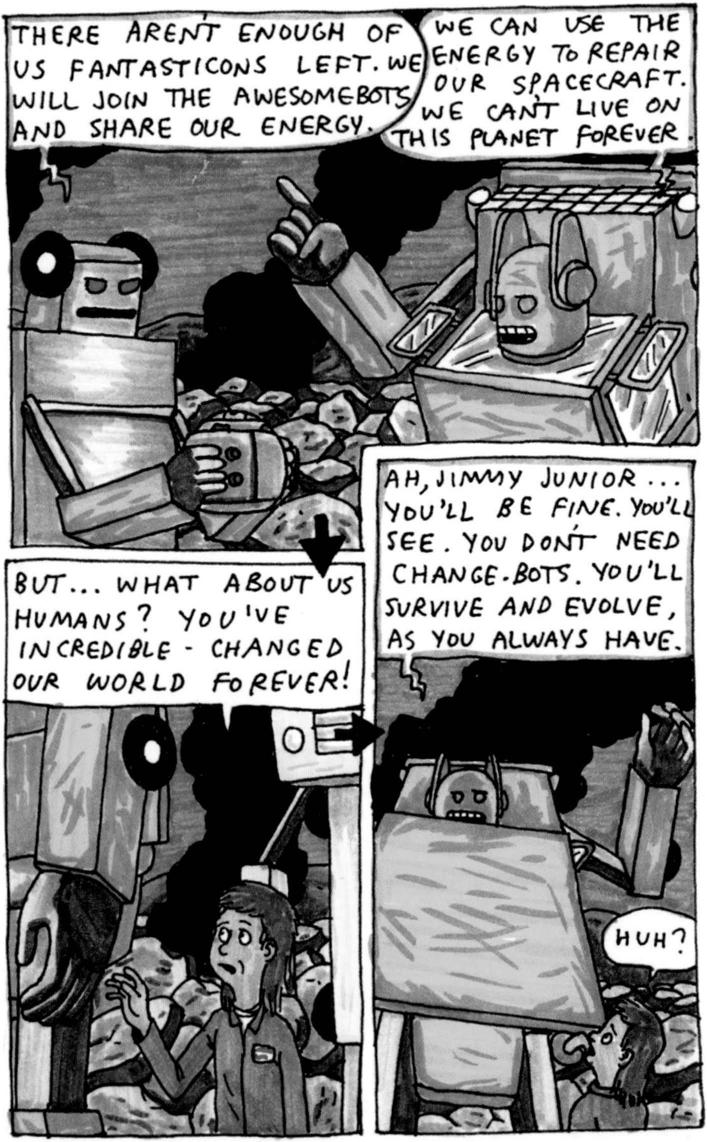
THERE AREN'T ENOUGH OF US FANTASTICONS LEFT. WE WILL JOIN THE AWESOMEBOTS AND SHARE OUR ENERGY.
WE CAN USE THE ENERGY TO REPAIR OUR SPACECRAFT. WE CAN'T LIVE ON THIS PLANET FOREVER.
BUT... WHAT ABOUT US HUMANS? YOU'VE INCREDIBLE - CHANGED OUR WORLD FOREVER!
AH, JIMMY JUNIOR... YOU'LL BE FINE. YOU'LL SEE. YOU DON'T NEED CHANGE-BOTS. YOU'LL SURVIVE AND EVOLVE, AS YOU ALWAYS HAVE.
HUH?

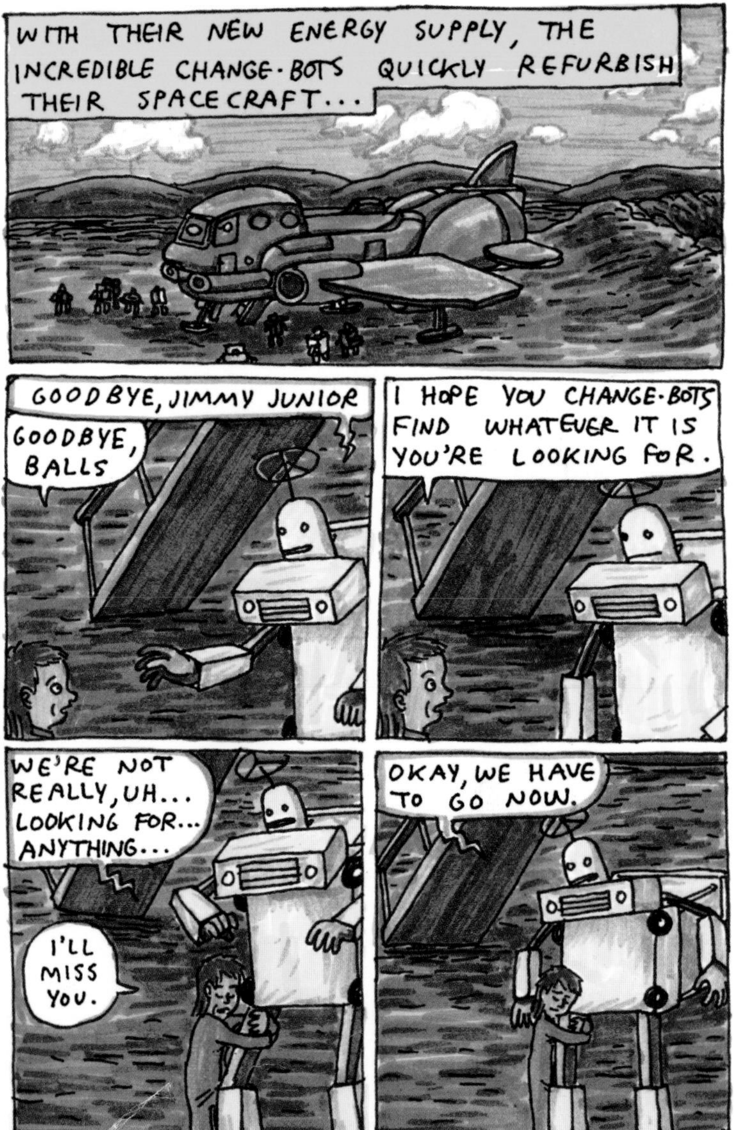
WITH THEIR NEW ENERGY SUPPLY, THE INCREDIBLE CHANGE-BOTS QUICKLY REFURBISH THEIR SPACECRAFT...
GOODBYE, JIMMY JUNIOR
GOODBYE, BALLS
I HOPE YOU CHANGE-BOTS FIND WHATEVER IT IS YOU'RE LOOKING FOR.
WE'RE NOT REALLY, UH... LOOKING FOR... ANYTHING...
I'LL MISS YOU.
OKAY, WE HAVE TO GO NOW.

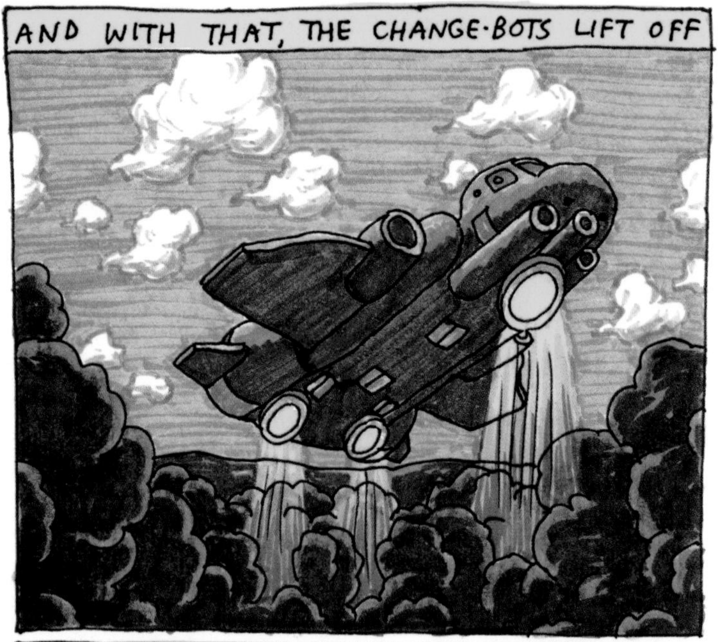
AND WITH THAT, THE CHANGE-BOTS LIFT OFF

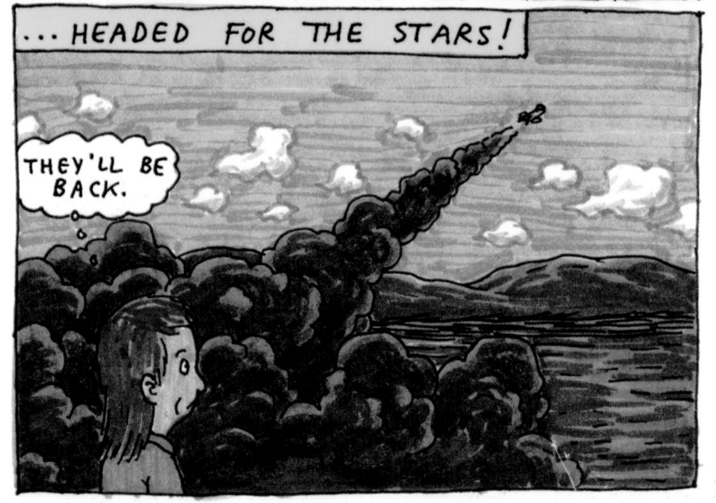
... HEADED FOR THE STARS!
THEY'LL BE BACK.

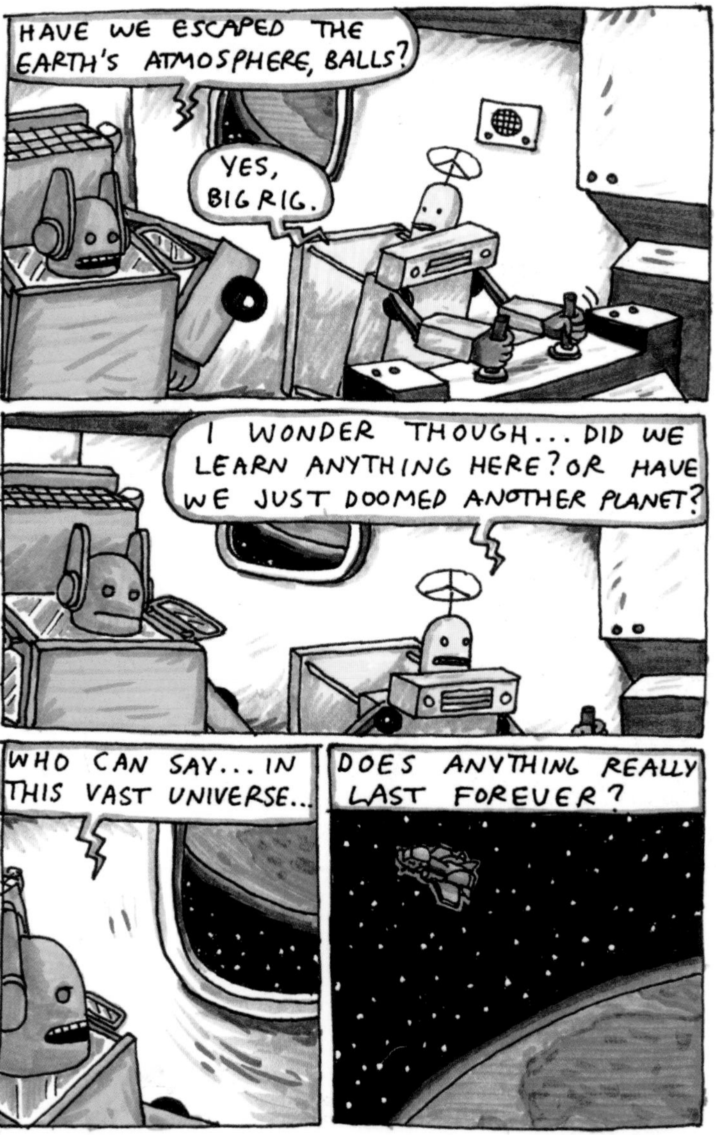
HAVE WE ESCAPED THE EARTH'S ATMOSPHERE, BALLS?
YES, BIG RIG.
I WONDER THOUGH... DID WE LEARN ANYTHING HERE? OR HAVE WE JUST DOOMED ANOTHER PLANET?
WHO CAN SAY... IN THIS VAST UNIVERSE...
DOES ANYTHING REALLY LAST FOREVER?

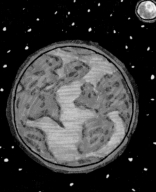

THE END!

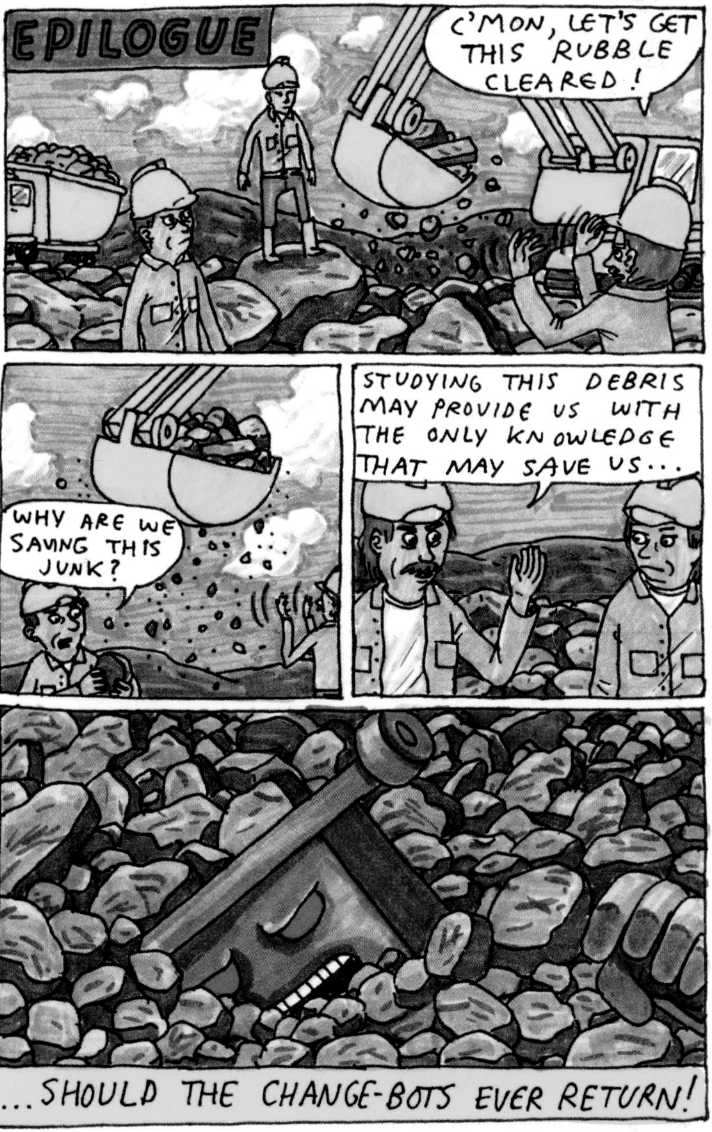
EPILOGUE
C'MON, LET'S GET THIS RUBBLE CLEARED!
WHY ARE WE SAVING THIS JUNK?
STUDYING THIS DEBRIS MAY PROVIDE US WITH THE ONLY KNOWLEDGE THAT MAY SAVE US...
...SHOULD THE CHANGE-BOTS EVER RETURN!

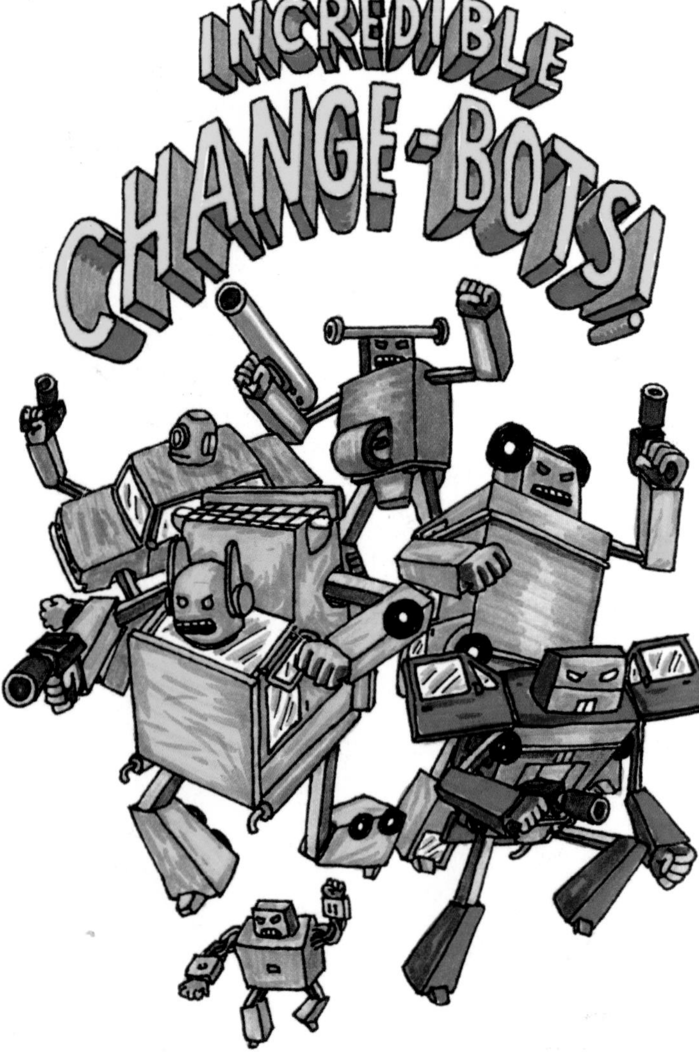
INCREDIBLE
CHANGE-BOTS!

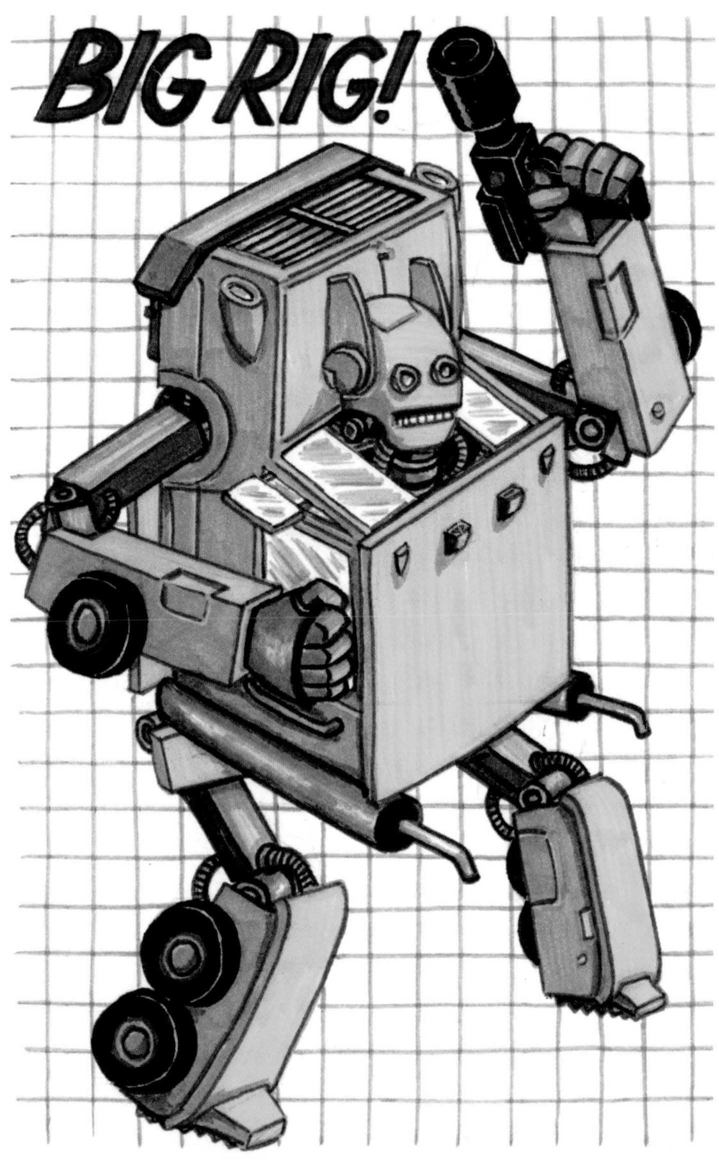
BIG RIG!

ABOUT THE AUTHOR

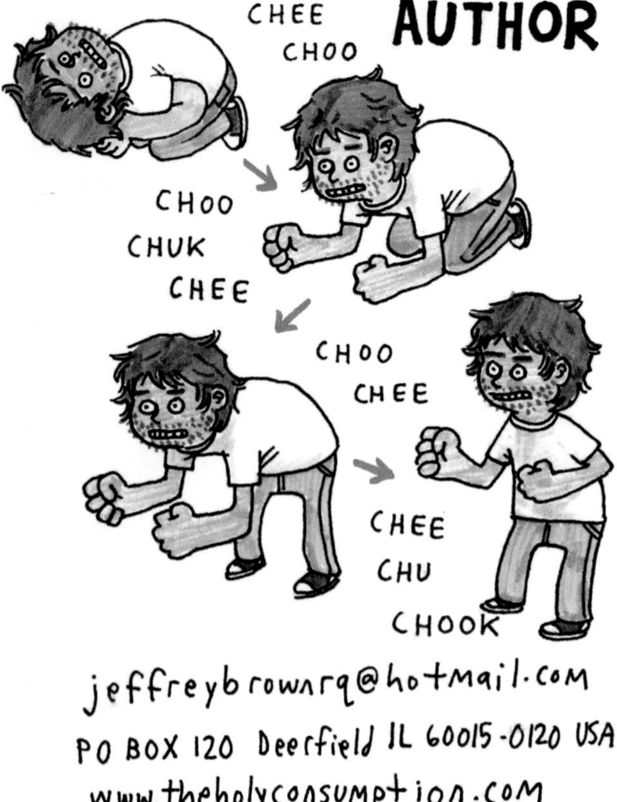
CHEE CHOO
CHOO CHUK CHEE
CHOO CHEE
CHEE CHU CHOOK

jeffreybrownrq@hotmail.com

PO BOX 120 Deerfield IL 60015-0120 USA

www.theholyconsumption.com